# Body²
## (Body Cubed or Body to th
### Introduction

This book is a collection of 15 articles published in Massage Magazine between 1997 and 2000 (and reprinted with their kind permission). Together they constitute a bodywide tour of structural anatomy and related somatic issues.

This is not a complete anatomy text; many areas are left under-explored, and having a good anatomy atlas at hand is often helpful. The book has nevertheless proven popular with all types of manual therapists, movements and yoga teachers, and even psychotherapists with an interest in the body.

Body³ was updated in 2014 for clarity to serve as a textbook for our training courses.

Many people contributed to the ideas in this book, but let me thank a few: Karen Menehan, the tireless editor at Massage Magazine, who shepherded the articles through publication; Tom Bowman, whose lively illustrations contributed so much to the series; my colleagues in the Life Sciences Faculty of the Rolf Institute and now my own teaching faculty, whose different points of view have broadened my knowledge.

Some of these ideas are expanded in published books: *Anatomy Trains* (Elsevier 2001, 2009, 2014, 2020), and *Fascial Release for Structural Balance* (Lotus, 2017). We also self-publish two other article collections which expand these ideas in other directions: *Anatomists's Corner*, from Massage & Bodywork Magazine, and *Structural Integration: Collected Journal Articles*, from the Journal of BodyWork and Movement Therapies.

We hope you enjoy it.
Tom

Thomas Myers is the cartographer of *Anatomy Trains* (Elsevier, 2001, 2009, 2014, 2020), the co-author of *Fascial Release for Structural Balance* (Lotus, 2017), and numerous chapters and journal articles that have been collected in the books *The Anatomist's Corner*, and *Structural Integration: Collected Journal Articles*. He has also produced over 16 videos and various webinars, with more forthcoming, on BodyReading® visual assessment, Fascial Release Technique®, and the applications of fascial research to body training.

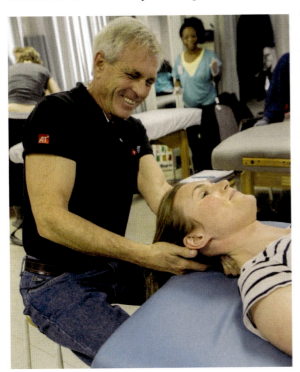

Tom and his faculty provide continuing education in Anatomy Trains and holistic myofascial strategies for a variety of movement and manual therapy professionals worldwide, as well as professional certification in Structural Integration based on the Anatomy Trains Myofascial Meridians. Tom studied directly with Drs. Ida Rolf, Moshe Feldenkrais, and Buckminster Fuller. He has also studied with movement teachers Judith Aston, Emilie Conrad, and in the martial arts. His Structural Integration programme is influenced by cranial, visceral, and intrinsic movement studies with European schools of osteopathy.

An inveterate traveler, Tom has practiced integrative manual therapy for over 40 years in a variety of clinical and cultural settings. He is a member of the International Association of Structural Integrators (IASI) and a member of the Health Advisory Board for Equinox. A certified Touch-in-Parenting instructor, Tom retains a strong interest in perinatal issues relating to movement. Tom lives, writes and sails on the coast of Maine.

*Thomas Myers • PO Box 78 • Walpole ME • USA 04573 • info@AnatomyTrains.com*

# BODY³ CUBED

## by Thomas Myers

This book is an article compilation that develops a three-dimensional understanding of what is under therapists' hands—moving up the body from feet to head. It is my contention that a felt anatomical understanding will enhance the intuitive skills of therapists in any of the modalities in our diverse field. These ideas come out of years of experience in reaching palpatory anatomy for hands-on and movement therapists–massage therapists, yoga teachers and integrative bodywork students in particular (see interview, "Thomas Myers' Vision for Bodywork in the Next Millennium," Issue #67, May/June 1997).

Although a few practical and clinical tips will be offered here, the articles are designed to deepen, through palpatory certainty, whatever practice you are already engaged in, rather than to add specific moves to your bag of tricks. It is my hope that these articles will further develop your freedom to play usefully in the vast field of the human body.

In my experience, the level of anatomical expertise given by the industry standard of 500-hour professional trainings is sufficient to do no harm, but insufficient to soar to the heights available to hands-on therapy (the standard is even lower for yoga teachers and most movement therapists). While I had a couple of short courses in locomotor anatomy at the beginning of my career, most of my knowledge was gained through on-the-job training, working in out-of-the-way places where information from colleagues and teachers was not readily available. Clients would show up with strange patterns, like the bunions described in this first chapter, or the locked knees of the second, and off I would go to my textbooks to try to make sense out of what was happening—and what might be done to correct the problem. The self-taught nature of my way of learning is helpful, I believe, in presenting this to other therapists, as is the emphasis on a kinesthetic, felt-sense approach. But co-teaching with my colleagues at the Rolf Institute, and later with other teaches in various modalities, has also been a rich source of information, so it gives me great pleasure to acknowledge how much my clients, students, and colleagues (and now my own faculty) have given me in terms of questions.

Moving back and forth from the map (books) to the territory (the body), is recommended. Netter's *Atlas of Human Anatomy*, Biel's *Trail Guide to the Body*, or other anatomy atlases such as Muscolino, Sobotta, Platzer, or Theime can all be helpful, but any detailed anatomy atlas would suffice to supplement the written text and the limited illustrations included here.

And with you right now is that other invaluable tool for learning anatomy—your own body. As you read this book, make sure that you can find the referenced landmarks and muscles in your own body, and your clients'. Doing so will deepen your grasp and do more than any other single technique to make the information part of your easily available working knowledge.

## Illustrations by Tom Bowman

# Table of Contents

1. The Foot: Understanding the Arches ............................................. 1
2. Knee and Thigh ............................................. 11
3. Fans of the Hip Joint ............................................. 19
4. Poise: Psoas - Piriformis Balance ............................................. 31
5. The Abdominal Balloon, Part 1: The Dynamics of the Abdomen ... 41
6. The Abdominal Balloon: Part 2: Gut-Level Strategies ............................................. 53
7. The River of Life, Part 1: Breath and the Rib Basket ............................................. 65
8. The River of Life, Part 2: A Front View of the Ribs ............................................. 73
9. Hanging Out with the Shoulder ............................................. 83
10. The Spine, Part 1: The Spring in Spine's Step ............................................. 93
11. The Spine, Part 2: Tensegrity Continuum ............................................. 101
12. The Neck and Cranium, Part 1: Touring the Motor Cylinder ............................................. 111
13. The Neck, Part 2: The Visceral Voice ............................................. 121
14. Moving in the World ............................................. 131
15. Moving On ............................................. 139

# Chapter 1: The Foot
## Understanding the Arches

**The need to understand the foot** is obvious—the feet have to "understand" all the rest of us! Even when we are simply standing, the feet act as a very dynamic foundation, requiring constant adaptation to shifting weight patterns from above as we move (which we are always doing, even when we are seemingly standing still). If the feet are not well-founded on the most basic structural level, it is difficult to balance in the body above them. On a more psychic level, the feet are a microcosmic map of our whole selves, as reflexologists have told us for years. In esoteric anatomy, the "karma" in the foot is said to be the "fear of being our true selves." At every level, then, getting the feet more balanced, aligned, grounded and graceful will help the overall person.

The foot, however, is a complicated bag of more than a couple of dozen bones, stringy with tendons and ligaments, often as tough and scaly as a dragon on the bottom. Other than soothing the poor things—stuck in their leather coffins all day—how are we massage therapists to make much of a difference?

One key to improved function in the feet is balanced and well-sprung arches. In this chapter we approach balancing the arches from several different angles, to give massage therapists more insight and a hands-on feel for making significant change in the feet.

### The uniqueness of the human foot

Four-legged creatures walk around, for the most part, on the balls of their feet. When we crawl around on "all fours," we are nowhere near a cat's or dog's walk. To imitate them we would have to lift our palms off the ground so that we were balanced on the "balls" of our fingers. Likewise, we must lift the heel and walk on the balls of our toes.

Not so easy, is it? Well, that is not too surprising—our hands and feet have changed a lot since they were adapted to this kind of locomotion. Four-legged animals walk on their paws with their heels high in the air. And they, of course, show similar awkwardness (frightening, in the case of a rearing horse, or cute, in a circus dog) when they temporarily try to assume our two-legged posture.

From a paw, the next stage leading to our feet is that of the monkey swinging through the trees.

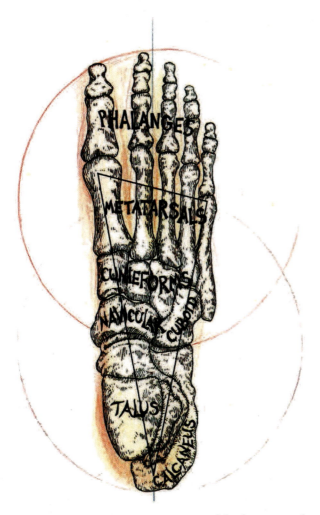

***Figure 1:*** *With the inner geometry of the foot mapped out, all these little bones make sense.*

**The Foot**

*Figure 2: From a house-like structure four points of support, a segmented "ridgepole" of a spine, and the head and tail cantilevered off either end, we see the development toward a tower—all the weights stacked on top of each other with a high center of gravity supported on two tiny triangles.*

The metacarpals, metatarsals and phalangeal bones elongated and separated to give both hands and feet more ability to grasp branches. A monkey will rest on its heel, usually somewhat supported by the arms, but rarely goes in for much sustained upright walking, due to changes yet to come in the pelvis and spine. In the move from an ape foot to a human foot, two small structural changes produced a huge functional difference: the loss of the opposable digits (our toes are all stuck going in pretty much the same direction), and the development of sustained longitudinal arches.

### The foot arch as another secondary curve

When we bring the heel down firmly on the ground and support ourselves above it exclusively on our hind legs, long-term walking and standing become possible. From four single points of support (four paws), we have moved to two tiny triangles of support (Figure 2). (With the center of gravity far above them in the belly—that is why the support has to be so dynamic: we are built like a radio tower, with all the supporting guy wires attaching to the feet.) The points of contact are the ball of the big toe, the ball of the little toe, and the heel.

Although we pay most attention to the medial longitudinal arch—the one that goes from the heel to the ball of the big toe there are actually three arches in the human foot. Between each of the points of contact lies an arch, so there is the familiar medial arch, but also the lateral longitudinal arch between the heel and little toe, and the transverse arch between the balls of the big and little toe (Figure 1). Each of these arches functions like a leaf spring in an old Model T Ford, providing the spring in our step, absorbing ground shock and helping us adapt to uneven surfaces.

Great arches are made, not born. We all arrive on the planet with flat feet. Arches are created in the acts of standing up and walking. In this sense, arches are like the secondary curves of the spine (the lumbar and the cervical), which start out as part of the primary flexion curve and are pulled into their normal adult reverse curvatures by the actions of our muscles. Similarly, the foot arches are pulled into being by the intrinsic muscles of the foot and the more distant action of the calf muscles, which create the tension necessary to reshape the bony relationships.

In fact, we have found it clinically useful to consider the foot arches as part of the primary-secondary wave that makes up human structure. In this expanded view of spinal mechanics, the primary flexion curve is expressed in the cranial, thoracic and sacrococcygeal sections of the spine, and as well in the primary, rounded curve of the heel and toe ball. The secondary curves can be seen in the cervical and lumbar curves, the unlocked knees and the foot arches. Thus, hyperextended knees, a common postural problem, can be seen as a primary-secondary imbalance. Likewise, we may postulate that the fallen or high arch is a similar primary-secondary imbalance. The cervical curve comes into being through picking up our head to look around, especially while in the prone position. The lumbar curve develops by means of the changes in tonus to the spinal erectors and

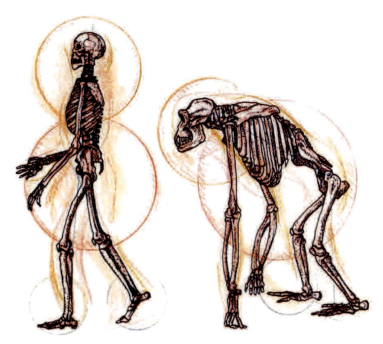

*Figure 3: In two ticks of the evolutionary clock, the same bones and muscles find a totally different architecture, including brand new foot arches.*

psoas muscle induced by crawling. The knee curve should be there when we stand up, and finally the arches develop as we "find our feet" in dealing with the forces of walking.

To understand the arches, let us do a quick review of the basic anatomy involved. We will review the many bones that make up the feet, the joints that allow their movement, a few of the major soft-tissue pieces that support the arches from below, and the calf muscles that provide a crucial lift to the arches from above.

### The bones: as easy as 1, 2, 3 ... 4, 5

In the thigh, the leg is built around one bone, the femur. In the lower leg, there are two bones, the tibia and fibula, wrapped in one tough piece of material composed of both periostea and the interosseous membrane. It is as if God could not be bothered to wrap both bones separately, so he simply wrapped them both with one piece and ran a couple of fingers up between them to seal the two layers together. The interosseous membrane allows more surface area for muscles to attach, and the fiber directions in the wrapping allows us to change the relationship between the two bones (Netter plate 483).

So, from one to two, we expect the next piece of the leg to have three bones, and indeed it does—and this is a crucial element for bodyworkers. The posterior part of the tarsus of the foot, the part that receives and distributes the weight of the body, consists of three bones: the talus, the calcaneus and the navicular. These three join together to form the sub-talar joint, which we will discuss below, and also distribute weight to the two longitudinal arches. For now, get the idea that these three are a unit working together (Netter plates 492, 493, 494).

Now, from three to four. The next layer of bones is clearly a line of four when you look at the foot from above: the three cuneiforms and the cuboid. The three cuneiforms all butt up against the navicular, but the cuboid butts up against the forward end of the calcaneus. Proceeding from this line, we come to the five metatarsals, one for each cuneiform, and two butting up against the cuboid (Figure 1).

If the pattern kept going from here, we could expect six toes, but of course we have made do with five, with three phalangeal bones in each of the smaller toes, but only two in the big one, so that each foot consists of 3+4+5+5+5+4=26 bones (not counting any of the little sesamoid bones like the ones under the first metatarsal).

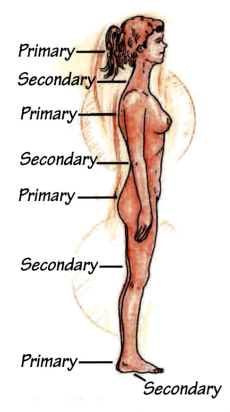

*Figure 4: To achieve this precarious upright posture, we live in a sea of counterbalancing waves.*

**The Foot**  3

## The Joints— alternating hinges and spirals

If we turn around and journey backward along the spaces between the bones, we find that the interphalangeal joints in the toes are all basically hinges. The five joints that make up the ball of the foot are capable of hinging, and they commonly do so in unison when we take a step, but they are also capable of some rotation. You can feel them do it as you roll your weight from the inside to outside of the ball, or try drawing a tiny circle with just your big toe.

The tarso-metatarsal joints (about halfway up the foot) also act like hinges but they have to. Look at the proximal end of the metatarsals and you will see they are squared off, and so incapable of rotation, only of a minor amount of hinging. Also, please note that the second one is more indented into the cuneiforms— the second metatarsal is longer and the second cuneiform shorter—which prevents the front of the foot from shearing when stressed by, say, a bad landing while playing basketball (Figure 1).

The mid-tarsal joints glide only a little, mostly helping the next joint with any real movement: the sub-talar joint (or talo-calcaneo-navicular joint, if you like long words). At least the long word tells you exactly where it is: in this joint the bottom of the talus moves on the calcaneus and the navicular, producing inversion/eversion (sometimes called pronation and supination). Cup the heel in your hand while your free foot does this movement, and you will see now complex this movement is. At the front of this joint, the navicular moves on the rounded head of the talus, which, coupled with the mid-tarsal glide, allows the sole of the foot to point down and in or up and out.

It is important to distinguish the sub-talar joint from the ankle itself (or tibio-talar joint), which is a hinge allowing dorsi- and plantar-flexion only. The top part of the talus, the trochlea, is like a semi-cylinder fitting into the corresponding "crescent wrench" space created by the bottom of the tibia and fibula—the talus is allowed very little side-to-side movement in the ankle joint. So, when you move the toe end of your foot in a big circle, you are combining the dorsi- and plantar-flexion hinge of the ankle joint with the inversion/eversion range of the subtalar joint (Netter plates 484, 495).

So when someone comes into your practice saying, "I have a pronated ankle: you will know to look below the ankle at the balance in the sub-talar complex. And when someone comes in with a sprained ankle, it is the sub-talar joint which has been taken violently into inversion or supination. This will, however, affect the ability to dorsi- and plantar-flex, since several ligaments (and thus the swelling) cross both joints.

**Figure 5:** *The movements of what we often call the ankle actually combine the hinge motion of the tibia-talar joint with the complex spiral of the sub-talar joint.*

Thus we see a pattern in the joints of the foot, generally alternating between a hinge motion or simple motion, and the more complex rotational motion, which allows the foot to adjust both to our movements above it and also to the wide variety of surfaces the earth provides (Figure 5).

## What holds up the arches?

The foot can be described as a tetrahedron, a three-sided pyramid, with the top of the talus in the ankle joint as the top of the pyramid. The heel, the ball of the big toe, and the ball of the little toe are the three points at the base of the pyramid, and there is a springy, shock-absorbing arch between each of these three base points—the medial longitudinal arch, the lateral longitudinal arch and the transverse arch.

Sustaining working arches throughout our lives depends on the balance in three inner elements that support them: the shape of the bones, the plantar ligaments and muscles, and the balanced upward pull from the muscles in the lower leg.

The last two elements can definitely be affected by the manipulative therapist, and though the shapes of the bones are beyond our control, we need to understand them to be able to work with the other two.

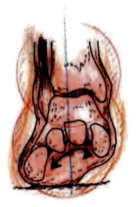

**Figure 6:** *The transverse arch has two distinct portions—the distal at the ball of the foot, and a proximal portion through the tarsal bones.*

### The transverse arch

We need to look at the transverse arch in two places: a transverse cut through the end of the metatarsals, the ball of the foot; and another section further back through the "4" section of the foot—the three cuneiforms and the cuboid (Figure 6).

If we look at the more proximal section first, we see that the three cuneiform bones are all wedge-shaped. (Remember back in Ancient History 101, the Phoenicians, a sea-trading people, kept their accounts on clay tablets with little wedge-shaped marks called "cuneiform" writing?) Because the wedges all point down, the bones themselves make a natural arch, leaning on the cuboid.

Looking at the ends of the metatarsals, we see rounded bones that hardly touch each other. This part of the transverse arch is certainly not held in place by the shapes of the bones, and depends on the integrity of the ligaments and the strength of the muscles, particularly the adductor hallucis, to maintain it.

Practice tip: How can you tell if the anterior portion of a client's transverse arch has fallen? Here is an easy clue: In a normal arch, the calluses under the balls of the foot will be most evident under the balls of the first and the fifth toe. In a foot where this arch has fallen, the callus will be visible or palpable under the second, third or fourth toe. Although this is not a serious problem, the client can often restore this arch to optimal function by strengthening the second element in our set of three: the plantar soft tissues. Tried and true methods include picking up jacks or small pebbles with the toes, or placing a towel or small rug on a slippery floor and scrunching it under the toes inch by inch. With daily perseverance, this can actually change the pattern in a relatively short time (with some dependence, of course, on the general integrity elsewhere in the foot and leg).

### The longitudinal arches

The lateral longitudinal arch consists of the calcaneus, the cuboid, and the fourth and fifth metatarsal. Looked at from the lateral side, the cuboid is not exactly cuboid—it is trapezoidal, with the wider dimension at the top. This allows the cuboid to act exactly like the keystone in a Roman arch. With the calcaneus butting up on one side, and the metatarsals on the other, the cuboid is held in place well off the ground (Netter plates 493, 494 & 495). The lateral arch is thus very stable. Even though many clients have continuous contact of flesh to ground along the outer edge of the foot, that does not mean that there is any problem with the lateral arch. In 20 years of practice, I have seen only a few collapsed lateral arches, and those were only in cases of severe trauma (a head-on collision in a Ferrari, a half-opened parachute) or foot deformity.

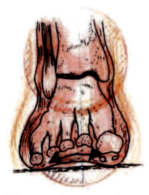

The rest of the bones of the foot are involved in the more troublesome, complicated, weight-bearing medial longitudinal arch. The talus, bearing the weight of the body from above, leads from its rounded forward end into the navicular, which in turn provides the support for the three cuneiforms and their three metatarsals. Thus, the first three toes are associated with the medial arch, while the lateral two little toes are associated with the lateral arch (Figure 1). You can argue that the calcaneus should be considered part of the medial arch, and it certainly seems so on first glance, but the more classic view has the heel bone tied to the lateral arch with the medial arch sitting atop it. Look at how the calcaneus supports the talus and you will see why: The talus sits primarily on the sustentaculum tali, a piece of the calcaneus that juts medially from the main body of the calcaneus. In other words, the heel holds the ankle bone like a waiter holds a tray (Netter plate 494). We will see

**The Foot**

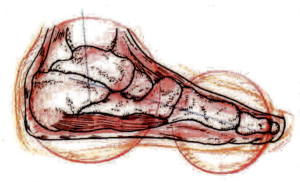

*Figure 7: In the medial arch, the first cuneiform is a weak spot that requires extra support.*

explain the "why" of this awkward arrangement when we look at the muscles that support the arch. If we take a cross section through the medial arch, it is very evident where the weak point is. The first cuneiform is not, like the cuboid, wider at the top than at the bottom. It is slightly the opposite—wider at the bottom than at the top, and is thus prone to slip downward, dropping the medial arch and taking the foundation out of the support for the inner leg.

To summarize, the shapes of the bones are very significant in the support of the proximal portion of the transverse arch, and in the lateral arch, but are less than sterling in the medial arch and the distal portion of the transverse arch.

A dancer friend taught us another terminology for the medial and lateral arch, which, while not technically kosher, is nevertheless accurate in feeling, function and usefulness to the bodyworker: The medial arch construction is the "toe foot," and the lateral arch is the "heel foot." The "toe foot" takes weight from the tibia to the talus and transmits weight through to the first three toes. This will be very evident if you look at an x-ray of a ballet dancer *sur les pointes*. The "heel foot" is the balancer, the outrigger on the canoe, with smaller bones designed not to bear weight so much as balance and distribute it. In this model, the lateral arch is connected to the fibula, which is also a non-weight-bearing force distributor.

### The plantar tissues

The second element necessary sustain our arches are all the soft tissues—muscles, fasciae and ligaments—that span the plantar surface of the foot. Chief among these is the plantar fascia, which goes from the heel bone to each of the five toes (metatarsal heads, actually—with a sixth string to the fifth metatarsal base to support the lateral arch), and acts like the bowstring to the "bow" of bones. Each time the weight comes down on the ankle, the two ends of the bow—the heel and the ball—want to move apart from each other and let the arches collapse. The plantar fascia prevents that, providing a tensional spring (Netter plate 500).

The plantar fascia is merely the first in a set of supports. There are three layers of musculature, thick with fasciae, that travel shorter spans between the plantar surface and the underside of the bones, all of which help support the variable forces coming through the foot in different positions. The long and short plantar ligaments are worth a mention, and the shortest of these supports—the calcaneonavicular, or spring ligament—provides a kind of trampoline for the talus as our weight comes down on top of it (Netter plates 501, 502, 503, 496). Without going into great detail, the variety of these springs and trampolines provide support from below for the vault of the foot, which is, after all, a very dynamic and responsive complex in constant motion, not a static architectural configuration.

Practice tip: Do not neglect the lateral portion of the plantar fascia, which runs from the outer edge of the heel bone over to the fifth metatarsal base (the bump about halfway back on the side of the foot). Lengthening this piece can help (along with re-education) in people who carry their weight on the outside edges of their feet.

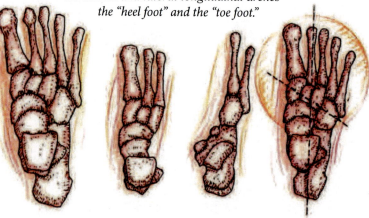

*Figure 8: The foot divides quite neatly into the bones of the medial and lateral longitudinal arches— the "heel foot" and the "toe foot."*

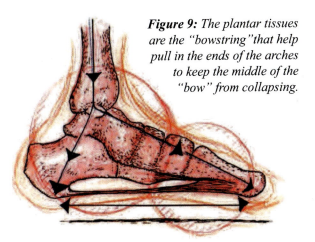

*Figure 9: The plantar tissues are the "bowstring" that help pull in the ends of the arches to keep the middle of the "bow" from collapsing.*

### The calf muscles

The last piece that supports the arches is the balance of upward pulls from specific muscles in the calf. Although this effect has been discounted in some texts, we have found it very useful in practice to restore fallen or painful arches. Perhaps it is the "little bit extra" necessary to put an almost-functioning arch into the "oh, yes" category. In any case, it is the element most amenable to manipulative effort.

The primary support for the medial arch comes from the tibialis anterior (Figure 10), which arises from the anterior compartment just lateral to the tibia, and passes just in front of the ankle joint to attach into the joint between the first cuneiform and first metatarsal bones. (Anatomy books often show the tendon split to attach to the two bones. This reflects the current scientific prejudice that muscles go from bone to bone. In fact, the collagen of the tendon is indistinguishable from and blends into the collagen of the ligamentous joint capsule and the periostea of the two bones.) This junction, as we pointed out above, is exactly the weakest point in the medial arch, so that the strong pull of the tibialis anterior serves as a muscular reinforcement to the health of the medial arch (Netter plates 488, 496).

Just lateral to the tibialis anterior, separated into the lateral compartment of the calf by a fascial intermuscular septum, lies the peroneus longus (Figure 10). The peroneus longus arises from the fibular head and passes down behind the lateral malleolus. Here it dives more deeply, running right under the cuboid in a channel specifically for that purpose, and finally attaching right on the lateral side of the first cuneiform-first metatatarsal joint. Again, the tendon is often shown split between the two bones, though dissection shows that the tendon blends into the ligaments and periostea just as the tibialis anterior does on the other side (Netter plates 490, 491, 496).

Thus we can say (as others have said before us) that the peroneus longus and tibialis anterior form a sling or a stirrup around the bottom of each foot, a continuous band of myofascial tissue attached at either end and in the middle at this tarso-metatarsal joint.

The action of the peroneus longus on the arches is twofold: it supports the lateral arch by lifting up against the cuboid, and it tends to evert or pronate the medial arch. The combined action of the sling is to support the lateral and transverse arches (by squeezing the cuboids and the cuneiform together), but the effect on the medial arch can be positive or negative depending on the balance between its two myofascial components—peroneus and tibialis. For a pronated or fallen medial arch, it is worth testing the relative strength and tonicity of these two muscles, and, using whatever techniques you have in your bag of tricks, relax and loosen the peroneus longus, and wake up and strengthen the tibialis anterior.

The tibialis posterior arises from the deepest portion of the calf behind the interosseous membrane, passing down behind the medial malleolus to grab onto nearly anything it can find under the sole of the foot, like a hand reaching under the tarsum to pull it

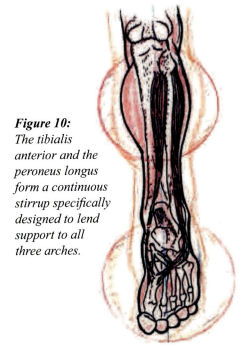

*Figure 10: The tibialis anterior and the peroneus longus form a continuous stirrup specifically designed to lend support to all three arches.*

**The Foot**

up. In this way it supports the medial arch, and interacts with the peroneus longus to produce a kind of fireman's carry for the arches (Netter plates 484, 486, 491 & 496).

The peroneus brevis comes from the lower part of the fibula behind the lateral malleolus to the base of the fifth metatarsal. Its job is to pull the fifth metatarsal firmly into the cuboid, helping to support the lateral arch (Netter plates 490, 491 & 495).

Again, these all work in a dynamic balance as the forces going through the foot are constantly shifting with walking and running. Before we discuss the fifth in our series of arch-supporting muscles, it is also useful to understand the action of the calf muscles on the two ankle joints we talked about: the tibio-talar joint (which does plantar and dorsi-flexion) and the sub-talar joint (which does inversion and eversion).

A full understanding of the action of the muscles of the calf on the foot depends on three factors:

1) How to locate them and work with them depends on their origin and fascial compartment in the calf;
2) Their action on the arches depends on the insertion and the direction the tendon pulls; but
3) Their action on the ankle depends on neither of those two but only on exactly where they pass the ankle.

So in Figure 11 we are looking down at our own right ankle. The tendons surround the ankle at all points of the compass. They are divided into groups by the axes of the two movements available through these two ankle joints. Thus everything to the left of the "north-south" line will be involved in inversion; those to the right could all help with eversion.

All those in front of the "east-west" line are dorsi-flexors; all those behind will be plantar-flexors. So, are tibialis anterior and tibialis posterior antagonists? The answer is, "Yes, they are for dorsi- and plantar-flexion, but they both work together to create inversion." Once this chart is clear to you, you can work on tendencies in foot stance through easing the appropriate muscles. Also, please note that the farther the line of a tendon is from the axial line, the more leverage it has. Thus, the soleus, attaching through the Achilles tendon to the heel, is a very strong plantar flexor, but exerts only a very weak inversion force.

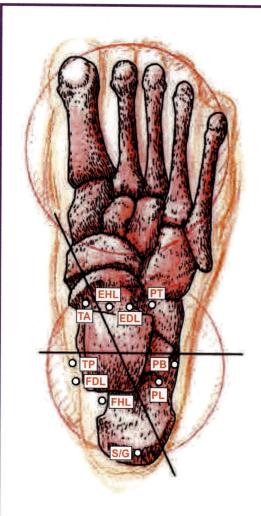

*Figure 11: Ankle tendon chart*
*Knowing where the tendons pass the ankle is key to understanding their actions.*

**TA** - Tibialis Anterior
**EHL** - Extensor Hallucis Longus
**PT** - Peroneus Tertius
**PB** - Peroneus Brevis
**PL** - Peroneus Longus
**S/G** - Soleus/Gastrocnemius
**FHL** - Flexor Hallucis Longus
**FDL** - Flexor Digitorum Longus
**TP** - Tibialis Posterior

### Your left foot

The final of the five muscles stands a bit apart from the others in function. The flexor hallucis longus comes from the deep posterior compartment, from the back of the fibula, but it runs right behind the talus and under the sustentaculum tali—in other words, right underneath the spot where the medial arch rests on the lateral arch. From here, it spans the underside of the foot, inserting into the big toe, which it can thus flex very strongly.

If you take a step, the daily function of this muscle will be very evident. As you step forward with your right foot, the left heel leaves the ground and the toes are hyperextended. When you push off with your left foot, all the toe flexors flex, but the bulk of the work, as you will feel, is done by this flexor hallucis longus. When we contract this muscle, the tendon tightens across the bottom of the foot and provides major bowstring-like support for the medial arch at the moment when it is thrusting the entire weight of the body forward. Looked at from behind, the calcaneus is not really situated under the talus; it is the upward pull of this muscle that really does the job of supporting that inner arch as you walk or run (Netter places 492 & 496).

### Bunion soup

While we are talking about this muscle, we ought to include its role in bunions. The strong pull of the flexor hallucis longus is, as we have said, straight across the medial arch, and straight across the metacarpo phalangeal (ball of the big toe) joint. As the tendon passes under this latter joint, it would be pinned to the floor, at the moment we push off, by our entire body weight. Under this kind of stress, it would not last a lifetime; it would fray, tear and pop. So God put two little sesamoid bones on either side of the tendon to make a little tunnel for the tendon to run through, and the weight is borne primarily by the bones, not the tendon (Netter plates 502, 503, 504 & 505).

The problem comes when accident, heredity —or those beautiful-but-hardly functional pointy-toed Italian shoes—push the big toe toward the little toe. Then the strong pull on the tendon goes through the big toe joint a little bit off center, a little bit toward the middle of the foot. Over time, the continued strong tension on this tendon pulls the tip of the big toe closer and closer to the little toe—sometimes even causing the toes to stack up one way or the other, and pushing the ball of the big toe farther and farther away from its mates—often causing a callosity on the medial side of the joint, and eventually causing the bones themselves to change shape.

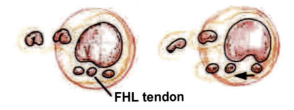

*Figure 12:* Under the ball of the big toe, two little sesamoid bones act like pillars to keep the weight off the flexor hallucis longus tendon. If the tendon moves laterally, it is like Simon, strong enough to pull the pillars out from under the first metatarsal, and the temple crashes into the beginning of a bunion.

Though the problem is relatively easy to understand, it is maddeningly hard to treat manipulatively. If it is caught early, fixing a wad of cotton between the toes can sometimes reset the course of the tendon. If you attempt to treat a middling case, aggressive balancing of all the myofascial units we have discussed, plus a radical change in footwear, can sometimes turn the corner. The problem is that the strength of the pull with each step often overcomes your best efforts within minutes or hours after the completion of treatment. In advanced cases, the wisest course is to simply balance the body as best you can on top of this problem. There is the surgery option, of course, but as I often see the failures in my office, I take a dim view of this course in all but the most painful cases.

### High arches

We often hear about "high" arches, but I have yet to see one in 20 years of practice. What is called a high arch is another pattern entirely. The next time you see or hear about a high arch, have the client sit down with the foot crossed over the other knee so that it can totally relax. Now cover the front part of the foot and look at the arch. Dollars to doughnuts it looks about normal relative to the ankle and calf. Now uncover the front part of the foot and see how the metatarsals bend down to put the balls and toes at a different plane than the heel.

It is not, then, that the arch is too high; it is that the metatarsals are too plantar-flexed (at the tarso-metatarsal joints). When you put this foot on a weight-bearing position on the floor, the balls and the heels are forced into the same plane, and the arch looks high. But the treatment for this pattern lies almost entirely in the deep plantar myofasciae, not in the tendon balance we have been discussing.

### Connections

An analysis like this depends on artificially separating the foot and lower leg from the influences coming from above, but then any analysis involves separating the truthful whole into digestible "lies." If integrating the feet depends on understanding the skeletal arrangement, plantar tissues and calf muscle balance we have outlined here, it also depends on knowing the connections through the rest of the body. But do not let that stop you from applying your vision and technique to changing your clients' connection to the earth. The power of bodywork to reshape the feet and thus change the groundedness, lightness, balance, poise and grace of our clients is not to be underestimated.

Finally, it is very important that our clients notice the changes we have made. When you return to the room after the client is dressed, direct their attention to their feet, and have them notice where their weight is falling. Have them sway a little and feel all the changes the feet make, and see if they feel comfortable in their shoes.

### Speaking of shoes...

Clients often ask about shoes. The choice of shoes is largely a matter of taste and extended comfort, although those two vectors only occasionally intersect. My own solution is to change shoes often, so that my feet keep adapting to different forces, and do not get too fixated. The criteria we suggest are three-fold:

1) Is the sole pliable? A stiff sole, such as in most business shoes, fixes the foot too much.
2) Is the area at the ball of the foot wide enough? The ball of the foot should not be squeezed, except gently in sport shoes.
3) Does your heel sit at right angles to the floor in the shoe? If the shoe tends to angle in or out, buy that shoe only if you want trouble.

The use of arch supports and orthotics is highly individual, and can change over time. Although I do not recommend them in my own practice, some clients benefit from them.

Some years ago when I worked in London, a certain American film director was sent to my practice by his cameraman because he had terrible feet. Like many Yanks with some cash, he had gone down to Saville Row and ordered up some "bespoke" clothes—made to order by England's finest tailors. Because he had bad feet, he also went to Lobb's, where casts were made of his feet and shoes made lovingly around them for a mere £325 a pair (about $1,200 total for the two pair he bought). When he came to me, I saw this trim, athletic man with feet like an arthritic chicken, and so I set to work on them. I thought I had done a pretty good job, but when l finished making notes and throwing the sheet in the hamper and went out to the hall, he was sitting on the chair with his forehead in one hand and this beautiful shoe in the other. The session had widened and lengthened his foot by one full size! I asked him when he had picked up his new shoes. "Yesterday," he groaned.

"Take them back," I urged, "This isn't America. They won't believe they made such a mistake."

And indeed this was true. With characteristic British manners and a "Terribly sorry, sir," a new cast was made and new shoes crafted. To this day, when I am asked if there is a hidden cost to manipulative bodywork, I always tell clients that they may find they want a new pair of shoes. ∎

---

**Reference**
Netter, Frank, M.D., *Atlas of Human Anatomy*. CIBA-Geigy, New Jersey, 1989.

# Chapter 2:
## The Knee and Thigh

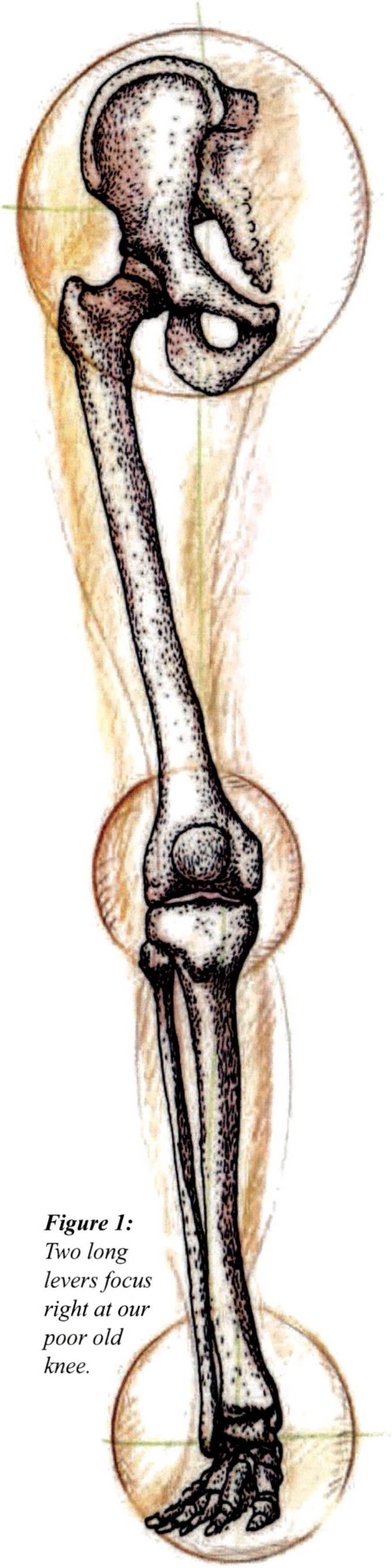

In the first chapter of this book, we dealt with issues in the tissues below the knee in relation to the foot. In this chapter we will concentrate on the movers and de-shakers that cross the knee from above, as well as the joint itself. We recognize the absurdity of dividing the body into parts like this, but practicality demands it.

We have included a few crucial illustrations, but for those who want to refresh their anatomy or improve their three-dimensional grasp of our wonderful soft machine, we include plate references for Frank Netter's Atlas of Human Anatomy, published by CIBA-Geigy, although you can follow along with any good anatomy atlas.

**The knee** is the most common response to the challenge, "Quick, name a joint!" Most people think of it as a simple hinge joint, with the kneecap as "something that keeps the knee from bending backward" (this is based on informal but extensive research by the author). In expression, the knee is a great indicator of grace or awkwardness: the knock-kneed toe-scuffing of the shy introvert, the bowlegged clomp of the inveterate horse rider, the jaunty bandy knees that mark the rolling gait of the sailor. And the knees indicate social and power positions: we fall to our knees to ask for forgiveness, as in "I'm down on my knees for ya, baby," to ask for pardon, for a hand in marriage, or to indicate surrender. The brave brace up at the knee, not allowing them to knock together in fear as Ichabod Crane's did.

In esoteric anatomy, knees store the fear of death, associated with Capricorn and Saturn: the Grim Reaper whose scythe eventually cuts us off at the knees.

In function, the human knee is our principal means of shortening the leg, either to lift the foot to clear a stair or a rock, or to get the center of gravity closer to the ground, as in squatting or sitting. The knee is a marvel of construction that has to deliver more range of motion than the "knees" of four legged animals, while resisting far greater stresses due to all our body weight getting placed on top of it. The knees of horses and dogs, for example, do not have to carry so much relative weight—most of their bulk is carried by

*Figure 1: Two long levers focus right at our poor old knee.*

*Figure 2:*
*The upright posture multiplies the strain on our knees.*

the shoulder girdle and foreleg—so they can be held in a flexed position most of the time, which makes their knees easy to stabilize (Figure 2).

Our upright posture means that the entire weight of the upper body must be handled by the pelvis, and thus by the knee also. To bear this weight successfully, the knee must hang out most of the time in a fully extended, gravity-resisting position, and yet still be able to flex fully enough for us to sit on our heels. Further, our upright position mandates that there be some rotation in our knee that our four-legged friends do not need.

Making a knee that can handle all this safely has been a difficult track to navigate for evolution, so perhaps we can give evolution some help.

Bodywork therapists know the knee as a troublesome locus of easily sustained and difficult-to-heal injuries, infested with ligaments and cartilage we cannot palpate, and surrounded by tissue that is too tough to change. What can we do here?

While we may not be able to reach into the joint (arthroscopic surgery, while not perfect, is getting better and better at that), we hands-on practitioners can affect the knee by playing with the tissues around it, and by adjusting the "guy wires" of the myofascial units above and below the joint. But first let us look at the situation of the knee itself.

The first crucial factor in considering the knee is that it lies smack dab in the middle between the two longest levers in the skeleton—the tibia and the femur. The femur sweeps down and in from the greater trochanter to the two large knobs on its distal end. These condyles have a poor fit with the relatively flat platform on the top of the tibia, which must bear all the weight while the fibula peeks out from under the tibia's wing. The kneecap (patella) floats like an afterthought above the tibia in a groove between the two femoral condyles. Small wonder the knee has to be tough—with long levers, a crooked angle between the bones and a bad fit, it almost seems as if the knee was designed by committee.

The knee has to handle stupendous forces during any vigorous game, or even a strenuous yoga session. Sudden augmentation of the forces on one of these levers or another can result in tearing in or around the joint itself. The wonder is not that the knee is subject to injury, the wonder is that it is not injured more often.

Slower-acting pressures also prey on the knee area. Caused by postural faults like locked knees, knock-knees, or torsions between the tibia and femur, these smaller but relentless forces work away at soft tissues (such as the many ligaments and interlocking cartilages of the knee), which are doing their best to accommodate these forces. The grinding, wearing or straining goes on below the conscious level until one day the camel's back breaks under just one more straw. The small skiing accident or the badly placed

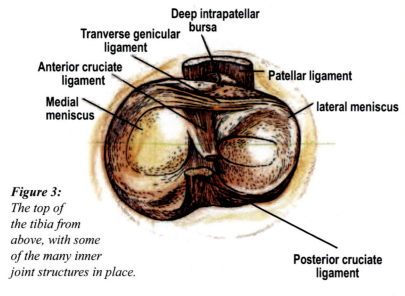

*Figure 3:*
*The top of the tibia from above, with some of the many inner joint structures in place.*

foot are blamed, but the actuality is that long-term strain assured that an accident would happen soon, no matter how careful the person was.

In those types of cases, postural rehabilitation is at least as necessary as the actual recovery from the presenting injury in preventing further degeneration.

Since we know that the ligaments are what primarily limit unwanted movements, and the cartilages absorb most of the shocks, let us look at them for a moment before we move on up to the muscles that make the movements we want in the knee (Figure 3).

## Ligaments and cartilages

It is good to remember that the ligaments we are going to discuss are all thickenings of the unitary fibrous capsule, lest we get the mistaken idea that what is in the books is actually what is going on in the body. The books give a wonderful idea about what is going on, but the map is not the territory. To get a medial collateral ligament, or even the cruciate ligaments, separate from the capsule, you have to use a knife. All the following ligaments, except the lateral collateral ligament, which is truly extra-capsular, are embedded in, and integral to, the entire sleeve, or muff, that fits around the whole joint.

The medial or tibial collateral ligament supports the inside of the knee by running vertically from the femur to the tibia and preventing the femur and the joint from collapsing medially toward the other leg. The lateral collateral ligament does the same for the outside of the knee, except that its lower end attaches to the head of the fibula. Both of these ligaments are further supported by muscles (and their fascia) that run outside of them, which we will look at a little later. These ligaments obviously prevent abduction and adduction of the knee, and permit only a very small transverse motion, which is used by craniosacral and other osteopathically trained practitioners in working with the natural motility of the knee (Netter plates 476-479).

Inside the knee joint (but still part of the complexly folded capsule) are the two cruciate ligaments. The biomechanics of these ligaments are wonderfully complicated, but we will summarize here by saying that they prevent the knee from hyperextending very far beyond a straight knee, and they act in concert to keep the surface of the femur from rolling or sliding off the knee in all its various positions (Figure 4).

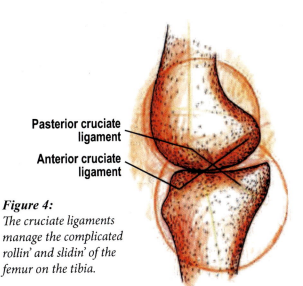

*Figure 4:*
*The cruciate ligaments manage the complicated rollin' and slidin' of the femur on the tibia.*

All of these ligaments are in the fully stretched position when the knee is extended (when the leg is straight). When the knee is flexed, the ligaments are more relaxed and allow the knee to have a moderate degree of rotation. You can feel and see this movement if you are sitting in a chair with your knee flexed, with your weight on the ball of your foot. Now move the heel in and out and you will be rotating the tibia under the femur at the knee. If you then try this standing up, you will still be able to swing the heel back and forth, but not from the knee: these ligaments will restrict you to rotating at the hip. Put your hand on your trochanter and you will feel it rotate in and out, as it will not if you are sitting with the knee flexed.

Even in flexion, and certainly in extension, the ligaments all combine to discourage medial rotation of the tibia on the femur. For this reason, it is much more common to see a misalignment in which the tibia (and thus the foot) faces outward while the kneecap (reflecting the femoral position) faces inward than to see the opposite pattern.

Inside the joint (Figure 3), on either side of the cruciates lie the semilunar cartilages, or menisci, designed to solve the problem of the bad fit between the rounded ends of the femur and the flat top of the tibia. These cartilages need to move to provide this tight fit from extension (where they sit anteriorly in the joint) to flexion (where they sit more posteriorly and squeezed into a tighter curve). Although they are primarily attached at either end of their crescent within the joint, they also have attachments into the tendons of the semimembranosus (medial

**The Knee and Thigh**

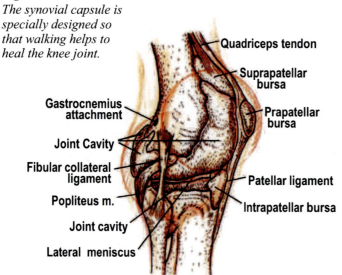

*Figure 5:*
*The synovial capsule is specially designed so that walking helps to heal the knee joint.*

hamstring) and the popliteus muscle (both of which draw the menisci posteriorly), and through the patella to the quadriceps (which draws them anteriorly). These connections open the intriguing possibility of affecting the middle of the joint by means of working the muscles.

The menisci and the ligaments are put into substantial strain by a very common movement that humans need: rotating the body while the foot remains planted. As an example: you are running to make a forehand shot out of a lob that is headed for the baseline. You plant your foot and swing around to send the ball zinging back over the net. You win the point, but your cartilages or ligaments may lose.

These cartilages—like all cartilage in our bodies, including the very thick ones on the end of the tibia and femur—have little or no blood supply. Being avascular, they tend to heal slowly, as they depend for their nutrition and repair on the proteins in the egg-white-like substance that lubricates all our synovial joints. And hereby hangs a wonderful little tale of the ingenuity of the body's design (Figure 5).

The synovial capsule of the knee is hemmed in on either side by the collateral ligaments, but it extends forward under the patella, to lubricate its travel, and backward between the femoral condyles and the heads of the gastrocnemius muscle that come from the heel. The ingenious part here is that as you put your foot out to take a walk, the knee straightens as the quadriceps tightens, pushing the patella against the underlying fluid, squeezing it back to the part of the capsule under the gastrocnemius. Later in the very same step, as you push off the ground with your toes, you contract the gastrocnemius, squeezing the fluid back past the cartilages—all of them—so that extra fluid rests again under the patella, awaiting your next step. This simple and efficient arrangement ensures that the cartilages are bathed with restorative nourishment every time you take a step—but, of course, you must get up and do it. Walking provides a better cartilage bath than running, and of course puts a lot less pressure on the cartilages as well (Netter plate 480).

Having looked a bit at the inside of the joint, let us return to more familiar territory for the massage therapist: the muscles that cross the joint to move it and stabilize it.

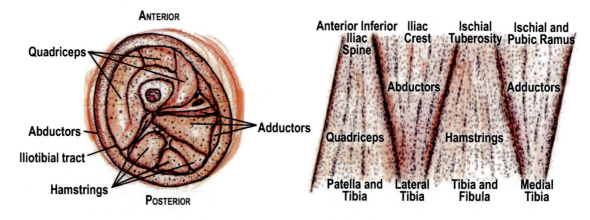

*Figure 6:* *This mid-thigh cross-section shows the dominance of the quadriceps group, while the diagram to the upper-right shows the structural layout of the thigh muscles.*

14  Body³: A Therapist's Anatomy Reader

### The muscles' role

Functionally, the muscles above the knee divide nearly into four groups: the abductors—the three gluteals and the tensor fasciae latae; the adductors, of which only the gracilis crosses the knee; the quadriceps, which act to extend the knee; and the hamstrings, the knee flexors (Figure 6). Little sartorius sits in a fascial plane all its own—the superficial plane of the whole fascia latae of the thigh—and assists in flexion and lateral rotation of the knee, though its main function is to serve and protect the femoral neurovascular bundle that runs underneath it between the quadriceps and adductors (Netter plates 462-465, 475).

Structurally, the vastii muscles of the quadriceps are very greedy, grabbing for themselves nearly the whole shaft of the femur, leaving the others to vie for space on the thin linea aspera (rough line) on the back of the femur, or giving up and looking for someplace to attach on the pelvis (Figure 6). These muscles, obviously, will affect the movements at the hip as well—but we will leave that discussion for another time, and concentrate for now on their effect on the knee.

If we were to unwrap these muscles from the bone, we find that the groups alternate between being wide at the bottom and narrow at the top, with the next group being narrow at the bottom and wide at the top (Figure 6). We will begin by looking at the two groups that are wide at the hip end and narrow at the knee end, both of which act to stabilize the knee joint more than moving it.

Of the abductor group, only three participate with the knee. The tensor fasciae latae, the upper fibers of the gluteus maximus, and the gluteus medius (from inside) all attach to the iliotibial tract, a strong fascial band that starts from the entire iliac crest, blends with these three muscles, and cups the greater trochanter in a sling as it passes down over the vastus lateralis to attach to the lateral tibial condyle below the knee (Netter plate 464).

On its way, the iliotibial tract passes near the lateral collateral ligament, so that all these muscles, working through the tract, can be helpful in keeping the knee from breaking outward laterally. Even the vastus lateralis can help, because when it contracts, it bunches up and pushes out against the iliotibial tract, keeping it right and stabilizing the joint.

On the inside of the knee, the medial collateral ligament is covered over and similarly supported by a three-tendon complex, which looked to some dissactor like a goose's foot when he pulled on it, and hence its name, pes anserinus. Although all three tendons help support the joint, they all go to very different places. The most anterior tendon, the

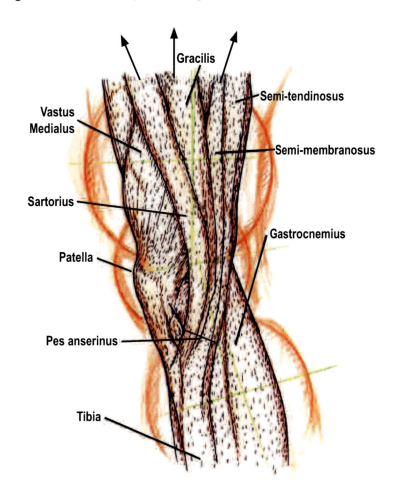

**Figure 7:** *The inside of the knee is stabilized to the very front, the bottom, and the very back of the pelvis.*

**The Knee and Thigh**

sartorius, goes up along the groove between the quadriceps and adductor group, attaching to the anterior superior iliac spine, the most forward part of the pelvis. The middle tendon, the gracilis, goes straight up to the pelvic ramus, the most inferior part of the pelvis. The posterior tendon is one of the hamstrings, the semitendinosus, and it travels up the back of the leg to the ischial tuberosity, one of the most posterior points on the pelvis. Thus the inside of the knee can be stabilized from all points of the pelvis. One only has to think of a skater doing a sustained arabesque on one skate to see the usefulness of this arrangement (Netter plane 476) (Figure 7).

All of these medial and lateral muscles that we have designated as stabilizers can get involved in knee flexion once the movement is under way, and can also help produce the rotation of the tibia on the femur that is possible when the knee is flexed.

Now we will consider the muscles that principally produce the strong flexion and extension of the knee that we use so much in running, kicking, walking and swimming.

The quadriceps may have "four heads," but it has only one foot. They start proximally from a narrow purchase on the anterior pelvis and the shaft of the femur, getting bulkier and more demanding as they move down the femur. Then all of their motive power is focused through the kneecap, which floats in their combined tendon and acts as a pulley to give the muscle more leverage on the knee. The patella is firmly attached to the tibial tuberosity on the front of the tibia, and can be considered a parallel structure to the olecranon (tip of the elbow) of the ulna, with the triceps as a parallel to the quadriceps. (Hold your arm out in front of your shoulder with your forearm and hand hanging down in front of your chest and you will immediately see the parallel.)

These muscles, which are nearly three times as strong as the hamstrings, act powerfully to extend the knee, and are often held tightly when there is a habitual posture of 'locked knees,' or hyperextension. They can also help stabilize the knee as well as extend it through the action of the two patellar retinacula that run like a bridle down and out from the patella to the sides of the knee joint.

The hamstrings, the principal flexors of the knee, are also powerful but highly tendinous muscles, and there are three and one-half of them.

Two of the three—the semitendinosus and the semimembranosus—arise from the ischial tuberosity (your sitting bone) and pass down to the medial side of the knee. The third, the biceps femoris, comes from the back side of the ischial tuberosity and goes to the lateral part of the leg, helping to reinforce the lateral collateral ligament. These muscles are also used to produce the rotation available with a flexed knee—the two "semis" producing medial rotation of the tibia, while the biceps produces lateral rotation (Netter plate 465).

The lower attachment of the biceps femoris—the fibular head just outside the lateral collateral ligament—puts it in a unique position vis-a-vis the fibula. The poor fibula has eight muscles that pull down on it—the peroneals and the soleus to name a few—and it is tucked under the tibia where it has no real "hook" to prevent it from falling. Thank goodness the biceps is pulling up on it, hooking the fibula directly to the sacrum (by means of the sacroruberous ligament, the superficial part of which is an extension of the biceps femoris).

But what about "three and one-half" muscles? The "fourth hamstring" has been neglected by bodyworkers, and it should not be. The short head of the biceps arises from the lower two-thirds of the linea aspera of the femur, and joins the tendon of the rest of the biceps. Thus this smaller muscle crosses only the knee joint, whereas the rest of the hamstrings cross both knee and hip. But look just across the linea aspera and see what leads up to the short head of biceps: the middle section of adductor magnus. These two muscles—adductor magnus and the short head of the biceps—act together as a deep fourth hamstring that often restricts forward bending in the way the rest of the hamstrings do (Figure 8). So in doing your hamstring work, extend your eyes and hands around to the inside of the thigh, and see if you do not get some joy from working on the adductor-short head complex (Netter plate 465).

### Everything's connected

I hope that this tour around the knee has been helpful in giving you some new ideas and the three-dimensional feel that Body$^3$ is aspiring to achieve. But let us not forget that however accurate we can get with our anatomy, we must always leave room for the unexplainable connection. If you will permit a story:

*Figure 8:* *The middle part of the adductor magnus and the short head of the biceps are usefully considered as "the fourth hamsrtring." (See also Figure 6)*

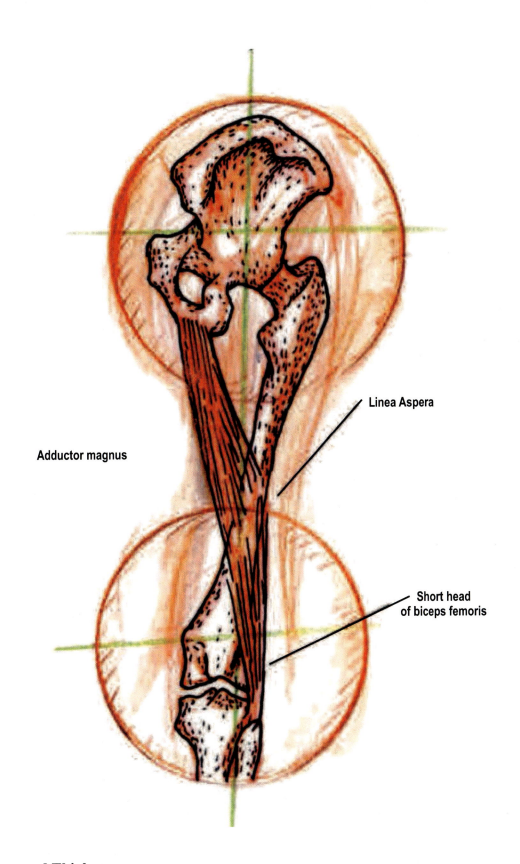

**The Knee and Thigh** 17

Early in my career as a Rolfing® practitioner, I was visited by an older woman of great dignity, a former opera diva. She would undress in the bathroom, and emerge wrapped in a sheet (still in her underwear, as is the custom during a Rolfing session), with a large beehive hairdo coming out of one end and small patent leather shoes peeking out the other. She would leave her shoes by the table, but retain the sheet, so that I was compelled to do all my work by feel only—no visual analysis possible.

She had come because she had worn all the cartilage off the back of her kneecap, and the bone rubbing on bone was very painful when she climbed stairs and when she reflexively bent her legs while sleeping. Rolfing structural integration was a last-ditch effort before surgery.

It was immediately evident to me what was going on: her quadriceps were so tight that it rubbed the back of the patella hard against the femur—so hard that, in her advancing years, the cartilage had all been worn away faster than it could be replaced. So any hope of a solution lay in relaxing the quadriceps.

With this in mind I preceded through the 10-session protocol that characterizes the Rolfing approach, but in every session I tucked in work on the quads. To no avail. They remained solidly contracted, no matter how hard or how skillfully I worked. Frustrated, I moved outward, thinking that perhaps the solution lay in the antagonists (the hamstrings) or the counter-antagonists in the calf, so I worked with all of these quite thoroughly as well.

She was quite pleased with what was going on—her migraines improved and she was feeling "perky" again and in good humor, but, "My knees, young man, when are you going to do something about my knees?"

We came to the session when, in the normal course of Rolfing events, I would work on her neck and head. This sometimes includes work in the mouth, and I had no idea whether this woman of another generation would accept this idea, but it was, "Oh, well, if that is what you do, go right ahead." On inspection, her palate was like a Gothic cathedral, high and arched. Since a high palate is sometimes connected with migraines, and since she was not singing professionally anymore, I began to work the palate toward a more normal configuration. "You know, I can feel that in my knee," she said, but I paid little attention. Focused as I was on maintaining my professional cool, I continued to the other side (which she also felt in her knee) and went on to complete the session. It was the only session where I did not go near her knees.

She called me up the next morning: "Young man, you've done it!" The pain, while not gone, was much reduced. Ida Rolf was still alive at this time, and I risked calling her up. "Dr. Rolf," I ventured a play on one of our frequent classroom jokes, "I have found the naso-patellar ligament."

But of course there is no naso-patellar ligament, and as we discussed what had gone on, we came jointly to the theory that perhaps, during voice training, this woman had somehow associated her singing, perhaps the high notes which bounce off the palate, with a reflex tightening of the quads. The reflex somehow required contact with the nerves in the palate to be released. Well, it is a hypothesis, at least, but I really have no idea how it worked. And work it did, for I heard through a mutual friend that she was still singing the Rolfing techniques praises some seven years later. I thank my guiding angels and commend the idea to you that everything is connected to everything else, and sometimes the connections are more mysterious than we can even imagine. ∎

# Chapter 3:
# Fans of the Hip Joint

**Do these guys get hip replacements at the same rate we do?**

**In the last chapter we considered the forces and the muscles at play around the knee joint. This time, we are going to take a particular and slightly eccentric look at the mighty array of muscles around the immensely stronger hip joint.**

**For those who want to refresh or deepen their visual grasp of this material, we include references to Frank Netter's Atlas of Human Anatomy, published by CIBA-Geigy, although you can follow along with any good anatomy atlas.**

Because of the deeply cupped way this ball-and-socket joint fits together, and the strength of the muscles around it, the effects of trauma or injury to this part of the body often get pushed into the knee or the lower back, rather than showing up directly in the hip. Likewise, postural imbalances in the hip tend to force problems or pain to occur either north or south of this super-strong joint. Ida Rolf calls the hip "the joint that determines symmetry," because small tilts, twists or body "attitudes" here can lead to painful compensations almost anywhere else. The lesson for us? We need to look at the functional health of the hip joint in all our clients, not just those who complain about that area.

The joint is also subject to slow wear and tear, as the number of late-in-life hip replacements attests. Does this indicate a widespread misuse of the hip joint in the Western world—when our hip joint does not last as long as we do? Or is it just our lot as humans for having stood up and put more of our weight on the hip, where four-legged creatures put more of their weight on the shoulder girdle? Should we be sitting less and squatting more? Exercising more or exercising less? Getting more massages maybe, so that tight muscles are not pulling the irreplaceable cartilaginous surfaces so firmly together? (Both sedentary and overactive folks often seem in our experience to be candidates for hip replacements. Is there a movement repatterning or preventative exercise regime that would save these hips?)

Our thesis in this chapter is this: No matter what the activity level of the hip you are working on, the working life of that hip depends on an even balance of tone in the 30 or so "myofascial units" (muscles) arranged around the femur and the hip bone. In school we tend to study the hip muscles as individuals or in small groups like the gluteals or lateral rotators. But who can remember all their Latin names, exact attachments and multiple functions when we are out there actually working on someone's tight butt? And yet we want to be specifically helpful.

There is a solution. Here we will zoom above these individual trees for a look at the forest: the hip muscles are (in fact, as opposed to in school) arranged around the joint in three large, sweeping and interconnected fans—and we can balance the hip joint by balancing within and among these fans. Our goal in this chapter is to corral this seemingly incomprehensible gaggle of muscles, through this metaphor of a fan, into an easily understood continuum.

We will first examine briefly the structure of the joint itself, and then take on the part we hands-on therapists can play with to enhance hip health and balance: the musculature around the hip. So, fans of the hip joint, let's go look at the fans of the hip joint.

### First, the bones

The hip joint is the classic ball-and-socket joint. The shaft of the femur sweeps up from the knee to the two knobbly trochanters, the greater provides attachment for the gluteals, the lesser for the iliopsoas. From the top of the shaft, the neck of the femur angles gracefully in toward the hip, giving the femur its characteristic "seven" shape, with the nearly perfect ball-peen hammer of the head on its end. The socket, or acetabulum (it comes from the Latin meaning "vinegar cup"), is formed at the intersection of three bones: the illium, which constutates the whole superior portion of the hip bone; the ischium, which includes our sitting bones; and the pubis (you know where that is). These three bones have fused into one by the time a baby starts to walk, but because they begin as three separate bones, their names persist in the adult body—e.g. iliac crest, ischial tuberosity, pubic symphysis.

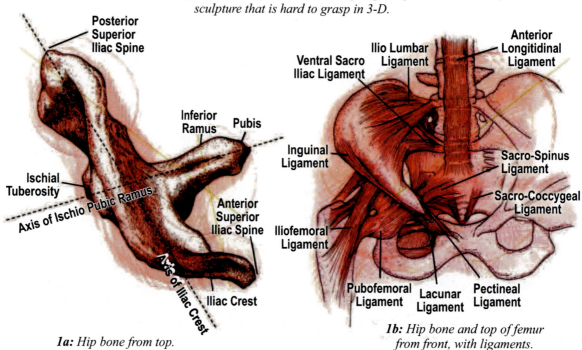

*Figure 1:* The hip bone is an intriguing bit of sculpture that is hard to grasp in 3-D.

*1a:* Hip bone from top.

*1b:* Hip bone and top of femur from front, with ligaments.

Although the Latin name for the fused bones is *os inominata*, we are sticking with "hip bone" here (Netter plate 457).

The hip bone is a difficult one to visualize in three dimensions. It is worthwhile to find a skeleton and hold the hip bone in your hands for a while to get a true sense of its shape. Since we are trapped in two dimensions between the pages of this magazine, we commend the idea to you that each hip bone is like a twisted figure-eight, or a two-blade propeller.

The mid-point, or axis, of the propeller is right where the femur sits into the acetabulum. One blade reaches up—that is the iliac portion, with the iliac crest as the tip of the blade. The other reaches down from the acetabulum to the ischial and pubic ramus, the tip of the second blade. These blades, as we will see, provide the attachment points for all these muscles that cross and move the hip.

In addition to having two blades and an axis, the blades are also twisted like a propeller's. Look down from the top on a single hip bone. The iliac crest is angled at 45 degrees, moving out from the spine and widening at the front. The ramus at the bottom of the pelvis is wide at the back, coming medially as it comes forward until it meets its opposite number at the pubic symphysis. Though the resemblance is intriguing, it is not being suggested here that the hip bone acts like a propeller; we offer this image only as an easy way to help visualize the three-dimensional complexity of the two hip bones.

Besides being joined by a fibrocartilage disc at the pubic symphysis, each hip is joined to the sacrum at the left and right sacroiliac joint. Since the majority of muscles we will discuss in this issue cross only the hip joint, we will save our discussion of the complicated sacroiliac joint, and the effect of the psoas and piriformis muscles on this joint, for the next issue.

### Then, the ligaments

The femur is joined to the hip bone by a set of

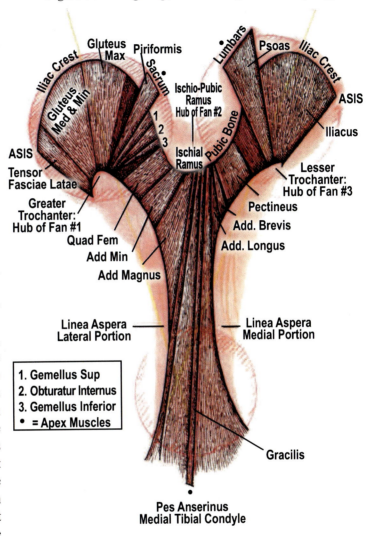

*Figure 2:* This figure shows all the fan muscles from one hip joint in diagrammatic form. The ASIS on the left side of the diagram is the same ASIS as on the right. To get a feel of how it works in 3-D, mentally wrap it all the way aroumd the bones in Figure 6 (except that Figure 6 is the right hip, and this diagram is the left hip).

ligaments that wind around the neck of the femur like a twisted towel. The towel is twisted in such a way that it is unwound as we flex the joint, and wound tighter as we try to hyperextend the joint. Thus, if you lean back to look at the sky with your knees straight, or lift the front of your pelvis away from the leg, you soon find that your attempt to go backward is stopped by these ligaments (and maybe the hip flexors too; have you been doing your stretching?)

Likewise, if you stand on one leg and put the other foot way back behind you in a lunge, or warrior pose, you will find that you are stretching

**Fans of the Hip Joint**

the groin: the muscles, and eventually the ligaments, that run right in front of the hip joint. If we take a very large step, we are likely to have to arch the lower back into a swayback or lordosis to achieve this long stride, again because hip hyperextension is limited by these ligaments. In full extension, these ligaments also limit lateral rotation, which saves us from dislocating the ball out of the relatively shallow front of the socket (Netter plate 458).

### And finally, the muscles

In spite of the ligamentous restrictions, the hip joint is quite mobile through many degrees of circumduction and rotation. Because of the ball-and-socket arrangement with its slick cartilage and synovial lubricant, it is also very slippery and easily movable. Thus it is necessary to have muscles coming from every direction to provide the stability and control necessary to balance the entire upper body, as well as the precision of movement to this all-important joint. And we would further expect these muscles to be triangular in shape, as triangular muscles provide precise control across a wide set of angles. (Look at how many triangular muscles surround the highly movable shoulder: traps, lats, pects, and delts, for instance.)

In fact, the hip sports not only a preponderance of triangular muscles, but these muscles are further arranged in a series of triangular fans, which interconnect with and counterbalance each other. It is simple once you see it: understand these fans and you understand how to balance the hip joint. Each of these fans has an axis, or a hub, where several muscles insert close together. Each has an outer edge, or a rim, where the same muscles attach along a longer line. Each of the fans has an "apex" muscle—a muscle about in the middle of each fan that goes "farther" than the other ones in terms of joints crossed.

Each of these muscular fans performs a variety of functions—flexion, abduction, rotation, etc., but they all work cooperatively together, or should, at least, to achieve both mobility and stability. Getting this complex in balance is part of our job, and the goal of any good stretching, exercise or rehabilitation program. Taken altogether, the three fans comprise about 20 muscles, depending on how you count them, so we will try to break them down into digestible mouthfuls.

### The trochanteric fan

This fan includes:
Tensor fasciae latae
Gluteus minimus
Gluteus medius
Gluteus maximus, superior fibers
Apex: Piriformis
Superior gemellus
Obturator internus
Inferior gemellus
Obturator externus
Transition: Quadratus femoris

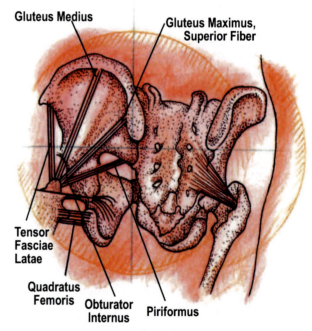

**Figure 3:** *The trochanteric fan spreads around the greater trochanter from the ASIS to the Ischial Tuberosity.*

The fans are named for their hub, or axis, and the axis of the first fan is the greater trochanter, the large knob of bone on the outside of the thigh a couple of inches below the hip. The rim is the iliac crest, running from the anterior superior iliac spine (ASIS) around to the lateral edge of the sacrum, down the sacrotuberous ligament and onto the ischial tuberosity (IT) (Netter plate 461).

You are familiar with the muscles of this fan as the abductor group and the lateral rotators, but we are going to try to persuade you to see these as parts of an integrated whole that play a dual role: they all help move the femur in the socket when that is what is required.

For instance, when we stroke off a skate or a rollerblade, these muscles are used in a smooth continuum (which is why these sports are so good at toning our buns). They stabilize the hip bone (and thus the whole upper body) on the leg when we are standing or sitting, or whenever we are in a posture that requires the lower body to be a stationary platform for movements of the upper body.

The functional role is perhaps more important to sports massage and rehabilitative therapists. The postural role—the habitual tone of these muscles in standing or sitting—is of great interest to structural bodyworkers.

To trace this first fan, begin with the front of the abductor group: the tensor fasciae latae (TFL), which joins the outside edge of the ASIS to the front face of the greater trochanter (and of course to the iliotibial band). Because of its forward position the TFL can function as a flexor and medial rotator, as well as an abductor (Netter plates 464-465).

Continue with the gluteus medius and minimus that go to the outside of the top of the trochanter, and act to abduct and to medially or laterally rotate, depending on which part of the muscle is used (just like the deltoid in the shoulder).

It is useful to look at these functions in both functional and postural ways. We will explain it fully here, then bring it up briefly, later, with some other muscles. But doing a little analysis like this is useful with nearly every muscle in the body. The gluteals perform abduction, and are therefore useful when we want to kick someone walking beside us on the street. Since that situation hopefully does not come up too often, their postural function is much more common, and occurs with every step you take.

Stand up and put your fingers firmly into the gluteals—out at the side, below your belt but above your pocket—and begin to walk. The muscles on either side under your hand alternately contract and loosen. Which side tightens, the leg you are standing on or the leg you are swinging forward?

If you are somewhere near normal, the abductors will tighten on the side where your weight is supported. As we walk, our supporting leg shifts from right to left, but the center of gravity in our lower belly does not shift nearly so much. Thus, the tendency would be for the upper body to fall away from the supporting leg, sliding on that slippery ball and socket.

### Palpatory Certainty - The piriformis, obturator internus, quadratus femoris

Most of the muscles in this first trochanteric fan are familiar and easily found by most massage therapists. In our teaching experience, the last three muscles named above are often not worked on specifically, because, since they are under the gluteus maximus , they are not always easy to feel clearly. This is a shame, because each of these muscles is so important to the structural balance of the pelvis. So here are fail-safe instructions on how to find these three muscles and be sure you are working on them, even if you cannot feel any guitar string twang under your fingers (all these can best be found with the client lying face-down).

### Piriformis:

First, find the top of the trochanter as specifically as you can. Press in a bit, sometimes the amount of flesh around the hip can fool you. Leave one finger there, pressed down against the superior aspect.

With your other hand, put a thumb and index finger along the body's midline at the top and bottom of the sacrum (for reasons of client privacy, do not include the tail bone). The best place to find the piriformis is in the center of the triangle made by your three fingers. Too close to the sacrum (medial) and you will not feel it, for the muscle runs deep to the sacrum. Too close to the trochanter (lateral) and the little stringy tendon disappears with all the others headed for the trochanter. If you strum across the fibers of the muscle, you will often feel it twanging, and even if you do not, you can be sure you are working on it through the gluteus.

### Obturator internus:

Find the bottom of the ischial tuberosity (IT). With your fingers firmly touching the bone, walk your fingers up the bone straight towards the head. You will go up the "mountain" of the IT and down into a valley" on the superior side of the IT. The softer part in this shallow valley is the obturator internus as it turns the corner from the internal part of the pelvis around the back of the IT headed for the trochanteric fossa of the femur. As you go

**Fans of the Hip Joint**

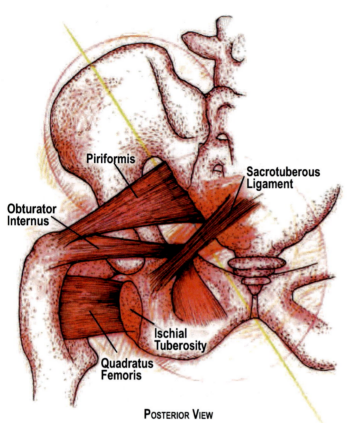

**Figure 4:** *Lateral rotators from Platzer: The small size of these deep hip muscles belies their importance.*

straight out laterally from here, you can often follow the tendon by twanging up and down over the fibers, again through the gluteus maximus. You may or may not be able to distinguish one or two other separate tendons, which would be the gemellus superior and inferior accompanying the obturator.

### Quadratus femoris:

Again, find the IT. Go just lateral to the lower aspect of the IT onto the back lower part of the trochanter. Strum up and down, but do not expect a twang—in most people this quadrate muscle feels like a little mound on the back side of the trochanter. Do not go lower than the lower aspect of the IT, or you will find yourself palpating the attachment of gluteus maximus instead.

### The adductors

In finding your way around the confusing territory of the inner thigh, try this mnemonic: First have your client lie on their side with the topside hip flexed so that the inner side of the lying-on-the-table leg is accessible. Now put your same hand on that thigh (i.e. your left hand on their left thigh or vice versa) with your middle finger running about straight up and down the axis of their leg, and your fingers lightly spread. With allowances for large thighs and small hands or the reverse, you will find that your thumb falls on the line of the satorius, that thin little muscle that covers the sulcus between the quadriceps and adductors.

Your index finger can easily find the tendonous bulk of the adductor longus. Your middle finger will then lie on the thin vertical line of the gracilis, your ring finger on the adductor magnus, and your little finger makes it all the way over to the hamstrings.

Thus the gluteals' main function is to contract to prevent that "adduction" that gravity would otherwise perform on us. That postural contraction is so automatic with us that it is difficult to take a step without contracting them. If you manage to do it, you will find yourself having to adopt a strange gait—either a "dropped hip" gait or throwing your weight from leg to leg—common to those with cerebral palsy or some other disease that robs someone of the unnoticed but essential postural role of the gluteals.

We can include the upper fibers of the gluteus maximus in this fan, as they travel from the posterior portion of the iliac crest to the back outside of the trochanter, but the lower fibers, from the sacrum and sacrotuberous ligament, go so far down the shaft of the femur that they really can not be thought of as part of the trochanteric fan, but more as a separate extensor muscle for running.

Right next to the posterior edge of the gluteus medius, and deep to the gluteus maximus, comes the next muscle in our fan series—usually thought of as a member of another group, but in actual function part of this trochanteric fan continuum: the piriformis.

The piriformis comes from the anterior surface of the sacrum, deep within the body, and, coming out through the same opening as the sciatic nerve, goes to the very inside top of the greater trochanter. It is usually listed as one of the lateral rotators, but this is so far from its real function that we will devote the entire next Body[3] chapter to the piriformis and its friend and competitor, the psoas (Netter plates 473 & 466).

For now, we will content ourselves by noting that the piriformis, located about halfway through this first fan, is the apex muscle of this fan. Even though the piriformis is not that long if measured by a ruler, it is "longer" than the other muscles because it crosses not only the hip joint but also the sacroiliac joint.

With this slight bow to the most holy piriformis, we keep going around our fan to the obturator internus and its two friends, gemellus superior and inferior. Since the tendons of these three often cluster together into one, we can consider them together. Of the three, the obturator is by far the strongest, and also the most important because, as we will learn in more detail next time around, it goes around the corner of the ischium into the inside of the pelvis and has a strong connection to the pelvic floor. For now, we note that these three are tied to the inside back of trochanter and thus very much part of our fan.

The next muscle is the last of this first fan and the first muscle of the next fan, a transitional point of fixation between the one fan and the other. The quadratus femoris is a small square of muscle covering the small distance from the outside of the ischial tuberosity to the back side of the trochanter. God uses square muscles where she needs stability.

Although this muscle is listed in the group of lateral rotators, once again its main function is not to turn the femur, but to stabilize the pelvis on the femur, preventing the hip from falling into flexion —and preventing the joint between these two fans from being too loose.

In fact, this whole fan around the greater trochanter provides great stability against the tendency of the hip to adduct and flex from the fully extended position required by upright standing. Although the so-called lateral rotators are capable of laterally rotating the femur, they actually function much more as extensors of the hip. They keep the pelvis (and thus the spine and head) from falling forward into a four-legged position. Balance in this fan is thus a hallmark of easy upright posture.

There is one other muscle usually included in the lateral rotator group. The obturator externus lies deep to the quadratus femoris, starting from the deep back of the trochanter and passing under the

*Figure 5:* Diagram of the ramic fan. A view of the ramic fan shows how the adductors join the two trochanters by way of the knee.

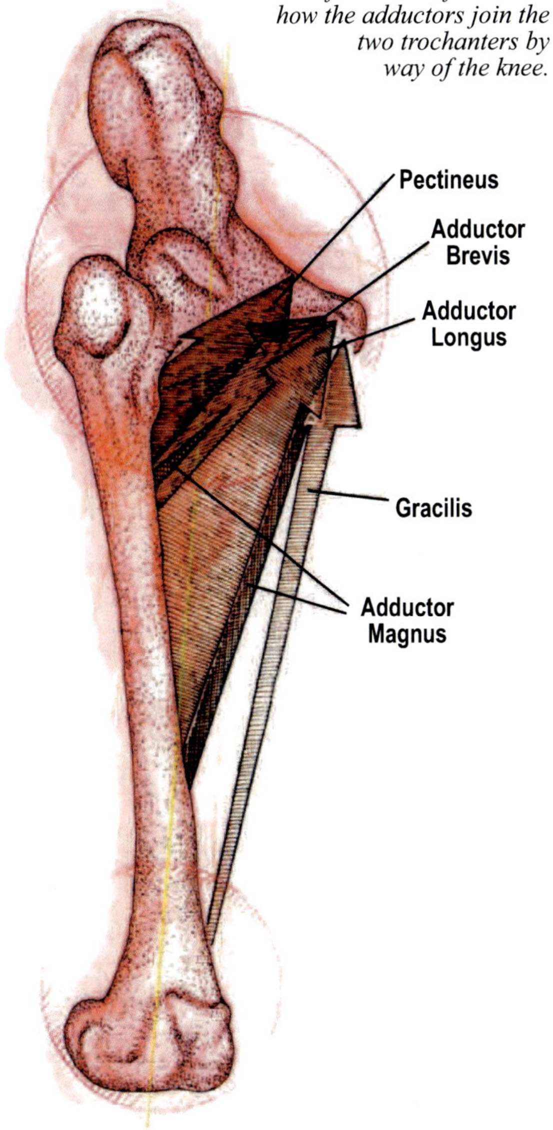

- Pectineus
- Adductor Brevis
- Adductor Longus
- Gracilis
- Adductor Magnus

neck of the femur to the outside face of the lower "propeller blade" of the hip bone. It is very hard to feel directly. Having ignored this muscle for many years, this practitioner is now very hot on its functional importance. It is not really part of this fan, nor is it primarily a lateral rotator, but it connects inside to outside through the complicated obturator membrane. The gory details are beyond the scope of this chapter, but think of this muscle as a kind of trampoline for the upper body's weight on the hip joint (Netter 463 & 465).

It is so hard to find an accurate rendering of this muscle in the anatomy atlases, which are, after all, taken from dead and supine corpses. This muscle comes into its own only in a living, standing

**Fans of the Hip Joint**

body. The best way to say this that we have found to date—and this is by no means the only gem in these excellent resources for massage therapists—is in *The Video Atlas of Human Anatomy* by Robert Acland, M.D.

### The ramic fan
This fan includes:
Transition: Quadratus femoris
Adductor minimus
Adductor magnus, middle part
Adductor magnus, lower part
Apex: Gracilis
Add longus
Adductor brevis
Transition: Pectineus

The second fan is a little harder to see, it has a confusing set of functions, and it lies in an area with a degree of taboo about it. So listen up, because understanding this fan could radically simplify and clarify your work on the inner thigh.

The second fan is called the Ramic fan because its hub or axis is the bone that runs along the bottom of the pelvis from the IT to the pubic symphysis, known as the ischial and pubic ramus—but let us just call it the ramus (meaning "branch") for short.

If the hub is the ramus, the rim of this fan is the linea aspera, the rough line that sweeps down the posterior shaft of the femur from below the trochanters to the medial epicondyle above the knee. The rest of the shaft of the femur—the outside, anterior and medial portions—is taken up by the strong and greedy quadriceps, leaving all the adductors and the short head of the biceps to scramble for attachment space along this fairly thin line that is (remember!) on the back of the femur, not the medial edge. (Netter plate 461)

"Wait a minute," you may be saying, "the first fan looked like a fan, with a hub and a sweeping rim. The linea aspera does not sweep around like the rim of a fan."

"Ah," I will tell you, "this sneaky little fan sweeps down one side of the linea aspera and up the other. Maybe it looks a little more like a feather or a folded-up fan, but it keeps with the idea of these three fans that stabilize the hip joint. Watch. From the greater trochanter, we will go down the back side (literally the lateral side) of the linea aspera, and up the front (or medial) side to the lesser trochanter."

The second fan begins right where the first fan left off: the quadratus femoris. The distal attachment of the quadratus defines the beginning of the linea aspera, which continues downward from the greater trochanter to the distal attachment of adductor minimus. The adductor minimus is a part of the adductor magus, which is a muscle as huge as its name. This anatomist would prefer that it be broken down into three muscles to define its differing parts and functions, but for now let us just call them the top, middle and bottom parts. The adductor minimus, when it is separated from the rest of the muscle, is the top part. (Netter plate 463)

All three parts originate from the underside (OK, OK, the inferior aspect) of the IT, as opposed to the hamstrings which attach to the back side of the IT. Thus the adductor magnus is as far posterior on the ramus as we can get, and we will be working our way forward from here.

The difference between the hamstring and adductor magnus tendons can be distinguished by doing the following: have the client lie on his or her side, with the top leg flexed at the hip and with the knee lying on a pillow—this gives you access to their inner thigh. Find the IT and feel the tendonous attachments coming off from it. Put your fingers against the back of the trochanter, or just below it, and ask the client to extend the hip ("Bring your knee back against me" is a good cue) and put a leg on your other arm in such a place as to offer resistance to their extension. You will feel the tendons of the hamstrings pop up against your palpating fingers at the IT.

Now put your fingers under the IT, and this time call for adduction ("Bring the inside of your foot to the ceiling" usually works for us) and feel the adductor magnus tendon pop into your hands. This clarifies the difference between these two adjacent muscles, and the small crevice in between is the intermuscular septum that separates the adductor group and the hamstring group all the way down to the knee.

The middle part of the adductor magnus inserts farther down the linea aspera from the adductor minimus part, and forms a living functional continuity with the short head of the biceps femoris (see Body[3], "The Knee and Thigh," Issue #70, Sept./Oct. 1997). Below this middle part, there is a hiatus (or hole) through the adductor magnus to allow the neuro-vascular bundle to pass from the front to the back of the leg, and then we get to the lowest section of the adductor magnus, which attaches very strongly to the medial femoral epicondyle. You can feel this lump and the attaching tendon very clearly on the inside of your knee about an inch above the joint.

The next muscle, the gracilis, is the apex muscle of this second fan, and like the others of its kind it goes farther than the rest of its fan-mates. The gracilis (literally, "thin") originates on the ramus just a little in front of the adductor magnus, and runs on top of the magnus straight down across the knee and into the pes anserinus on the inside of the tibia. (Again, for a discussion of the pes, see Body[3], "The Knee and Thigh," Issue #70, Sept./Oct. 1997). The gracilis thus crosses two joints, both the hip and knee. (Netter plate 462)

Having come down one side of the linea aspera with the adductor magnus complex, and beyond the linea altogether with the gracilis, let us go up the other (more medial or frontal portion of the linea, though remember it is still on the back side of the femur) toward the groin and the lesser trochanter.

The adductor longus has its distal attachment about halfway down the femur, parallel to but in front of the middle part of adductor magnus. The proximal attachment is more forward on the pubic ramus than that of gracilis. You can always feel this one: it is the big, hunky tendon that you can feel on everyone on the front inside of the leg, and the one readily visible in most people when they sit cross-legged in a bathing suit.

Deep to adductor longus, but still on the "front" side of this adductor fan, is the adductor brevis, another triangular muscle that can be divided into separate parts like the adductor magnus on the "back" side of the fan.

This muscle breaks up the fan a little bit, because although it is clearly

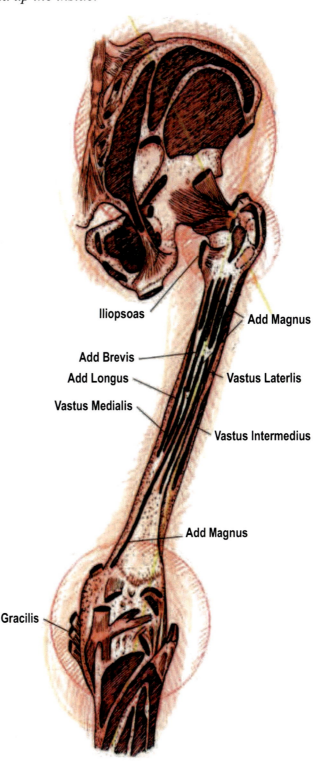

**Figure 6:** *Femur and hip from behind with linea aspera. Many muscles fight for attachment room on the back of the femur. It makes sense if you see them coming down the outside of the line and up the inside.*

**Fans of the Hip Joint**

the next muscle along the rim of this fan as we come up the front of the linea aspera, adductor brevis has its ramic attachment a little bit posterior and inferior to the adductor longus, between gracilis and longus. Noting this little "fudge factor," we carry on to the transitional muscle to the next fan.

Before we do, we need to say something about adductor function and adductor fact. Sadly, our beautifully laid-out scheme is rarely what you find when you put your hand on the leg. The adductors are very often a confused and tightly bunched up set of muscles, which is why we have been offering these palpatory clues for finding the muscles with confidence. They are not as easily delineated as the quadricep or hamstrings. Why is this? There are three reasons that make sense to us:

(1) The inside of the leg is a charged area due to the proximity of sexuality. A lot of emotions can get stored as chronic tension in the adductors, especially sexual fears and impotent rage. Proceed with caution, tenderness and awareness.
(2) Like the abductors, the adductors are primarily used posturally to keep the body steady while other actions are going on. One only has to do the occasional horse ride to discover how sore the adductor get when they are really actively used. So postural difficulties in the spine, upper body or pelvis get shifted down onto the adductors (because the other thigh muscles have to be free to move us in walking, kicking, swimming, or whatever).
(3) The adductors are pinch hitters—they are capable of substituting for or augmenting the actions of the other muscles of the thigh. The adductor magnus can pinch hit as an extensor, the brevis and longus can aid in flexion. Furthermore, depending on the position of the hip joint, the adductors can assist in medial or lateral rotation. This is a controversial notion, and would again involve a long and complicated discussion. The main points are clearly summarized in the section on adductor function in *Kendall & McCreary's Muscles: Testing and Function*. The adductors are especially active in returning the femur to a normal position from an extreme—i.e., the longus and brevis work best as flexors when returning the femur from a fully extended or hyperextended position.

For all these reasons or combinations, these muscles and their fasciae can get bound up with each other, and especially the insertions on the linea aspera can be tied in together like so much tangled hair. As with your daughter's tangled hair, it is best just to take a small bit each time and brush and comb it out, rather than taking on the whole inside of the leg at once.

OK, hip joint fans, we have made it to the last of the hip joint fans, and our transitional muscle is (May I have the envelope, please?) the pectineus! Yes, the pectineus, like the quadratus femoris that won the last award as transition between two fans, is a squarish kind of muscle, but with a very hip function. It hails from a band of tendon that defines the top edge of the inner part of the linea aspera, bringing that part of the line to the lesser trochanter just as the quadratus insertion defined the transition between the linea aspera and the greater trochanter (Netter plate 462).

The upper attachment of pectineus goes beyond the ramus to that top branch of bone just beside the pubic symphysis. You can find your own pectineus by sitting cross-legged and putting your fingers right up against the fold of your leg, finding the big, obvious tendon of adductor longus. Put your fingers into the hole just in front of and lateral to the tendon, staying very close to the fold between your leg and your trunk. Since pectineus is both a flexor and abductor, if you lift your knee up and in, you should feel the pectineus pushing out against your fingers. It is a touchy area to go for in clients if you have never done it before, but it is rewarding to get used to it (and get them used to it) because the pectineus can be so involved in the anterior pelvic tilts that form the basis of so much bad posture.

But let us get the whole picture, because pectineus may be the transition muscle, but it is also very much involved in the third and last fan of the hip joint, which should, by our own rules, be called the lesser trochanter fan. We have dubbed it "The Inguinal Fan" instead. In our even-less-formal-than-usual moments we call it the "leg pit," for these next set of muscles define the armpit of the leg.

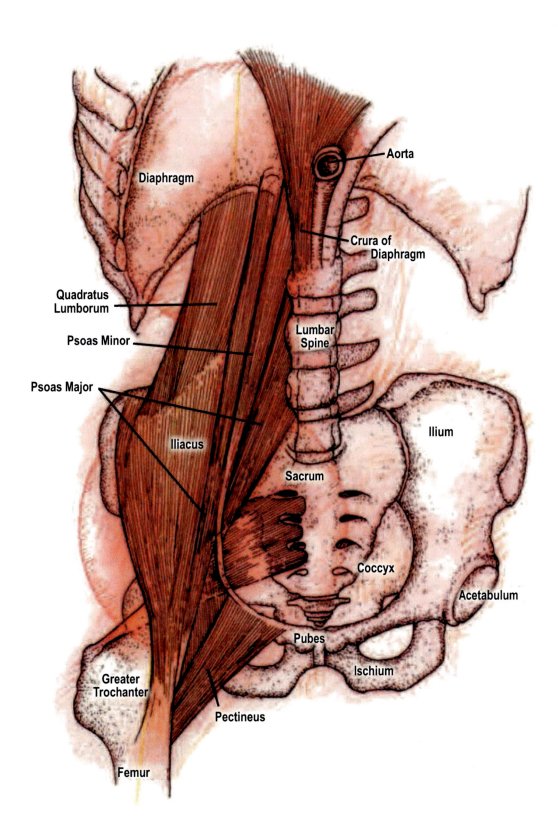

*Figure 7:* The Inguinal Fan centers around the lesser trochanter, includes some strong hip flexors, and completes the circle of the fans.

**Fans of the Hip Joint**

## The inguinal fan

This fan includes:
Pectineus
Apex: Psoas
Iliacus

The hub of our last fan is the lesser trochanter, that little nub of bone tucked on the inside corner of the "seven" of the femur. The first muscle, pectineus, has a band of tendon that comes up to the lesser trochanter from below, then the psoas and the iliacus both have attachments right into the knob of the trochanter itself.

The rim of this fan is not as easy to define as a single line, but it covers the front of the pelvis from the pubic bone to the ASIS. The pectineus has a wide, flat origin that stretches along the pelvic rim from the pubic symphysis out about an inch toward the ASIS. The psoas covers the next area, but, being the apex muscle of this fan, stretches beyond the single joint to cover the sacroiliac and lower lumbar joints as well. The iliopectineal bursa makes sure that the psoas slides over this part of the pelvis rather than attaching here. The iliacus, the third and last muscle of this fan, fills the inside of the iliac bone, essentially attaching along the rim of the pelvis from the sacral promontory all the way over to the ASIS (Netter plate 246, 462, 466).

All three of these muscles flex the hip, and although there are arguments to the contrary, we find them all to be lateral rotators as well. They are all located in the "leg pit"—more formally, the femoral triangle: a space defined by the inguinal ligament on the superior side, the adductor longus on the medial side, and the sartorius on the lateral side. They can all be palpated and worked on in this area, and they can all affect pelvic tilt and resulting curvature in the spine.

Everybody bows down before the psoas, and this anatomist is no exception. We will devote our next column to the psoas almost exclusively. In the matter of anterior pelvic tilt, however, do not neglect the pectineus and iliacus, which, being one-joint muscles, are single-minded about pulling the femur into flexion toward the pelvis. When one is standing up and the femur is fixed, they can be just as single-minded about pulling the pelvis down in the front toward the femur. The iliacus needs to be considered with the muscle that continues from it up to the 12th rib, the quadratus lumborum. For a full discussion of myofascial continuities of this sort, please see "The Anatomy Trains" by this author in the *Journal of Bodywork and Movement Therapies*, Vol. 1, No's 2 & 3, published by Churchill Livingstone.

We have come full circle around the "propeller" of the hip bone, from the tensor fasciae latae on the outside tip of the ASIS to the iliacus on the inside tip of the ASIS. To get there, we had to travel out and back and down on the iliac crest, around the ischial tuberosity and along the ramus to the pubic bone, and out along the superior ramus to the ASIS.

Thus it becomes evident that the musculature around the hip acts in a sweeping continuum, which can be conveniently divided into the three fans we have described. Generally speaking, we look for a consistency of tension among all these guy wires, like the cables on a suspension bridge.

Isolated pockets of higher or lower tension lead to imbalance in the affected hip (which leads eventually to joint degeneration of some kind) or imbalance between the hips, which can manifest at the sacroiliac joint or farther afield.

The special muscles within the fans call for a little extra attention. The transitional muscles, the quadratus femoris and the pectineus, generally clamp down when there is a severe postural distortion. The quadratus will work very hard in cases of posterior pelvic tilt or in postural lateral rotation of the femur; the pectineus gets slam-dunked in anterior tilt and medial femoral roration.

The apex muscles—the psoas, piriformis, and gracilis—are more delicately poised, fall into imbalance more easily, and require patient care and feeding. The balance of the gracilis relates to the balance of tendon pull at the pes anserinus (we discussed in the last chapter), but the ramifications of the psoas and piriformis are so profound to our upright balance that we will bring our discussion to a close here and draw breath for giving it a full airing in the next chapter. ∎

# Chapter 4:
# Poise: Psoas-Piriformis Balance

**Poise is an elusive quality of posture or movement. Fred Astaire had it. Jackie O. had it. Princess Diana, bless her soul, was going for it. We can argue about who has it now, but we will probably agree that very few of us or our clients really possess poise nowadays. But—what is it?**

As we are hands-on therapists, let us attempt to define poise in its physical sense, not the mental components of urbanity and quick wits we often associate with it. If we stick to what poise means in the body, can we get close to something that we can get our hands on, or even help to bring about through our work?

(To assist you in getting a more complete picture than we can provide here, we include references to Frank Netter's *Atlas of Human Anatomy*, published by CIBA-Geigy, although you can follow along with any good anatomy atlas.)

Surely part of our assumption as massage therapists is that if we bring something about in the body, we also bring it to the rest of us (whatever our beliefs about what constitutes "the rest of us"). When we bring about relaxation in tight muscles, the whole person relaxes. New behaviors become possible for them, like a deep releasing breath. The same is true when we relieve chronic pain: clients change how they relate to the world and the people around them. Likewise, if we can produce poise in a physical sense, we can expect it to express itself in the being as well.

The basis of this chapter is the bald hypothesis that poise can be spelled out in a very specific somatic sense: a dynamic, fully lengthened balance of the psoas and piriformis across the sacroiliac joint. When this delicate balance is achieved, poise appears. When this relationship goes wrong, these two muscles necessarily tighten up during standing regardless of how much havoc that wreaks, on all their other biomechanical functions. After that happens, it may still be possible to have strength, competence, coordination or sturdiness, but the calm, fluid, ready-for-any-eventuality we call poise will be missing.

This poise, this psoas-piriformis balance, is part of the potential birthright of easy uprightness for each of us. But like so many of our potentialities, very few actually achieve it in full. Since posture in humans is a learned experience more than in any other animal, it is, unfortunately, subject to mislearning. At the end of our first year of life, we stand however we learned to stand, but the process is often not completed, not fully matured—and the most we get for instruction from then on is a fairly useless "Stand up straight!" or "Get your shoulders back, will you?"

Poise, however, is not dependent on pleasing Mom, athletic ability, sweating heavily, twisting yourself into a yogic pretzel, or any other kind of effort. To the contrary, one of its chief characteristics is that it looks easy and is in fact effortless. This is because poise is built not on power but on a deep kinesthetic knowledge—conscious or unconscious—learned or natural, which leads to balance in our core being.

When we speak of the core of our being, we are not speaking of our soul or something ethereal, but of a tangible, physical core that steadies our lower spine on our legs. Poise comes when the psoas-piriformis balance handles this job, leaving the other muscles free and ready to move us in any direction. Sadly, few people have the full openness in the hip area that allows for this very particular balance. Psoas-piriformis balance is one of the first places to be adversely affected by any postural defect, often never to be recovered in a lifetime of moving.

In fact, the psoas-piriformis relationship is so stubbornly out of balance in most of our clients that many a massage therapist has grimaced in frustration as we find that once again the muscles we eased and smoothed in last week's session have returned to their taut, hair-trigger state. These muscles seem to be the first to go and the last to come back to normal in any pelvic dysfunction, and very resistant to sustained health, besides being difficult to reach and release with confidence.

Some kind of balance between these two muscles is absolutely necessary for any kind of upright standing, but 99 percent of the time the balance we end up achieving involves these muscles being chronically tight, and the sacroiliac joint in between being locked or at least under increased strain. An additional component to this core contraction is nearly always compensatory tightness of other surrounding muscles, such as the abdominals, when the delicate dynamics of this antagonistic relationship start to go haywire.[1]

### A few words on the nature of antagonism

"Antagonist" is an unfortunate choice of terms for our understanding the relationship between muscles. Even dedicated antagonists like the triceps and biceps must cooperate to produce the steadiness of the upper arm so necessary to a bodyworker's daily motions. So the first unfortunate aspect of this term is that all antagonists are, in reality, coworkers.

A second assumption lies in the word: many of us presume that if one wins by becoming short and hard, the other must lose by becoming weak and soft. The truth is that in an imbalanced situation, they both lose: one gets bunched up and tense (let's use a Rolfing colleague's term, "locked short"), the other one gets strained and tense (let's call it "locked long"). They both end up feeling tense and hard and working at way less than their optimum (Figure 1). The pain and trigger points will almost always be in the strained, locked-long muscle, the place that needs connective tissue release work is most often the silent, locked-short muscle. The area all around both muscles' fascial planes will be pulled out of place.

A third cause of our antagonism to the word antagonist is that many muscles often play a part in counterbalancing the action of any one. Also, muscles that are antagonists now might not be antagonists even a microsecond later, due to the shifting balance of forces in the body. The term 'antagonist' implies a one-to-one correspondence not found in the real world, so the term must be strictly limited to a specific action being discussed. For example, the anterior and posterior deltoids are antagonists for horizontal flexion and extension, but both are also prime movers for abduction, antagonized by the lats and the pects, which themselves are antagonists for protraction and retraction of the shoulder—and so on. Try to analyze a living body in terms of counterbalancing antagonists, and you are off on a long and frustrating journey. Too many massage therapists presume that muscles that are named antagonists for one movement are opposing each other all the time. They are not.

## The components of this balance

With these cautions in mind, let us explore this very particular, sometimes antagonistic—but secretly cooperative—relationship deep within the pelvis. To understand the balance of forces that produces length, ease and poise here, we will need to fill in our sketchy knowledge of the sacroiliac (SI) joint, touch on the pelvic floor and lateral rotators, and focus very closely on the details of our two major muscular

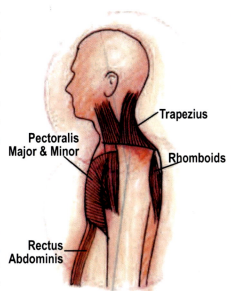

*Figure 1:* If the front of the shoulder is "locked short", the antagonists on the back of the shoulder are most likely "locked long."

components of this core. When we have the elements in place, we can bring them together and point to some applications in daily bodywork.

Many massage therapists have had little cause to study the sacroiliac joint—the major 'motor mount' for our walking engine—leaving SI joint manipulations to the chiropractors and osteopaths. Although, as a soft-tissue practitioner, this author does not manipulate SI joints in the usual high-velocity-thrust manner, nevertheless we bodyworkers can aid in the natural easing and repositioning of these joints through a systematic application of the understanding outlined below.

## An evolutionary moment

A brief look at the mechanics of upright standing will help clarify how these elements work together in the uniquely human situation.

In a four-legged creature, the spine is horizontal, and most of the weight is supported by the shoulder girdle (Figure 2). The weight of the spine, ribs, head and organs bears down on the forelegs. Since the shoulder assembly of most four-legged creatures—a horse, for example—does not connect to the rest of the skeleton by any joint, because they do not have a collar bone, the torso rests on a sling made out of the serratus anterior muscles and its associated fasciae. This allows for a lot of motion at the shoulder, during a canter or gallop, as the trunk swings back and forth with in the sling.

The sling assembly also allows for maximum shock-absorbing effect. The weight of the whole forward part of the body comes down on the forefeet as they strike, and the 'serratus sling' acts as shock absorbers on a car. The weight-bearing aspect also requires that the foreleg be quite straight.

Down at the other end of the horse, the pelvis has a much easier job: it primarily provides attachment points for the large muscles of jumping and running. Because not so much weight comes down through

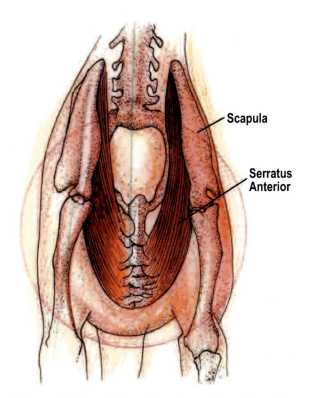

*Figure 2:* Most of the weight of a quadruped rests in a myofascial sling hung from the medial borders of their two scapulae.

**Poise: Psoas-Piriformis Balance**

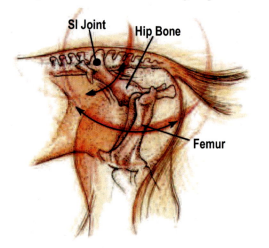

*Figure 3: The horse's hip bone rocks in time with the femur in the canter and the gallop.*

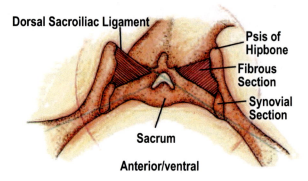

*Figure 4: Although not in the same loose sling, the back end of the quadruped also hangs from the inside upper edge of the hip bones.*

moveable than our own SI joints. They allow the hip bones to follow the pendulum-like movements of the femur, almost like the escape mechanism in an old grandfather clock (Figure 4).

What has to happen for this structure to stand up on its hind legs? Many things, of course. For one thing, all the shock absorbing aspect is shifted from these legs, they can be held in the series of right angles that allows for maximum power in jumping and kicking (Figure 3). A human runner's legs assume a similar position of mechanical advantage when she crouches into the starting blocks for a race.

In the horse's hips, the spine also hangs between the two hip bones at the SI joints, specifically from strong ligaments attached from the sacrum to the posterior superior iliac spines (PSIS). The sacroiliac joints of horses are less moveable than the sling we just looked at in its shoulder, but still much more the shoulder girdle to the pelvic girdle. We have already spoken in earlier chapters of this book about the shock-absorbing functions of foot arches and knee cartilages. Our SI joint also has a role in springing this shock, as we will see below.

The central aspect to our discussion now is that for upright posture, the pelvis must swing around on the hips from sharply-angled flexion to full extension, so that the pelvic bowl and spine face upward instead of forward, and the femurs are going straight toward the ground (Figure 5). This requires

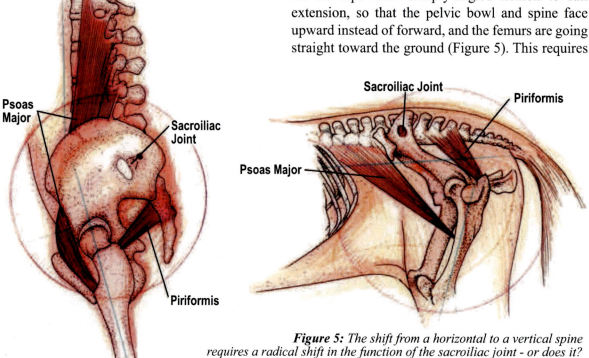

*Figure 5: The shift from a horizontal to a vertical spine requires a radical shift in the function of the sacroiliac joint - or does it?*

*Figure 6: Do not ignore the role of these three muscles in maintaining good posture.*

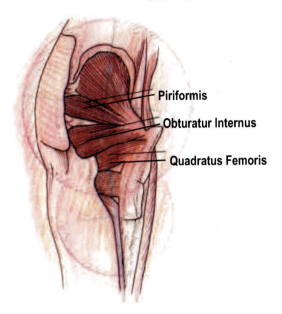

## Understanding the human sacroiliac joint

The essential point to understanding how our sacroiliac (SI) joint works is that, in spite of the radically different orientation, it does much the same as when we were quadrupeds: it hangs in the pelvic girdle, and it follows the femoral movement in walking.

Whoa! What do you mean, it hangs in the pelvic bones? Most of us, this author included, spend our working lives thinking of the sacrum as being wedged down into the two hip bone. "The sacrum is the arrowhead," I used to say to my students. "The spine is the arrow." (Figure 7) My point was to show how the iliolumbar and sacrospinous ligaments were necessary to keep the force of the arrow from splitting the hip hones apart. This view is still valid, but it is only part of the truth.

*Figure 7: The sacrum is wedged like an arrowhead from side-to-side, with the indicated ligaments keeping the arrow from "splitting" the pelvis.*

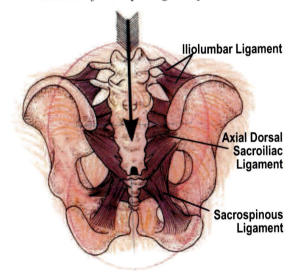

a lot of muscle power to pull the ischial tuberosities (ITs) and the sacrum closer to the back side of the femur in order to open the angle of the hip joint as well as to erect the spine and lift the head.

The hamstrings are in the position to do this, by pulling the ITs toward the back of the knee. The adductor magnus can help in that manner also. But the hamstrings cannot be doing this job all the time, because they need to be free to participate in running, walking, flexing and rotating the knee. The gluteus maximus would seem to be a good candidate, but myographic evidence shows that this muscle is almost totally silent during simple standing, and does not really get active until we are walking uphill.[2]

The lateral rotators, in spite of their name, are in a very good position to bring the back of the pelvis closer to the back of the femur, and this postural aspect of their function cannot be ignored (Figure 6). The obturatur internus and the quadratus femoris are particularly important in pulling the ITs down to create this extension at the hip joint. But of the lateral rotators, only the piriformis pulls directly down and forward on the sacrum, thus crossing and affecting the SI joint. The pelvic floor also has a role in this action, which we will address in a little while.

First we need to return to the SI joint, and see how it swings in humans.

As well as being wedged from side to side, it is also true to say that the spine—the sacrum part of it—still "hangs" in the hip girdle from top to bottom. Look at a coronal section through our SI joint. (Figure 8) It is not wedged in this dimension; rather it is wider at the bottom than it is at the top, and could conceivably fall out of the embrace of the hip bones.

What holds the sacrum in place is the same piece that holds it in the horse—a strong ligament going from our PSIS to the posterior edge of the second

**Poise: Psoas-Piriformis Balance**

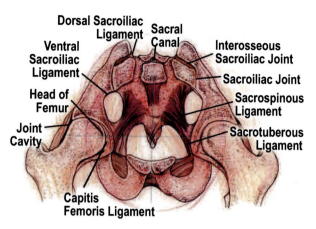

*Figure 8: A coronal section of the pelvis shows how weight is transferred between femur and spine, but also shows how the sacrum hangs between the hip bones, even in humans.*

sacral segment: the dorsal sacroiliac ligament. This ligament also becomes the axis, or hub, for a tiny but important arc of movement in our SI joint that is much like the horse's.

The SI joint has been considered a non-moving joint by many in the medical profession, although chiropractors and osteopaths have been moving it successfully for centuries. Do a dissection on the old and often misused bodies that come into the anatomy lab and you will find that the joint has fused as often as not. It would be our contention that this is not normal, and probably contributed to those people's pain or dysfunction before they died. You can live without movement of the SI Joint, but you cannot live or move fully without it, and without it you certainly cannot have poise. It is not a joint that we can voluntarily move, like our elbow, but if the passive rocking movement of the joint is not present, it can cause all kinds of pain and problems in the surrounding tissues, sometimes quite distant from the joint itself.

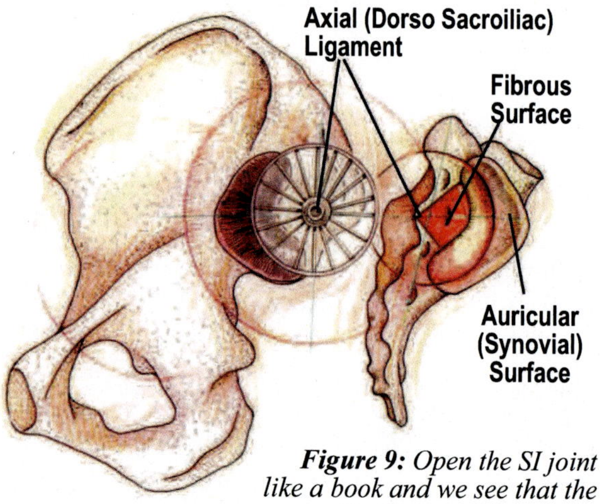

The SI joint is also confusing because it is a combination fibrous joint and synovial joint. How can it be both? And how does it move then? If we open the sacroiliac joint around the vertical axis like a book, all will be revealed.

Here we can see the two corresponding surfaces of the SI joint on the medial side of the hip bone and the lateral side of the sacrum. They can be seen roughly as arcs of a circle, like a piece of pie, with the dorsal sacroiliac ligament at the center of the circle, and the auricular surface—the synovial part of the joint—out at the edge of the circle.

To understand how it moves, think of the dorsal sacroiliac ligament as the hub, or axle, of a wheel, and the auricular[3] surface as part of the rim of the wheel—a wheel which, if it existed, would stick a couple of inches out of our backs. (Figure 9) If this image is somewhere near the truth, the hip bone could move like this wheel (there is argument about how much, but surely not more than a couple of degrees) on the sacrum around the fixed point of the ligament. Or, conversely, the sacrum could move in a similar way on the hip bone.

This image also explains how the synovial and fibrous parts of the joint could work in harmony. The hub, the dorsal sacroiliac ligament, does not move at all; it only twists a little. The inner part of the wheel has to move a little more, and this movement is accommodated by collagen fibers, just as the tiny movements of the skull bones are accommodated by the fibers of the sutures. The outer rim of the wheel has to move more, and thus requires the sliding cartilage surfaces and the lubricating synovial fluid.

In healthy walking, as the right femur flexes toward the hip in a step, the wheel of the right hip bone rotates posteriorly so that the acetabulum follows the movement of the femur slightly, and the iliac crest moves up and back. As we push through the step and the femur extends behind us, the hip bone rotates forward so that the acetabulum follows the femur back, with the iliac crest moving anterior and inferior. This is much the same movement as we saw in the horse, only smaller and with a more vertical orientation. If this tiny movement is either

*Figure 9: Open the SI joint like a book and we see that the sacrum moves on the ilium (or vice versa) like the movement of a wheel around a hub.*

hypermobile or absent, it can and does create problems for the walker and for the manipulator who tries to get it back into proper motion.

The above explanation—assuming the movement of the hip bones on a steady sacrum—is a bit oversimplified, but we need to start somewhere. As well as the hip bones moving on the sacrum, the sacrum itself performs a multidimensional, rotational dance in walking, and the two-joint complex is subject to getting stuck in a variety of ways and positions, some of them requiring sophisticated skills to untangle.

A similar but converse movement also takes place: the sacrum can also move between two stabilized hip bones. The freedom for this movement is well understood by craniosacral therapists, who feel for the nutation (nodding) of the sacral wheel powered by the tides of the cerebrospinal fluid and the pull of the dura on the second sacral segment—just in front of the wheel's hub.

However, if we have gotten this basic wheel part across, the antagonistic role of psoas and piriformis in poise will fall into place. If we look a little wider than the SI joint itself, we can see many muscles that could have an effect on the hip bone part of this relationship, as was discussed in the last chapter.

Two of these fan muscles, though, stand out as having very strong and specific leverage on the sacrum: the piriformis, just inferior to our SI wheel pulling forward and down on that spoke, and the psoas, just up the other way pulling forward and down on the lumbar spine spoke. See how they can be antagonists? Need a little more clarity? Read on.

### The muscular elements

The piriformis originates on the anterior surface of the lower part of the sacrum, usually with three slips from S2- S4, and passes out through the greater sciatic notch along with the sciatic nerve to attach to the inside of the very top of the greater trochanter (Netter plates 246, 337 & 465). The psoas originates on the transverse processes and bodies of the lumbar vertebrae, usually five or six slips from Tl2 - L5, and passes down and forward, staying behind all the organs and their peritoneal coverings. It comes closest to the surface of the body where it crosses the front of the pelvis at the groin just lateral to the pubic bone, and then goes inferiorly and posteriorly again to insert on the lesser trochanter (Netter plates 246 & 466).

Both of these muscles earn their importance through the many things that they connect. First, both connect the spine to the femur—both "jump over" the hip bones. That means they are connecting up and down in the body, both connect axial to appendicular in a big way, and they both go from deep inside to more outside parts of the body—therefore we can reach very deeply into the body's structure by affecting these muscles.

The actions of these muscles are a matter of some debate, which is why this author feels OK about throwing this new two cents' worth into the discussion. The piriformis has always been listed among the lateral rotator group, but because of the attachment position right at the top of the trochanter, it has never been in much of a position to rotate the femur laterally. In fact, there is some evidence to show that when the hip is really flexed, the piriformis could become a mild medial rotator.[4]

### The piriformis' postural performance

In fact, the piriformis is better considered as working from its insertion to its origin, as it could do whenever the femur (and thus the trochanter) is held stable. If we look at Figure 5, we can consider first the side-to-side action of the piriformis on the sacrum. It is a spinal balancer, and here is an image of how it works: Remember when you held a broom in the open palm of your hand, with the head of the broom up in the air? After a little practice you could keep the broom up there indefinitely by making little movements with your hand to steady it. The spine is like the broom, and your head like the head of the broom. The spine hangs into the sacroiliac joints, and the piriformis exerts its pull below the level of this joint. Thus as the spine leans to the left, the tail of the spine—the part of the sacrum below the SI and the coccyx—would tend to move to the right. The left piriformis can then exert a ligament-like restraint on this tendency, reducing strain on the SI joints.

Returning to the broom in your hand, what happens if the broom starts to tilt beyond what you can compensate for with the little adjustments of the palm? It will fall, unless you switch tactics and grab the lower end of the handle with one or both hands, thus saving the broom from falling all the way. This is what happens to the piriformis in many of our clients: the spine above the pelvis has a twist or a lean in one direction or another, and the piriformis grabs with all its might to prevent the spine from falling further. To be more precise, it grabs to prevent that spinal lean from overtaxing the SI ligaments. So as we work the piriformii (What *is* the plural of "piriformis"?) in our clients, they may relax while they are on the table, but as soon as their bodies are back in gravity, the piriformis says, in effect, "Hey, I can't afford to be this loose and relaxed, I gotta tighten up again to stabilize this spine o' mine" and the whole cycle begins again.

We will leave the broom metaphor here, but it is worthwhile to keep it in mind throughout the rest of our discussion.

We are not done, however, considering piriformis function (anyone who tells you that any part of the body serves only one function simply has not looked deeply enough). If we look at Figure 5, another job for the piriformis becomes apparent. In passing from the front of the sacrum to the top of the trochanter, the piriformis runs anteriorly. That means that it not only pulls side to side on the sacrum; it also pulls the tail forward and down. This essential piriformic action is the one we are hypothesizing is opposed by the psoas.

### Turning now to the psoas

Upright posture dictated a new and unique pathway for the psoas. Notice that in a quadruped the muscle does not touch the pelvis, going directly from the spine to the femur (Figure 5). When the hip joint is fully extended into our upright stance, the psoas takes a strange route forward from the spine to the front of the pelvis, where it touches but does not attach, and then back to the femur. This means that contraction of the muscle should pull the femur forward (into flexion) and the lumbar spine forward, while pushing the pelvis back (as if the psoas were a bowstring and the pelvis is the arrow).

However, the actions of the psoas muscle, like the piriformis, are multiple and open to question.[5] Everyone agrees that it is a hip flexor, and most agree that it produces lateral rotation, though

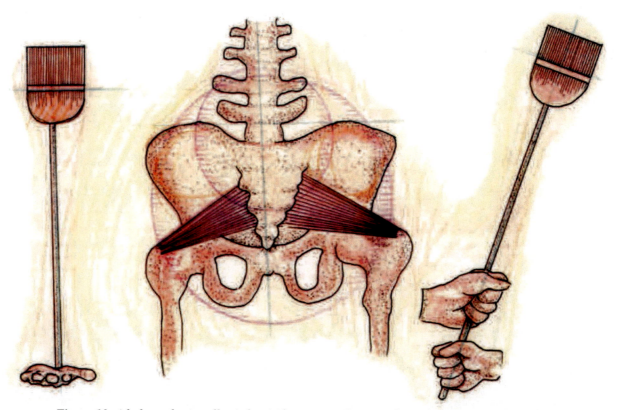

***Figure 10:*** *A balanced spine allows the piriformis to make periodic and temporary adjustments; an unbalanced spine requires dedicated tightness in the piriformis.*

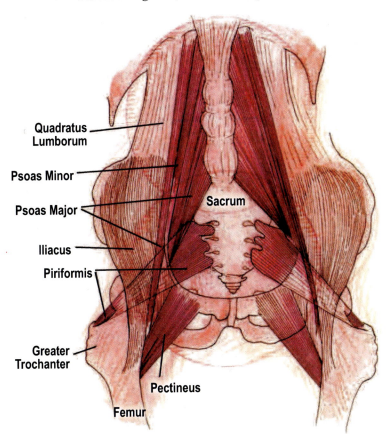

*Figure 11: The core structures from the front reveals a different relationship between the psoas and the piriformis than does Figure 5, the same area from the side.*

arguments can be made (with which this author disagrees) that it could produce medial rotation of the femur. It is axiomatic that the psoas produces extension and hyperextension in the lumbars, but we can also open that to question, in the manner described in the following paragraph.

The psoas is a triangular muscle, like, say, the deltoid. The insertion is practically a point—the lesser trochanter—but the origin stretches from the fifth lumbar to the 12th thoracic. Fibers from the bodies and the transverse processes of each of these vertebrae head directly toward the insertion on the femur. The human psoas does not look like a triangular muscle in the books because, in standing up, the longest fibers cover the shorter ones, so it appears to be (and feels like) a fusiform muscle. Look at the accompanying diagram (Figure 5) of the psoas in a quadruped (like a cow, where it forms the round steaks of the filet mignon) and its triangular nature is much clearer. As with the deltoid, one edge of a triangular muscle can make different movements from the other edge. What if this were true for the psoas as well? The lower fibers of the psoas clearly are going to pull L5 and L4 anteriorly and create lumbar hyperextension (Figure 5). The upper fibers of the psoas (and the muscular fibers of psoas minor, if present) are going to pull T12 and L1 toward the groin, which could conceivably push the middle and lower lumbars back, posteriorly, into lumbar flexion. Whether this will happen depends on the placement of the mechanical axis of the lumbars and where the upper lumbars are held relative to the hip joint. If it is true, we are led to the surprising proposition that the different segments of the psoas could counterbalance each other, supporting the lumbars in their proper curvature, leaving surrounding muscles free for movement.

[Author's note: the preceding paragraph is pure speculation, subject to experiment; however, this theory has worked well for the author clinically, in certain postural patterns. The author believes that this argument should be tested, because it has profound and practical implications for clinical treatment of lumbar lordosis or reverse lumbar curvature and the host of related ills that accompany either of those postural distortions.]

But for the rest of this chapter, let us assume the psoas as a whole—or at least the lower (and more medial) fibers—is producing a flexion, a forward-pulling of the lower lumbars, and thus dragging the sacrum along with it. Thus the psoas, like the piriformis, also affects the SI joint independently of the hip bone position.

We should say a few words here about the pelvic floor in this regard (Netter plates 337 & 338). The levator ani consists of three smaller muscles, all of which pull forward on the lower end of the sacrum, as we have seen in the piriformis—though these three pull on the sacrum by way of the less stable coccyx. But their role in keeping the sacrum in place, or contributing to a locked SI joint through hypertension, should not be ignored.

**Poise: Psoas-Piriformis Balance**

## Application

So let us summarize the picture we have presented here: To line up the pelvis, chest and head in gravity, humans must achieve full extension in the hip joint. This requires bringing the back of the femur and the back of the pelvis closer together. Hamstrings, adductor magnus, and the lateral rotators, most notably the quadratus femoris and the obturatur internus—all of these act to extend the hip bone on the femur. Only the piriformis and the pelvic floor act to pull the sacrum in a similar direction, called counter-nutation.

This extension of the hip is opposed by the iliacus, pectineus, and all the other hip flexors, which must release to allow full opening and the complete extension necessary to easy, upright poise. But only the psoas goes directly to the spine to oppose the piriformis. Only these two muscles jump from femur to spine.

We do not offer techniques in Body[3], we offer strategies, and invite you to match your bag of techniques to the strategies. Whether you use facilitated stretching, positional release, trigger points, deep tissue work or crystal vibrations, the strategy is the same:

1. Open the monarticular hip flexors, like the pectineus, iliacus and the anterior adductors;
2. Make sure the multi-articular hip flexors (the TFL, sartorius, rectus femoris) are also supple;
3. Seek balanced tone among the hip extensors (the hamstrings and lower lateral rotators);
4. In lordotic cases, ease the thoracico-lumbar fascia and lower deep transversospinalis muscles;
5. Free the psoas, especially the medial fibers—carefully, sensitively, but fully;
6. Seek ease in the piriformis, and see if it might not stick around a bit longer than usual;
7. Educate your clients about the front-back balance, and call their attention to the movements within the pelvis, so that they can reinforce your work with every step they take.

Poise? It's still elusive. As this balance becomes familiar to your clients, with the sacrum poised over the legs, well, they may not all become supermodels or Fred Astaire, but you can look for a more fluid confidence that comes from being poised "on top of their world." ■

---

**Footnotes:**

1. In the interests of space and simplicity we are leaving out of this chapter a fourth component of less-than-optimal structure in this area: rotation and torque. We consider sagittal issues: flexion extension in the hips, nutation and counter nutation in the sacroiliac joints, flexion and hyperextension in the lumbar spine.

These issues are often further complicated by rotational issues proceeding from functionally short legs or traumatic sequelae that lead to medially or laterally rotated femurs, separate patterns of tilt, flare or torque in the innominates, and rotational components in the sacrolumbar junction, in the lumbers themselves as allowed, and in the thoracic-lumbar junction. We will deal with rotations in the lumbers in the next chapter, but pelvic torque will remain beyond the scope of this series.

2. Kendall, Florence; and McReary, Elizabeth. *Muscles, Testing & Function*, third edition, 1983, Williams & Wilkins, Baltimore, Maryland.

3. Somebody thought it looked like an "ear."

4. Gorman, D. The Body Moveable, Vol. Ill, pg. 53, 1981, Ampersand Press, Guelph, Ontario, Canada.

5. Although it is often combined with the iliacus as the "iliopsoas." this author is adamant in separating the functions of the two muscles. The discussion here refers only to the actions of the psoas major muscle, except where otherwise designated.

# Chapter 5:
# The Abdominal Balloon, Part 1: THE DYNAMICS of the ABDOMEN

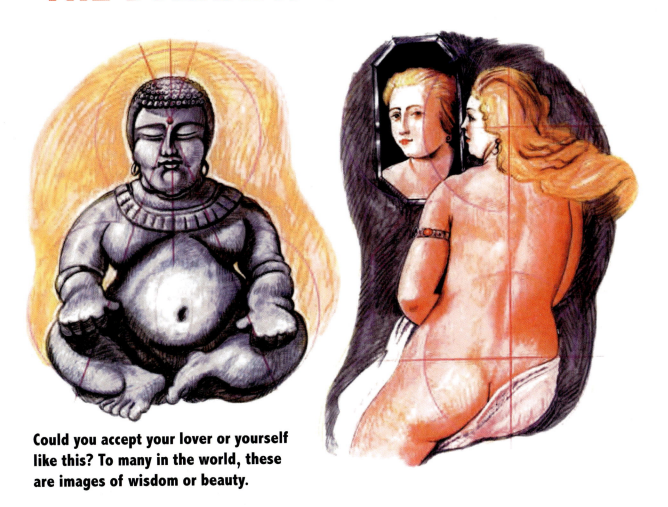

**Could you accept your lover or yourself like this? To many in the world, these are images of wisdom or beauty.**

**Tummies.** Everybody has one, and you wouldn't want to try to get along without it—but not very many of us are happy with our own. For some, the cause of unhappiness is how the organs inside are working, but for most of us entering the 21st century in the Western world's media bubble, it is a problem of our tummy's shape. This chapter is about how we can use our hands to help give our clients' abdominal area a more healthful contour. But to accomplish this, we first need to understand the area as a whole—the interwoven tapestry of the "abdominal balloon."

### Where's the beef?

In my experience, there are two groups of people who are quite content with the shape of their bellies—the very thin and the very fat. Many of the very thin, except for anorexics and others whose body image is distorted (and of course, let us not forget, the very hungry), are quite happy to be able to put a yardstick from hip bone to hip bone without touching any flab. Most of the rest of us are often heard complaining how we are about to get started on losing weight or gaining muscle tone.

Owners of huge round tummies, having given up the battle of the bulge some time ago, also seem, often enough, very satisfied with their accomplishment. They may give a few token complaints because they live in a culture that values being thin over anything other than being rich, but you can tell their hearts are not really in it. Secretly, they are proud. And having a large belly does lend a certain gravitas—one knows from the beginning that the thin little Peter Lorre will never be able to stand up to the magnificently rotund Sidney Greenstreet in *The Maltese Falcon*. And what about all those laughing Buddhas? They all have a substantial Buddha belly. Is it their karma or their dharma to be so large? Or is the cunenr dogma about being thin chasing the wrong karma?

Of course, not everyone wants to be thin. The African chief and the Arabian potentate both wanted their women as far as they were themselves, to show off their wealth and prowess as providers. The new Barbie, the Body Shop's "Ruby," and the return of the more zaftig woman even to Victoria's Secret catalogues are all indications that society may be letting go of its fascination with twig-like waifs and gaunt, "heroin-chic" supermodels.

If our clients are a bit neurotic about their bellies, we professionals have our own obsessions and prejudices about the abdomen that we might want to get over as well. The abdomen is a "touchy" place for many of us—client and practitioner alike. Many therapists ask their clients whether they want their abdomen worked on, and even if the answer is "yes", the work can be a bit tentative and restrict itself to the upper abdomen. Our circumspection is understandable—the belly is very sensitive, and rubbing it can awaken Aladdin's genie of sexual feelings. Besides, all those organs are in there— what if we did some damage by rubbing too hard?

### Postural issues

Human beings are strange animals for many reasons, several of which we have talked about in earlier Body³ chapters. Here is another one for this chapter: we humans take all our soft, sensitive bits and put them right up front in very vulnerable positions—where they can be seen, struck or bitten.

Most animals hide their soft underbelly and other woundable areas in the least accessible places, protected by their head, their limbs, their back or the ground. Not us: when you stand face to face with another person, the entire front line of the body, from throat to breasts to belly to groin, is within reach of that other person. This is an extraordinary act of postural trust, and it gives us an enormous potential for a profound, uniquely human sensitivity (see Figure 1).

This "up front" posture, however, also puts us in a constantly precarious and potentially defensive position psychologically. Anyone who has examined human structure has noticed that people contract, retract or immobilize themselves to try to protect one or more of these sensitive areas in response to perceived threat or distress—sometimes temporarily, sometimes more or less permanently. Whether the threat is physical or psychogenic, it can express itself as a forward head, hunched shoulders, a sunken chest, a tightly contracted or overly padded belly, and pelvic retraction or hip flexion to protect the groin and genitals. So while our wariness about doing deeper work on and in the belly is understandable, it is also unfortunate, because our organic self is the repository of so much feeling, and much can be done here to restore full expression and easy upright posture, us we shall see.

Our posture also makes hugging more intimate and fun than it is for any other animal. We all know people who lean forward to hug your collarbones, pat your back and peck the air by your cheek; how much they miss of a uniquely human treat!

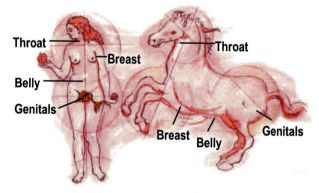

***Figure 1:*** *Shown here is comparison of places of vulnerability in two-leggeds and four-leggeds. Human posture is an extraordinary act of trust. Chronic tension and postural distortion are common in the indicated areas.*

### Is my belly "right"?

And then there is the "hard belly-soft belly" controversy, which is a little bit different from the "fat-thin" dichotomy. Our traditional body ideal is of a taut, flat washboard (as opposed to a washtub) abdomen, a "Bruce Lee" belly that reflects athletic trimness and seems to imply a certain ascetic godliness. This belly, we are told, provides support for the back and creates good posture. Bellies like this can be seen every late night on TV, pitching whatever new ab machine or diet plan some promoter thinks we are gullible enough to buy. The flat belly is promoted in nearly every athletic endeavor, except perhaps Sumo wrestling, and can be seen in the bodywork field in Ida Rolf's little boy logo with his pseudo-adult high chest and flat tummy.

The other prevalent body ideal floating around the bodywork world says, "Hey, relax—that trim belly is way too upright. You want your belly to be loose, man, so that you can breathe deeply and cultivate your chi. It's not how you look that's important; it's how you feel. A little roundness is natural and human—look at babies, what could be more natural then their little round bellies?" This "Buddha" belly is championed by body-centered therapists such as breath workers and Feldenkrais practitioners, and by many Oriental approaches. Is one of these ideal "right"? Is there some compromise position that incorporates them both? Which one do you promote, consciously or unconsciously, in your practice?

Body[3], ever a voice of moderation, recommends the middle way. We have certainly seen trim-as-a-stick runners, addicted to their 10 miles a day, who are hiding a wealth of feeling in their ever-taut bellies. They can be recognized by their emerging anger or depression as soon as they stop running for a few days. And we have seen soft, round bellies that seem to reflect not so much a fully rounded emotionality or a well-developed hara as a sloppy lack of self-discipline and postural collapse. These folks can often be recognized by their fondness for yummy creme rolls. Once we get the anatomical picture in place, we will lay out a strategy for the best of both worlds.

Now, if we let go of all the imagery around how other people (and even ourselves) want our tummies to look like from the outside, how do we want our belly to be from the inside? A few pounds here or there are really unimportant in terms of health and well-being, but we can make a short list of desirable components:

- That there be enough muscle tone around the abdominal balloon to support the organs in position, but not so much that they are cramped and therefore too compressed to do their jobs properly,

- That the abdominal muscles and the back muscles balance each other in standing, with an even tone that allows full movement and length, rather than compression, in the lumbar spine.

- That the movement of the diaphragm in breathing especially be unrestricted; and

- That any extra fat be carried evenly around the spine.

Now, the first three are definitely in our domain as hands-on therapists, and will occupy us for

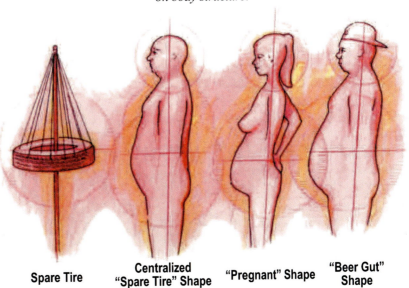

*Figure:2*: Keep weight centralized and you minimize its harmful effects on body structure.

Spare Tire     Centralized "Spare Tire" Shape     "Pregnant" Shape     "Beer Gut" Shape

**The Abdominal Balloon, Part 1**

the rest of this chapter—and for part of the next chapter's installment of "The Abdominal Balloon"—but let us look at the last point first. The author's unsubstantiated conviction, supported only by common sense, is that weight carried out in front of the body is much more damaging than weight carried evenly around the central supporting pole of the spine (see Figure 2).

We all know people who can be wildly overweight, who still dance all night with great skill and panache, and who walk so lightly and gracefully that they would not break an egg. Look at any of these folks and it's dollars to doughnuts that they are carrying their weight literally like a "spare tire"—evenly around the front, back and side. Then spy our someone with a beer belly or a "bay window," and watch them dance or walk. See how that configuration of extra fat distorts their movement, shapes the lower spine, and imagine how it drags literally on their heart.

While it is not always possible, in the author's experience, to change the configuration in which weight is carried around the body, it is definitely worth a try, because it will improve health even when the client is not willing or able to lose their excess weight. Achieving the muscle balances outlined throughout this chapter will move people toward this "spare tire" balance, though it may take a few months and some postural re-education to make the shift fully.

Women in the later stages of pregnancy also have to take care not to fall into a similar pattern of letting the baby get way out in front of them, shortening the lumbar muscles and straining the back. Massage and stretching can help maintain the balance of the upper body over the legs, reducing pain, strain and varicose veins. We will return to this and other pregnancy issues later in this chapter.

The rest of our list has to do with muscle tone, balance and resilience, and these issues are very much open to our help. In this chapter of Body³ we examine the individual myofascial components of the abdominal balloon's outer layer. In the next chapter we will put these elements together with the contents of the abdominal balloon to create some strategies for the best possible form and function in this area.

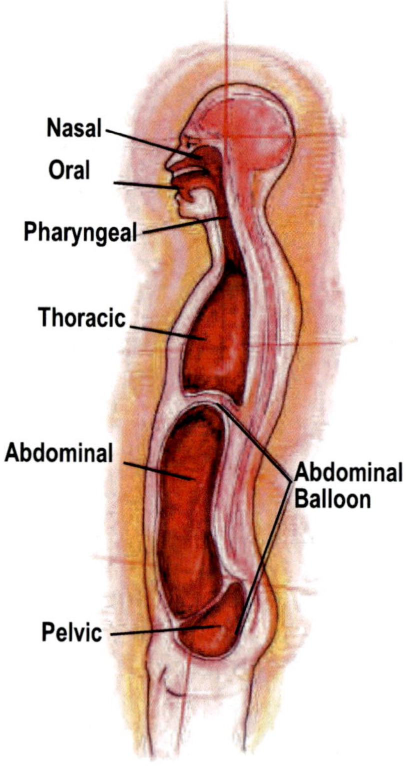

## The big picture

The abdominal balloon is part of the larger ventral cavity in the front of our body, which runs from our nose and mouth all the way down to the lower pelvic area (see Figure 3). The ventral cavity contains our most ancient self—the "gut body" and reproductive organs that can still run our lives, no matter what we may consciously wish, to this day. It is bounded by the ribs, spine, belly muscles and pelvis. We usually divide the ventral cavity into its nasal, oral, pharyngeal, thoracic, abdominal and pelvic parts. Our concern, for now, is limited to the balloon-like shape of the abdomino-pelvic section of the ventral cavity.

The abdominal balloon is a water balloon—the abdominal organs are more than 90 percent water, even in the adult. Like any water balloon, the contents are always exerting an outward pressure, which is restricted by the constricting tension of the membranes and the muscles that surround them in the walls of the ventral cavity. The organs and the membranes will be dealt with in the next chapter of "The Abdominal Balloon"; for now we are going to concentrate on the muscle balance around the balloon: the rectus abdominis, the diaphragm, the transversus ahdominis, the external and internal obliques, the levator ani or pelvic floor,

*Figure 3: The ventral cavity contains many spongy, hollow and muscular organs that maintain our "internal sea," keeping the homeostatic chemical balance intact by nourishing and cleaning the trillions of little cells that would otherwise be quickly isolated from such services. The intake valves are at the head end of the cavity. The pumps for metabolic process, the heart and lungs, lie in the thoracic cavity, but the surfaces of exchange for extracting food and water and sifting out waste are located in the abdominal cavity. The pelvic cavity contains the lower excretory end of these systems, as well as the specialized organs for making more of us.*

the quadratus lumborum, the psoas, the iliacus, the piriformis and the obturatur internus all interconnect to form the skin of the balloon.

In the next chapter we will also look at the coordination of these muscles with the paraspinal muscles behind the lumbar transverse processes—and the erector spinae and some other issues of soft-tissue strategies in this area.

The muscles surrounding the abdomen obviously work from second to second as a whole, coordinated with each other and with the rest of the body. To study them and their various functions, we have to look at them individually through particular lenses; thus we will be using a number of metaphors to clarify how these muscles function together in different ways. Don't confuse the map with the territory; the actual body is much more complex and wonderful than we can convey within a short column, but we trust that the images will lead you to ever more useful therapeutic work by giving you a more three-dimensional understanding. (To assist you in getting a more complete picture than we can provide here, we include references to Frank Netter's *Atlas of Human Anatomy*, published by CIBA-Geigy, although you can follow along with any good anatomy atlas.)

The long list of muscles shown to the right (see Figure 4) can be easily organized into four categories: the diaphragm, which forms the top of the box (see, we have switched metaphors on you already: the balloon has become a six-sided box!), and the pelvic floor, lateral rotators and iliacus, which form the bottom of the box. The psoas and quadratus lumborum, along with the lumbar vertebrae, line the back of the box; the abdominal muscles form the front and the two sides (Netter plate 246). We begin with the abdominals themselves.

The abdominals began life as the floor of the abdominal balloon. Look at a cat or a dog and you will see that the abdominals are directly responsible for holding up the organs, which hang in a sack from the spine. In humans, the organs still hang from the spine, but the abdominals have become the sides of the balloon-box. The muscles are arranged, in cats and dogs and us, like the layers in plywood: each successive muscle layer has a different "grain" to create the various lines of pull and resistance, lending extra strength to this highly mobile area (see Figure 5).

## The belt—the transversus abdominis

The deepest muscle, which wraps the organs horizontally, is the transversus abdominis (Netter plates 234, 246). The first thing to remember is that there are really two of them, a right one and a left one, joined by a fascial sheet across the front so that they act like one muscle. The second thing that folks

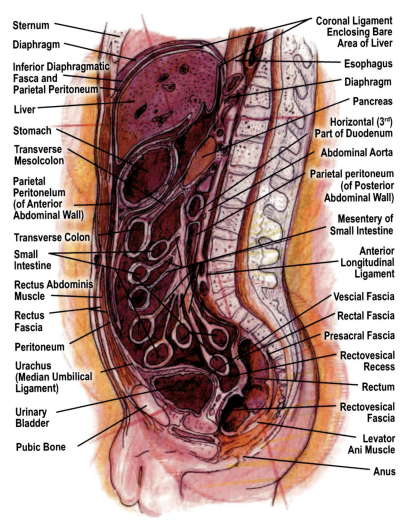

*Figure 4:* The abdominal cavity is lined with muscles that hold the organs in and up. In this view we can see the vertical belt around the circumference.

**The Abdominal Balloon, Part 1**

tend to forget, even after an anatomy class, is that the fasciae of the transversus (and the obliques as well) go all the way around the body to attach to the transverse processes of the lumbar vertebrae.

If we start from those strong attachments and move around laterally and forward, we see the muscle attaching superiorly to the bottom of the rib cage, and inferiorly to the iliac crest. As we pass the side of the body and start coming around to the front, the belt gets a lot wider, like those huge, flashy numbers favored by Elvis in his Vegas heyday.

The upper border stays with the rib cartilages of the subcostal arch; the lower border, having run out of iliac crest, wraps itself into the inguinal ligament (Netter plate 245).

Although the muscle fibers run out around the edge of the rectus abdominis, the fascia keeps going all the way to the linea alba at the midline in the front, where this myofascial unit is at its widest, running all the way from the xiphoid process down to the pubic bone (Netter plate 234).

This belt has a substantial effect on the pressure within the abdominal balloon. Proper tone in the transversus has a great deal to do with keeping the organs in place and supporting the lumbar spine. Low tone in this muscle allows the abdominal contents to loll forward and out over the sides of the ilia. A strong contraction of the transversus forces the water balloon to seek other openings, like squeezing the toothpaste tube, and thus accompanies throwing up, defecating, coughing and labor contractions (tightening it and the rest of the abdominal balloon is known as the Valsalva's maneuver). Contraction of the transversus also assists in creating forced exhalation, and thus is helpful in playing the clarinet, blowing up balloons and moving pianos (just try pushing an immovable object, and you will feel it contract). Chronic hypertonicity of the transversus compresses the organs and could predispose one toward a hiatal or inguinal hernia, urinary incontinence, hemorrhoids or any number of digestive troubles.

### The "x": the obliques

The external and internal obliques often work together and form an 'x', so we will consider them together (Netter plates 232 & 233). The internal oblique is just outside the transversus, and you can approximate its position and fiber direction by putting the heel of your hand on the top of your hip bone (the front edge of the iliac crest), with your elbows wide and your fingers spread out on your belly and pointing as vertically as you can manage (I never said this would be comfortable, just enlightening).

In this position, your thumbs should be going nearly straight up and down somewhere near your sides, and indeed the fibers of the internal oblique are nearly going straight up and down out here from hip to the lower ribs. Your splayed little finger may be horizontal or even heading down from the anterior superior iliac spine (ASIS) toward the pubic bone, and the fibers of the internal oblique do the same. In between these two, your three middle fingers are headed toward your belly button and the ribs on the other side, and that where the middle fibers go, fading into the same fascial sheets and the linea alba as the transversus.

When the internal obliques contract together they flex the trunk, and singly they can help the opposite external oblique rotate the trunk.

To approximate the position of the external obliques, put your hands into a couple of imaginary wind breaker pockets, with your fingers splayed as before—but this time your thumbs against the index

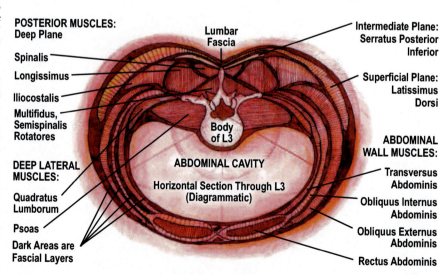

*Figure 5:* Understanding this picture is one key to getting both ease and control in abdominal posture.

fingers. Notice that once again, as with the internals, the lateral fibers (your little finger this time) are nearly vertical. Grab the side of your waist and you will be able to feel (unless you, too, are like Sidney Greenstreet) these fibers of both obliques, although the external is easier to feel, being more superficial. Why is this often such a ticklish spot?

The rest of the fibers of the external oblique head down to the pubic bone, and into the abdominal aponeurosis the other two deeper abdominals also joined. Thus the external oblique has three distinct lines of pull: down at the sides to create lateral flexion, down to the pubic bone to create forward flexion, and diagonally over to the opposite internal oblique to create trunk rotation (see Figure 6).

### The guy-rope: the rectus abdominis

The last of the abdominal muscles is the familiar rectus, abdominis which starts way up on the stable fifth rib and passes down, narrowing as it goes, to a round attachment right on top of the pubic bone (Netter plates 233 & 234).

How many joints does the rectus act on? The answer to this question, for any muscle, is "Let your fingers do the walking." On the skeleton, walk your fingers from the origin to the insertion; no fair making big jumps!—and every joint you cross is affected to some degree by the muscle.

If we do this mentally now with the rectus, we have to start on the fifth rib and walk around on it to the spine, crossing the costovertebral joint, and then passing down all the spinal facet joints from T5 to the sacrum, across the sacroiliac joint to the ilium, and then around to the pubis (Netter plate 231). All those joints, especially the spinal joints, are directly affected by the actions and relative tonus of the rectus, and many more joints, of course, can be affected indirectly.

The rectus is thus like a guy-rope that really has a large effect on all the structures above it, because it has such good leverage on the front of the rib cage. The muscle cannot choose, of course, whether it pulls the ribs toward the pubic bone or the pubic bone toward the ribs; it just pulls equally on both ends. The physics of the situation, in most cases, dictates that a hypertoned rectus will pull the ribs down toward the pubic bone, with a host of secondary results. This is the problematic part of the "Bruce Lee" belly—if the rectus overcomes other muscles and pulls the ribs out of shape, well, the belly may be flat, but a host of other problems, like kyphosis, neck pain, lumbar disc problems or restricted breathing, will eventually follow.

Why does the rectus have those tendinous inscriptions that create the washboard look so favored by the "Bruce Lee" belly advocates? Because this muscle passes over such a long empty space with no supporting bone underneath, it is more prone to tear if it were overstretched—in an overhead tennis smash, say. The sartorious, for example, which is even longer, is supported by the femur. But the rectus is safer as four smaller muscles than as a long thin strip out there on its own.

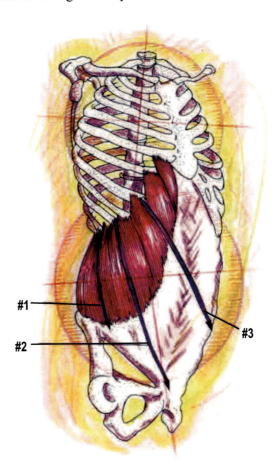

***Figure 6:*** *The external oblique anchors the ribs to the hip bone at the side (#1), the pubic bone in the middle (#2), and through the internal oblique on the other side to the opposite hip (#3). Each of these pulls is a follow-on from another muscle: #1 continues the pull of the latissimus, #2 continues the pull of the sarratus anterior, and #3 continues the pull of the pectoralis major. Just lateral to the pubic bone is the hole where men have the opening to the scrotum, which can be the site of an inguinal hernia.*

**The Abdominal Balloon, Part 1**

### The ourobouros

If the transversus is a horizontal belt, the rectus is part of another belt that runs vertically around the abdominal balloon. The image of a vertical belt is like the ourobouros—the cosmic snake that bites its own tail.

This belt includes most of the rest of the muscles of the abdominal balloon, from the rectus around the pelvic floor, up the front of the spine, onto the diaphragm and around to the back side of the rectus again (Figure 4, Netter plate 333). Before we get there, however, we need to consider the abdominal wall in terms of fascial layers, not just the muscles, because a funny thing happens on the way to the pubic bone.

The rectus is often characterized as the most superficial of the abdominal muscles, and in muscular terms, it is true: no muscle sits in front of the rectus. In terms of fascial layers, however, it is a different story. The books often show you the muscles minus the fascia, so it gets confusing, but in this area we need to be clear about it—but don't get neurotic about the abdominal aponeurosis. The rectus muscle sits in the rectus sheath, fascia which runs in front of the rectus and behind it, and is continuous with the sheets we talked about from the obliques and transversus (Figure 5).

Figure 7A shows you how the sheets are arranged for the upper part of the muscle, all the way down to below the navel. It is pretty straight forward and logical: the sheet that is the continuation of the external oblique runs in front of the rectus (so, in fascial terms the external oblique is the most superficial muscle). The internal oblique sheet splits around the rectus, part going in front and part going behind, and the entire sheet from the transversus goes behind the rectus. They all meet and tend to be tacked down together at the linea alba, the 'white line' that goes right from the xiphoid of the sternum down the middle of the belly to the pubic symphysis

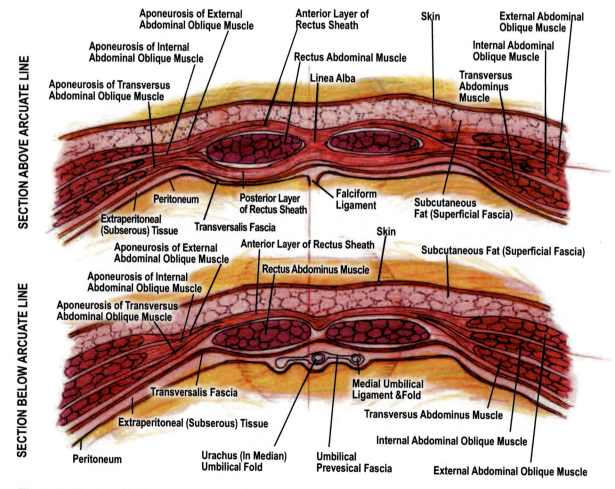

**Figure 7:** *The facial layers of the abdominal muscles in cross-section, A) above the hara, B) below the hara*

**48**  Body³: A Therapist's Anatomy Reader

(Netter plate 234 & 235).

Strangely, about two inches below the umbilicus at the level of the hara, the arrangement suddenly changes, and all the sheets—both obliques and the transversus, pass in front of the rectus (Figure 7B). So in "Mr. Muscle" terms—that chart on your wall—the rectus is still the most superficial, but in fascial terms, the lowest part of the rectus is now the deepest of the abdominal muscles.

So what? Here's what: The next part of the abdominal balloon we are going to look at is the pelvic floor. The 'what' is that if the rectus abdominis is the deepest abdominal muscle, then it interacts with the pelvic floor, and is thus a way to affect the pelvic floor, which can be a hard place to reach otherwise.

### The pelvic floor

Let us fill in some detail on the pelvic floor. We have already said that the abdominal wall is the organic "floor" in four-leggeds, and a "side-wall" in humans; the very opposite is true of the pelvic floor: it is a "side-wall" in a horse, but in humans it is, indeed, the floor that must hold everything else up. It is the funnel-shaped drain (if you will forgive the image) in the pelvic basin. The main consequence of this is that the pelvic floor is denser, tougher and thicker in humans—it has to be to prevent prolapse.

The most obvious difference for us shows up in childbirth. A large infant's head must pass this small and tough membrane, with results to which most mothers and all midwives can attest. Deep relaxation and tissue preparation through stretching and massage can help the birth process immensely. Birth in other animals is generally easier because the myofascia, being under less pressure, is not so tough and can stretch more easily. Those not familiar with farms may say "Yuck!" but it is relatively easy to reach into a mare to assist the birth of a foal, whereas reaching into a human mother with forceps is problematic and, according to some birth experts, so damaging that it should only be done when the life of the mother or baby are threatened.

After giving birth, restoring the pelvic floor can also be assisted by bodywork and exercise. It is here that the connection between the pelvic floor and the rectus becomes relevant. Sometimes, women find it hard to restore the pelvic floor after birth, leading to diminished sexual enjoyment and/or urinary

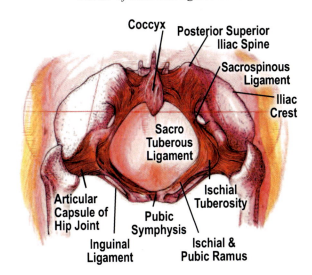

**Figure 8:** *The pelvic floor provides the bottom for pelvic basin, and is bordered by a roughly diamond-shaped border of bone and ligament.*

incontinence. This is sometimes accompanied by a small pouch of an unwelcome little belly at the bottom of the abdomen. Working on the lower abdomen in conjunction with exercise can help restore the balance in the muscle tone, often with many psychological side benefits.

The pelvic floor, or levator ani muscle, is a hammock composed of three muscles: the coccygeus, the iliococcygeus and the pubococcygeus (see Figure 8). Two lateral rotators, the piriformis and obturatur internus, are also part of the deep basin as well (but we have already covered these muscles in earlier Body³ columns, so we will leave them pretty much alone here). The coccygeus is the smallest, lying right over the sacrospinous ligament; this was the muscle that wagged our tail when we had one. The iliococcygeus comes in from the side and meets its opposite number in a raphe (wall) of connective tissue. This median raphe is what is cut and sewn back together in an episiotomy (Netter plates 337, 338 & 339).

These two muscles, as can be seen in Figures 9A and 9B, are shaped like a "U," looping from the front toward the tailbone and back to the front again (Netter plate 338). If these muscles tighten, they tend to pull the pelvic floor up toward the head, and pull the anus and whatever else you have—prostate or vagina—forward toward the pubic bone.

The iliococcygeus has a unique anatomic arrangement: from its central raphe it reaches forward and out toward the ischial rami, but that

**The Abdominal Balloon, Part 1**

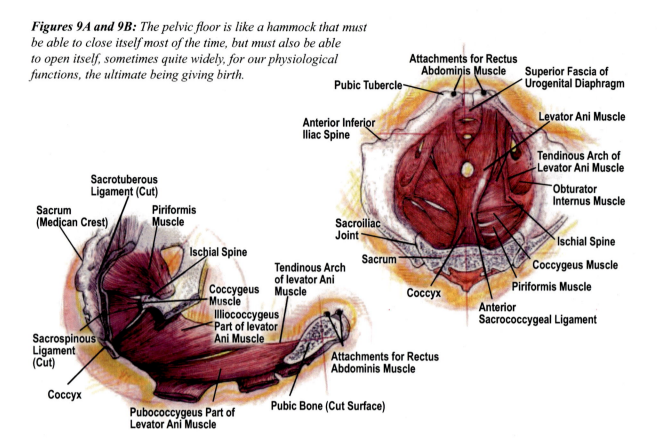

**Figures 9A and 9B:** The pelvic floor is like a hammock that must be able to close itself most of the time, but must also be able to open itself, sometimes quite widely, for our physiological functions, the ultimate being giving birth.

bone is covered by the obturatur internus. The iliococcygeus has no choice but to attach itself to the fascia of the obturatur, one of very few places in the body where a muscle originated solely on the fascia of another muscle (Netter plate 349). Thus, for the initiated (it is too complicated to explain the technique here, and besides it is pretty intimate), structural therapists can affect the pelvic floor by manipulating the obturatur internus.

A final, general comment about the pelvic floor is its relationship to breathing. If hypertonicity in the abdomen can restrict the downward movement of the diaphragm, so can tightness in the pelvic floor. This is easily demonstrated: either stand or sit up straight so that you are resting on your sitting bones, not your tail bone (this is generally good advice for most times). Now breathe in and notice how your breath feels, how deeply you can breathe, how easy it is, etc. Now simply tighten your anus and hold it so; this tightens the pelvic floor. Now breathe in again in the same way. How does it feel now? Need any more convincing of the importance of relaxed tone in the pelvic floor?

The last muscle, the pubococcygeus, runs from the tailbone beside the pelvic openings to the pubic bone, and is thus a continuation of the rectus abdominis, in terms of the line of pull. If we keep going in the same direction from the pubococcygeus, we go right onto the anterior longitudinal ligament, which runs all the way up the spine. The crura ("feet") of the diaphragm arise from this ligament in front of the lumbar bodies, and we can ride from there around on the central tendon of the diaphragm to the back of the rectus again, thus completing the circle of the vertical belt (see Figure 6 and Netter plate 246).

This also completes our basic tour of the muscles of the abdominal balloon. If you can "see" both the horizontal and vertical belts described here, you are ready to understand the strategy for giving your client's belly a relaxed and versatile new contour. In the next chapter we will proceed to these strategies, some considerations of how the organs "hang around" inside us, and some further general comments on the abdominal-lumbar relationship in Part Two of "The Abdominal Balloon."

## Some thoughts on muscle shape

The shapes of muscle's reveal their function. Although muscles come in many shapes, and all, of course, are shaped individually, most fall easily into four categories: triangular, fusiform, pennate and quadrate.

**TRIANGULAR   FUSIFORM   PENNIFORM   QUADRATE**

What unique function can a triangular muscle serve? All muscles contract, of course, and serve to move bones around joints, but what does a triangular muscle do in particular? It has a wide origin, narrowing down to a narrow insertion. Therefore it can control the movement of a joint over a wide range. Imagine raising a flagpole. The flagpole is fixed to the earth at one end, and a rope is tied to the other. Someone stands on the roof pulling on the rope to raise the pole. Can you see how it might swing left or right and be very hard to manage? Now imagine that we put three people on the roof, our original lifter plus one some feet to his left, the other some feet to his right. Each of them has a rope that goes to the far end of the pole also. Can you see how they will be able to control the pole easily now?

Think of some triangular muscles, and where they are used: traps, lats, pects and delts, for instance. These muscles, all basically triangular, surround the shoulder joint. The rotator cuff muscles, also, fit the picture. Where else? Gluteus medius, minimus, and piriformis and a bunch of other triangular muscles surround the hip. Now, both of these joints are ball-and-socket, they have many degrees of freedom and need wide-ranging control. Therefore there are lots of triangular muscles around the most freely moving joints of the body. In our model above, the flagpole is like the femur or the humerus. So with triangular muscles, you get great control.

Fusiform muscles are the cigar-shaped muscles they always put in diagrams of a generic muscle: it starts at one point, spreads out a bit through the belly of the muscle, then narrows again to attach at another point. These muscles have quite long fibers, so they have a very long range of available motion, and only one precise angle of pull (as opposed to the triangular muscles that pull over wide range of angles). Therefore fusiform muscles are most often used over hinge joints, where the pull can only be in one direction anyway. The rectus femoris, hamstrings, biceps, brachialis, triceps and tibialis anterior come to mind, working over the hinges of the elbow, knee and ankle. Thus the great advantage of fusiform muscles is range. (I know, I know—I can hear anatomist-readers everywhere sucking in their breaths to clamor our objections and exceptions. We are categorizing here, and categories are man-made inventions applied to a nature-made body. It is clear that nature has less use for categories than we do, but they can still be useful to us, even if inexact. Think of Myers-Briggs, or astrological signs.)

Penniform (feather-shaped) muscles have a long tendon that goes through the belly of the muscle, and the muscle fibers angle in toward the tendon. These muscles have short fibers, so their range is not as great as the fusiform muscles, but they have a high degree of strength for the amount of room they take up. This is because the strength of a muscle is determined by its cross-section. To measure the cross section of a fusiform muscle, since the fibers all run straight, we would just mentally cut it and measure the

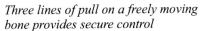
*Three lines of pull on a freely moving bone provides secure control*

**The Abdominal Balloon, Part 1**

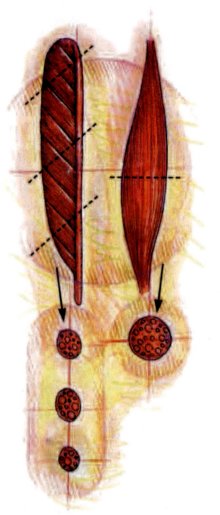

*The cross-section (and thus the relative strength) of a pennate muscle is surprisingly high.*

amount of area the muscle fibers make up. Since a penniform muscle has angled fibers though, we would have to make several angled cuts to include them all, and thus we would get a relatively larger cross-section. So with penniform muscles you get a lot of strength in a small package, at the cost of a greater range.

Where do we find penniform muscles? There are tons in the lower leg—tibialis posterior, the toe flexors, the gastrocnemius, and many of those finger and thumb movers in the forearm. We do not want huge muscles in the lower arm and leg, it would unbalance us. Not only would we look like Popeye, it would require even larger muscles in the thigh and upper arm to accelerate the extra weight in the lower limbs, and pretty soon we would all be as muscle bound as the Hulk. We do need a lot of strength in the lower limbs, to grip suitcases and to launch the whole body up on tippy-toes, and more. Penniform muscles provide that strength without taking up so much space.

But if penniform muscles have such a short range, how come we can move our fingers and feet through such a wide range of motion? The answer is that small movements in these muscles are translated around pulleys in the wrists and ankles to produce larger resulting motion at the end of the limbs.

Finally, we have quadrate muscles, shaped like a square or a rhomboid. Quadratus lumborum, the rhomboids, and quadratus femoris are all named for their quadrate shape. What do you think is their special function? Quadrate muscles can contract, of course, but their primary postural function is stabilization. The QL stabilizes the ribs on the pelvis, the rhomboids stabilize the scapula on the ribs. Stabilizing muscles tend to resist being stretched, rather than doing so much active shortening.

So what about these abdominal muscles we have been talking about? What are they? The transversus has a special shape all its own, but in form it is closest to a quadrate muscle. The rectus abdominis is almost a quadrate muscle, though it is a little wider at the top than it is at the bottom, so it might be considered a triangular muscle. It is about the same for the internal and external obliques, basically a sheet, but spread like a fan.

And in fact, if you think about it, this is exactly right, because these muscles have to split their functions between being stabilizing muscles and control muscles. When we are working with our arms or legs, during square dancing for example, the belly muscles have to stabilize the ribs to the pelvis. But when we do the hula or the twist, they have to act like triangular muscles, controlling the 'ball-and-socket' joint of the lumbothoracic spine. Pretty neat, huh? ∎

---

**Footnotes:**

1. I have not seen this idea laid out in any book. I worked it out for myself, but cannot believe that others have not also thought of it. I would be grateful if a reader can point out some similar discussion in a book somewhere.
— *Tom Myers*

# Chapter 6:
# The Abdominal Balloon, Part 2: GUT-LEVEL STRATEGIES

In the last chapter we outlined the myofascial components of the abdominal balloon, and set two strategic goals: one was how to balance more evenly around the spinal column any extra weight our clients are carrying; we also asked ourselves whether there was any way to toe the line between the soft belly desired for emotional openness and the strong back required for athletic endeavor.

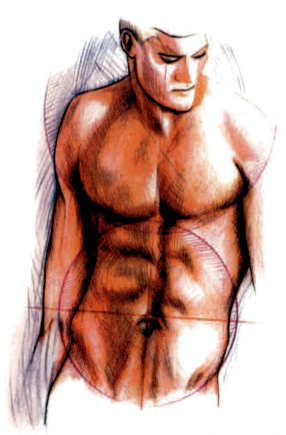

Our culture's "ideal" abdomen is taut and flat—but a "washboard" belly can lead to just as many structural difficulties as a "washtub" belly.

In reviewing the muscles and fasciae of the abdomino-pelvic cavity, we called attention to two "belts" within the balloon: a horizontal belt made up of the transversus muscles, which together gird in the belly from the left transverse processes of the lumbars all the way 'round to the right transverse processes (see Figure 1), and a vertical belt composed of the respiratory diaphragm, the back side of the rectus abdominis, the pelvic floor, and the anterior longitudinal ligament of the lumbars (see Figure 3).

We also called attention to the two crosses—the "+" cross of the rectus and transversus, and the "x" cross of the obliques, which both meet at the umbilicus.

These elements are keys to understanding the myofascial strategies that will allow us to achieve our goals. First, though, we will want to consider the importance of the sensitive umbilical area itself.

### The belly button—
### crossroads of our emotional life

A central point to our psychophysiology is the umbilicus, the belly button. For the first nine months of our life, first the embryonic yolk sac and then the umbilical cord were our total connection to all nourishment. We start life with our bellies wide, wide open to the front, but we gradually get longer in the back and close into the familiar fetal position. The navel is thus a focal place of development. Anatomically, our navel connects with all the muscles of both the "+" and the "x," (or "flag") (see Figure 2), as well as having connections through the peritoneum to the liver (the falciform ligament), the urinary bladder and the intestine (Netter plate 236). Thus, connections from the navel radiate out in all directions. (To assist you in getting a more complete picture, reference to Frank Netter's *Atlas of Human Anatomy*, published by CIBA-Geigy, are included

The Abdominal Balloon, Part 2

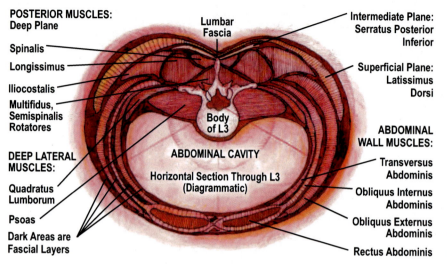

*Figure 1: A horizontal belt made up of the transversus muscles runs from the left transverse processes of the lumbars all the way around the viscera to the right transverse processes.*

throughout this chapter, although you can follow along with any good anatomy atlas.)

Baby's first breath—besides everything else it is spiritually and emotionally—is a dramatic mechanical event. After nine months of receiving both food and oxygen passively via the placenta and the mother's blood, the infant begins absorbing its chemical needs in a radically new way. The wet-paper-towel tissues of the lungs are suddenly pushed open by atmospheric pressure, the valve between the heart ventricles snaps shut, the ductus venosus and arteriosus collapse. All this is miraculous, sudden and normal.

When the baby is born, the pink and pulsing umbilical cord is still attached to the placenta, which is still attached to the wall of the uterus for about a quarter of an hour after birth. The umbilical cord is still able to do its job—but in our modern technocratic version of birth (don't get me started), the umbilical cord is cut very quickly, usually within seconds of the baby being born. It has to be clamped, because blood is still pulsing through it.

In the newly opened lungs there are 150 enzymatic reactions involved in getting the oxygen from the air to the hemoglobin bushes inside the red blood cells inside the alveolar capillaries. Could it be that it might take a minute or two to line up this 150-step bucket brigade through out the many square feet of the baby's lung surface? In other words, are we cutting the cord too soon? If we left the cord attached for a while, what would be the problem? Is it medical necessity, or simply fear and the need to control that power this procedure?

In home births, the cord is most often left attached, while the mother nurses the baby for the first time. The cord is always long enough for the baby to reach the breast. The stimulation of nursing helps to deliver the afterbirth. After some minutes, the cord goes greyish and stops pulsing, and ceases to look as if it is part of somebody. At that point it could be cut without clamping (although you do, to prevent sepsis), and we can rest assured that the baby is getting enough oxygen through its new method of breathing.

In our rush to control birth and separate the baby from its mother, are we as a society creating a feeling of lack, a feeling of deprivation, that stays with some children their entire lives, no matter what abundance they were born into? Is the predominance of this kind of medical procedure in part responsible for the desperate consumer culture we live in?

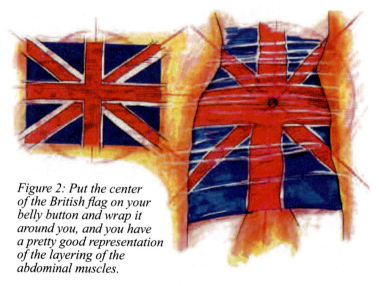

*Figure 2: Put the center of the British flag on your belly button and wrap it around you, and you have a pretty good representation of the layering of the abdominal muscles.*

Speculation, sure, but if you have a chance to hang around babies not born into the frantic rush of hospitals, you can feel the difference. As a therapist, this author has found the umbilical fasciae to be one of the most—if not the most—potent storage spots for feelings of lack, dependence, "starvation" and other emotional attitudes of deprivation. Thus sensitive exploration around the navel, especially the deeper parts, is a potent source of healing for these feelings.

Let me climb down off my soapbox here, so that we can proceed with our stated objectives.

### Balancing weight around the spine

We noted in the last issue that extra weight carried around the spine like a "spare tire" is less damaging to structure and function than weight that sits out front, like a beer belly. Can that really be changed? The answer is "yes," but not always, and it takes some time. When weight starts getting carried out front, it drags certain myofasciae with it. All of the following will need to be done several times; use your intuition and your eyes to tell you what needs work most. Here is a general "how to" (even so, there may be individual quirks you need to address beyond this overall program): first, you need to determine if the extra weight is carried inside or outside the abdominal muscle wall. Have your client pick up his head and upper chest as he lies on his back, so the abdomen is tensed. Palpate firmly through the fat to the muscle. If the rectus muscle is close to being parallel to the table, and you are going through considerable amounts of tissue to feel that, then you can proceed with the following program. (If, on the other hand, you find that when the client lifts his head that there is little fat between your hand and the muscle layer, and that the rectus is still arched like a Japanese bridge, then you must change tactics. In this case, the bulk is inside the muscle layer, either

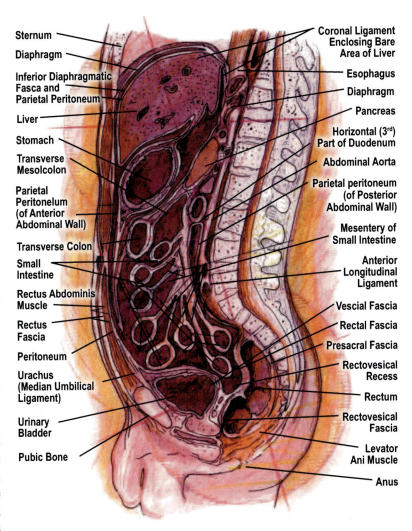

*Figure 3:* The abdomino-pelvic cavity also contains a vertical belt made up of the respiratory diaphragm, the back side of the rectus abdominis, the pelvic floor and the anterior longitudinal ligament of the lumbars.

in the omental fat or, more often, simply too much bulk is being carried in the gut. There is only one solution to this, and that is for the person to get used to eating less, in a sustained manner—and you can tell them I said so.)

Given that you had a positive "bay window" test, you can begin working: begin putting weight in its place by cleaning, clearing and moving the tissues back along the iliac crest from the anterior superior iliac spine (asis). Begin with the outer laminae of the abdominal fasciae, but you will eventually need to get into the inner laminae. To really reach the internal oblique and transversus fasciae and move them back, you need to be hooked onto the inner edge of the crest. You can do some

**The Abdominal Balloon, Part 2**

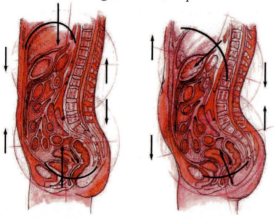

*Figure 4:* When the vertical belt is in balance (left), the respiratory and pelvic diaphragms can "feel" each other. When they are out of balance (right), things start to lock up.

of it with fingertips on your side-lying client, but using a knuckle or even an elbow (it looks worse than it feels) with the client on his back will usually be necessary to make a difference in these layers, especially if they are extra thick or tight.

Having the client reach across his body with the same arm can assist you in getting the most out of this move.

The lower ribs and sub-costal arch also needs to move back, so we do the same operation to the lower ribs. Much more caution and circumspection is necessary here, however, because of the fragility of the ends of the floating and near-floating ribs.

Begin just lateral to the rectus abdominis in the costal arch, moving tissue back along the ribs, being careful of the rib ends and cartilages, and moving the tissue right along the "grain" of the ribs and intercostal spaces. Again, the heavier and denser the tissue, the more firm or repetitive you must be. You may carry this out to the lateral line of the body, again being careful of the sensitive free end of the 11th rib.

The lumbar erector muscles are our next port of call, for they must be lengthened to keep pace with the changing belly. If the lumbar spinous processes are buried deep in a valley of band-like erectors, move the inner erectors out to each side as you lengthen them, making room for the lumbars to come back. Take the lateral edge of the erectors and move them up toward the head, taking care not to push on the 11th and 12th ribs in the process.

Since the rectus and belly wall will generally need some toning in these cases, we often give a modified version of a sit-up as client homework. Have the client lie on his back with his knees up. Have him lift his head and upper chest, so that most or all of the thoracic spine is off the table. His outstretched arms are on either side of his knees. The chin should be firmly tucked in; aching in the neck is a reason to stop the exercise. The client moves his hands about one inch along the legs (his head moving toward his knees) in a tiny "crunch" at a rate of about one per second. The goal is to do this 100 times, but the client can build toward that number. The exercise can be made harder by lifting one foot, then the other, then both, off the table while continuing the exercise. When 400 of these (100 in each position: both legs down, each leg up, both legs straight up) are nearly effortless, the muscle is well-toned—and both client and therapist will regard the effort as time well-spent in terms of shape-shifting. Other parts of the body may call out to you as part of this same pattern. If the head is held well forward of the rest of the body, the weight will resist the backward move. The groin can also get pulled down in this pattern, requiring work on the pectineus, iliacus, or the adductors to get full extension in the hip. The deep lateral rotators will require work in those with deeply buried lumbars (the design and treatment of all of these muscles was discussed in Chapter 3).

If you are firm in your intent and the tissues actually move, you and your client should see results in a lessening of strain on the back and neck, and increased energy and coordination, as well as the visual change of contour that was our original goal.

Clients with "bay windows" usually come with another accompanying problem, and that is that as the belly lengthens and the lower back shortens and the whole lumbar segment goes forward, the respiratory and pelvic diaphragms—the top and bottom of the abdominal balloon—get out of balance with each other (see Figure 4).

As you get the front and back of the balloon more balanced, the top and bottom will come into better relation with each other naturally. To test this, have your clients take a deep breath as they sit erect on the edge of the table; can they feel the response in the pelvic floor? Then have them sit on your hand, so that your hand is between their sitz bones (you can do this fully clothed for comfort); can you feel the response to inhalation in the pelvic floor? If you can, the client is on the road back toward healthy functioning.

Most of these folks will also benefit from the following discussion on balancing the lower back with the abdominals. The above sequence can also be applied to ease pressure and strain for pregnant women, but we hesitate to say so, because great sensitivity is required to work in this area in the later stages of pregnancy. In the earlier stage of pregnancy, one does run a slight risk of inducing a miscarriage, or being blamed for it even if you had nothing to do with it. So, please, if you carry these ideas to pregnant women, do so with clarity, experience and caution.

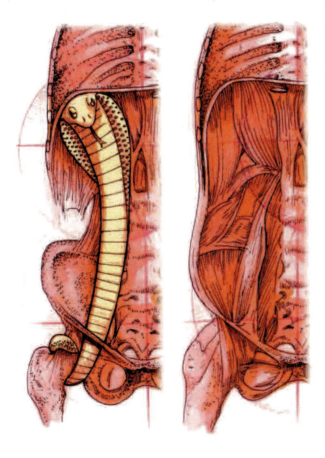

*Figure 5:* The relation between each psoas and each dome of the diaphragm is like a cobra: The tail arises from the distal end of the psoas, the lesser trochanter, curls up over the front of the pelvis, rears up behind the peritoneum to the lumbars, and the hood of the "cobra" is the dome of the diaphragm.

## The cobras

We have left the iliacus out of our discussion, because it has less to do with the abdominal balloon than the hip—and we covered that in Chapter 3. The psoas and the quadratus lumborum, however, form the back wall of the abdominal wall, and support the front of the lumbar spine. We are going to discuss how the psoas affects the lumbar spine in terms of rotation in a future column, and the same for the quadratus lumborum's effect on breathing.

For right now, we just want to raise just one more image, to help us understand the relationship between the psoas and the diaphragm. The diaphragm relates to breathing and the upper body; the psoas relates to walking and the lower body. The junction between them lies behind and between the kidneys and their adrenal caps, is associated with the solar plexus (the second biggest "brain" in our body) and sits right in front of the unique lumbodorsal junction of the spine. This is an essential area, crucial to coordination. It also carries a load of a psychological significance, relating to how we fulfill our needs.

The books, having scraped away all the fascia, give the appearance that the diaphragm and the psoas are quite separate, but in vivo this is not the case: they run right by each other—the psoas up to T12, the diaphragm down to about L3—and they are very much interconnected by both fascia and function.

Now, try this image on for size: The diaphragm is not one big dome, it is two—left and right. If you look at the relation between each psoas and each dome of the diaphragm, it is like two cobras: The tail arises from the distal end of the psoas, the lesser trochanter, curls up over the front of the pelvis, rears up behind the peritoneum to the lumbars, and the hood or each "cobra" is the dome of the diaphragm (see Figure 5 or Netter plate 246). The tail is the core of walking, and the head is the core of breathing; getting them to work in perfect concert is the work of a lifetime. This image has been helpful to me in seeing the balance of the core in my clients and getting it right. I hope it is helpful to you too.

## Balance around the balloon

Obviously, balance in both of the "belts" mentioned above is important for optimum function in the abdominal balloon. In terms of the horizontal belt, good tonus of the transversus is necessary to hold our organs firmly against the spine. We are

**The Abdominal Balloon, Part 2**

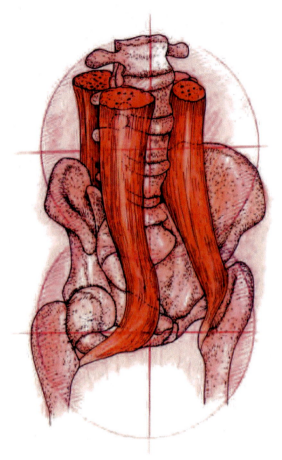

*Figure 6: The psoas can support the front of the spine so that the abdominals are free to breathe and be breathed.*

not going into breathing much here, as it will be the subject of our next chapter, but we do need to note one very important, often ignored fact: the abdominal contents, the organs, are generally still hung off the spine via the mesentery, as they are in the quadruped. In a human, the pelvic floor takes on an extra job of supporting them from below, as we noted before, but the diaphragm also takes on, out of necessity, an extra job of holding them up from above. We tend to forget, if we ever knew, that the liver and the stomach (or to be more precise, the bags that the liver and stomach come in) are firmly attached to the diaphragm from below (see sidebar, "The Peritoneum and Visceral Manipulation").

### Strength in the back, openness in the front

Our other goal was to see if we could find our way out of the conundrum between the athletic "Bruce Lee" belly, and the emotionally open, chi-filled "Buddha Belly." The athletic belly argument positsthat good abdominal tone, besides giving that socially desirable washboard look, helps support the lower back by counterbalancing the lumbar erectors. The trouble with this idea is that it ignores the three other layers of muscle in between.

Looking at Figure 1 (or Netter plate 332), we need to realize that the lumbar area is held not by only two sets of muscles—the rectus abdominis and the erectors, but by five sets of muscles: the erectors behind the spine; the abdominal fasciae, principally the transversus, just beside the spine; the quadratus lumborum, also beside the spine but in front of the abdominals; the psoas, just in front of the spine; and the rectus, way in front of the spine. If you get balance across the first four of these layers, the rectus is not necessary for good lumbar support.

The lumbar vertebrae viewed from above look a bit like the Egyptian symbol of life: the ankh, a cross with a circle at the top. The cross part creates four gullies, or grooves, around the spine. The erectors fill in the grooves in back of the spine, and the psoas fills in the grooves on the front side of the spine (see Figure 1 again), while the middle two layers hang onto the transverse processes. When you get lengthened balance among these four muscles, the abdominals, and the rectus abdominis in particular, are not necessary to maintain the proper curvature in the lower back.

The psoas, because of its triangular nature, creates hyperextension (lordosis) with its lower fibers, and lumbar flexion (flattening of the lower back) with its upper fibers (see "Chapter 3, for a discussion of this effect). The back muscles, the erectors and the transversospinalis, create lordosis and finally lumbar compression, if they clamp down too hard. If the psoas is too tight (which creates further lumbar compression), or too lax (offering no support at all), then you need to bring in the abdominals to make up for what the psoas is not doing. (See Figure 6. For a more sophisticated discussion of this model, see Chapter 4.)

If the psoas has a lengthened tone, then you can leave the abdominals to do their job of holding in the organs, aiding in our physiological pulsations, and assisting the back when we are lifting or pushing something really heavy. Otherwise, they are not necessary to posture. On the contrary, as you draw them into postural roles through excessive exercise or lack of tone in the psoas, they start a host of problems, such as forward head, kyphosis and respiratory restriction. If everything gets low-toned, the upper body collapses into the lower, with predictable results. The "best of both worlds" strategy—which gives maximum support while leaving the breathing mechanism free—has to involve lengthened tone of both psoas and erectors.

Such a balance is not independent of the rest of the body (see Figure 4). For breathing to work well, the two diaphragms—the respiratory diaphragm and the pelvic floor—must face each other functionally. If the pelvis is too anteriorly tipped, or the rib cage too posteriorly tipped, this reciprocity between the two diaphragms is lost, and breathing becomes shallow and labored (see Figure 4). This pattern is usually characterized by a very short lower back, but a very long line from sternum to pubes. This pattern requires substantial release work on the erector myofasciae, and toning work on the rectus and upper part of the psoas, using the modified sit-up outlined above.

Getting this kind of balance in the belly tends to fly in the face, for some, of the social image that people have of the belly. For others, there lies the possibility of awakening feelings that have been stored in the belly for time out of mind. But getting this balance is worth either of these, because the free flow of both fluid and feeling in the lower three chakras repays the work on both your part and the client's.

The bases of vitality, security, power, sexual expression and animal instinct—the foundations of our being—reside within the abdominal balloon. Leaving it out of our work because we are scared of its power is as criminal as bulldozing our way through it because we are unaware of its sensitivity. Visceral manipulation has shown an integrated way forward; let us build up our skills in this regard. Meanwhile, may the strategy of the lengthened balance through the four layers of the lumbar muscles be something you can play with usefully.

## The Peritoneum and Visceral Manipulation

For the first 15 years of my practice I treated the organs as a thing apart from my work. Oh, I knew they were in there, all right, sloshing around, and I paid lip service to the idea that reducing muscle tension or improving posture could have some salutary effect on organic function—but it was mostly prayer at best and hot air at worst. The closest I ever got to treating organs directly was to make sure I was going clockwise around the abdomen to help the flow of the large intestine, and, later on in my career, pressing gently on the ileocecal valve to ease inflammation (I hoped).

No more. These days the organs are an integral part of the whole person I treat. Not through diet, though diet is an obvious route; I simply do not know enough about it to intervene in that way beyond what everybody knows about water, vitamin C and "work harder than you eat." No, it is Jean-Pierre Barral, D.O., who has lighted the way for me, with his explorations in visceral manipulation. Visceral work is, in my opinion, the single most significant advance in manipulation in 100 years. Something very akin to Rolfing® bodywork can be seen on Greek bas-reliefs, and trigger points have been around for centuries-these and most of the other "new" bodywork methods are revivals and retellings of stuff that has been around for millennia.

The discovery of cranial motility by William Sutherland, D.O., at the beginning of this century and the organic motility of Barral at its end are truly groundbreaking. These approaches hold the promise of integrating the physiological with the mechanical, or structural. The research on these approaches is just beginning, but we should welcome them with open arms, as they point to a new way of healing and a new harmony of form and function.

Although I heartily recommend Barral's books and classes as a way to understand the complexities

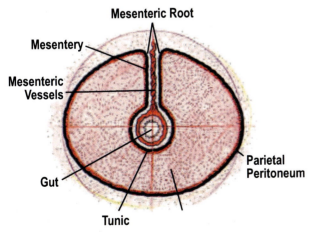

*Figure A:* This simplified diagram shows the relationship between the inner and outer parts of the peritoneum, and the gut and vessels it envelops. This fits into the open space in the middle of Figure 1.

**The Abdominal Balloon, Part 2**

of his theories, the basic premise is that the organs move in specific ways in response to the breath. In the abdominal cavity, the key to the axes of movement—the so-called mobility and motility of the organs—is the peritoneum and its attachments to the muscular wall. For the most part, all our guts lie within this peritoneal bag, but in a curious way. Imagine you have (or go to the kitchen and get) a plastic shopping bag and a vegetable, a long one, like a zucchini. Lay the bag on the table with the open end facing you. Lay the zucchini in the middle of the bag, with one end of the zucchini facing you. Now put your hands into the bag on either side of the zucchini, palms up, and then bring your hands together over the top of the zucchini.

Is the zucchini in the bag? Well, no...er, yes ...um, sort of (I quote my 10-year-old daughter when I asked her this question). This is how the peritoneal bag surrounds the alimentary tube. The part that is outside your hands is called the peritoneum. The part between your hands is called the mesentery; the part that goes right around the gut (zucchini) is called the tunic. But it is all one bag (Figure A).

The outer peritoneum forms the real skin of the abdominal balloon, and seals the space. (Breaking it through a perforated ulcer, burst appendix or bungled surgery can result in peritonitis.) The double-layered mesentery (remember, just a continuation of the same bag) carries the blood and lymphatic vessels between its two walls that fetch and carry nourishment to and from the intestine. The tunic forms the protective covering of the intestine itself (Netter plate 263).

How does the peritoneum come about? In the earliest stages of the embryo, two spaces form in the ventral cavity, with two bags to line them (Figure B). Notice how they enclose (moving from anterior toward the posterior) the liver in the front, the stomach (or further down, the intestine), the spleen, and then the pancreas, which is just in front of the back, with connections between each of these organs created by the walls of the two bags. In the course of normal development, the liver slides around to our right side, the stomach and spleen to our left, but the connections remain between them, and survive into adulthood (Figure C). The falciform ligament still connects the liver to the front wall of the abdomen; the lesser omentum connects the liver to the stomach, and so on (Netter plates 236, 258).

The liver, the gut and the spleen sink into these peritoneal bags, being nearly enclosed by them. The liver gets firmly but not quite snugly tied to the diaphragm by the coronal and triangular ligaments,

**Figure B & C:** *The top figure (B) shows the original position of the organs within the peritoneal cavity, at about six weeks in utero. The bottom figure (C) shows how they have moved by late pregnancy, much closer to normal adullt position.*

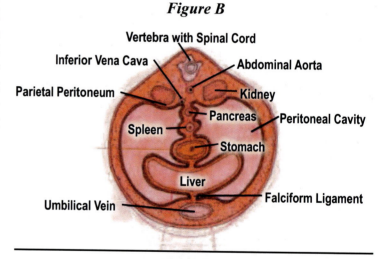

*Figure B*

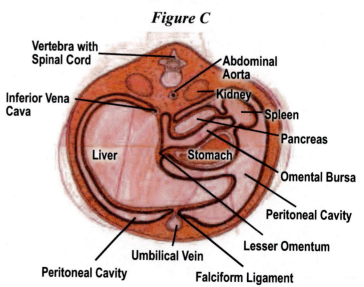

*Figure C*

Body³: A Therapist's Anatomy Reader

and so does the fundus of the stomach under the other dome of the diaphragm (Netter plate 270). The gall bladder, duodenum and large intestine are hung in their turn from the liver. The kidneys are located behind the whole peritoneal bag (retroperitoneal), along with the psoas and the big blood vessels, the aorta and vena cava (Netter plates 257. 315).

When the diaphragm descends on the inhale, it pushes the liver and the stomach down also, which pushes the rest of the organs down in their turn. (You have heard of the breath "massaging" the organs; well, this is it.) The exact excursion of any organ is determined by 1) the depth of the breath; 2) the connective tissue tie-ins to the peritoneal bag or other surroundings; and 3) any additional adhesions caused by disease, inflammation, trauma, surgery or pathological breakdown. It is these last that can be "melted" through treatment; Barral's genius is to have found a way to read the natural mobility of the organs so that any unnatural restriction can be detected simply by placing a knowing hand on the abdomen.

The kidneys, Barral tells us, travel several centimeters up and down in their connective tissue bag along the front of the psoas with every breath. This would add up to about three-quarters of a mile per day. "Nice idea," I thought, "but is it really true?" I was expressing my skepticism to one of my classes that included a radiologist. "Absolutely," he said, "I have to inject radiological dye into the pelvis of patients' kidneys to x-ray for kidney stones, with along hypodermic needle. If I get the needle placed properly, it swings wildly up and down with each breath. That's one of the ways I know I have it placed correctly." So much for that skepticism.

In addition to the mobility engendered by the breath, Barral has discovered what he calls motility, an inherent pulse of each organ somewhat similar to the inherent motion of the craniosacral system.

We have put forward a vastly simplified version of the peritoneum here (which is part of what is known as the triple-heater in Oriental medicine). With the large loop of the large intestine, the wavy loops of the small intestine, and the myriad twists and turns of other parts of the "organiarium" (my word), the pentoneum has an incredibly complicated three-dimensional shape (Netter plates 236, 253-8). If this introduction piques your interest, read *Visceral Manipulation*, by Jean-Pierre Barral and Pierre Mercier, 1988, Eastland Press, Seattle, Washington.

## Through the Alimentary Canal with Gun & Camera Left Side: The Seven Sacred Sphincters

Sphincters are round rings of muscle that punctuate the alimentary canal, allowing or discouraging the passage of food from section to section.

***The lips:*** The first sphincter is entirely voluntary, and it is the one that gets us in the most trouble: the mouth. The actual sphincter is the orbiculans oris muscle, but call it what you will, sometimes the best advice is to just keep it closed (Netter plate 21).

***The throat:*** The second sphincter is the pharyngeal constrictor. It is the gateway between the voluntary and the involuntary part of the food tube. You can feel it by starting the motions of swallowing; get past a certain point and the involuntary part of swallowing, which ensures that food goes onto the esophagus and not the trachea, takes over (Netter plate 61).

***The cardiac sphincter:*** Between the esophagus and the stomach, just below the surface of the diaphragm, is the cardiac sphincter, so named because it is close to the heart. It is designed to open to admit incoming food, and to close again to keep the acidic stomach contents from being pushed up.

This sphincter is up under the ribs, just to the left of the xiphoid process (the tip of the sternum) (Netter plate 259). Sometimes the sphincter and a bit of the stomach get pushed up past the diaphragm, resulting in reflux and heartburn—this is a hiatal hernia in the abdominal balloon.

***The pyloric sphincter:*** When food has been thoroughly "chewed" a second time by the strong peristalsis on the stomach, the pyloric sphincter opens and the chyme (partly digested food mixed with digestive secretions) is pushed into the duodenum. This sphincter is just to the right of center, just below the edge of the costal arch, but deep, behind the liver (Netter plate 260).

***The duodenal-jejunal junction:*** Though the duodenal-jejunal junction is not considered a sphincter on most texts, it can certainly act like one. The small intestine takes a sharp turn here into the long twists of the jejunum, and the turn is held up by a ligament called the Muscle of Treitz (or a

**The Abdominal Balloon, Part 2**

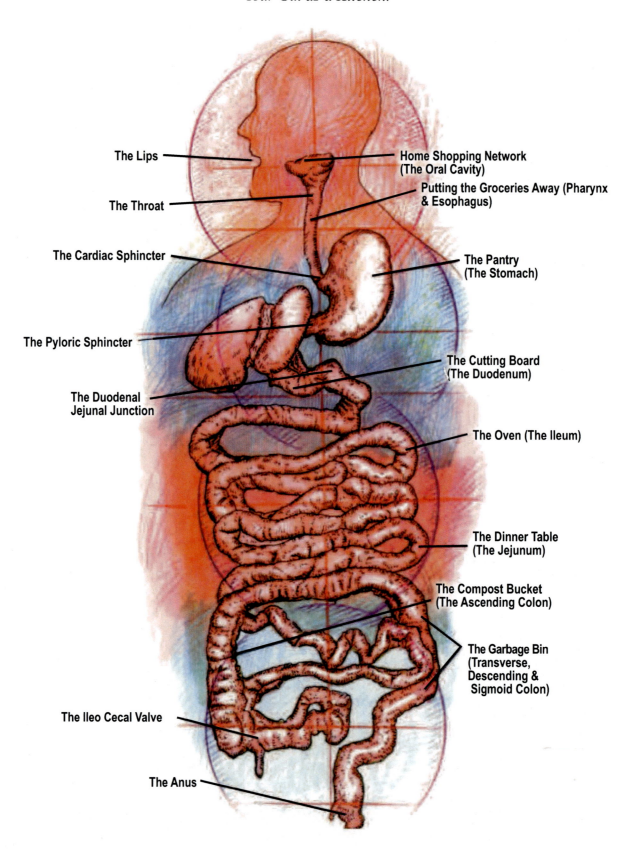

muscle called the Ligament of Treitz—go figure), that attaches up onto the muscular crura of the diaphragm near the aorta (Netter plate 253).

If the muscle, which is smooth and involuntary, contracts, which it can do in response to stress, especially respiratory stress, it can interfere with smooth digestion, so it acts like a sphincter. As a general guide, the duodenal-jejunal junction is two finger-widths up and two finger widths over to the left of the navel, though digestive health and volume of eating can affect the location somewhat (Netter plate 261).

***The ileocecal valve:*** This flapped sphincter mediates between the small intestine and the large intestine. Certain allergic reactions or inappropriate foods can trigger inflammation of the ileocecal valve, which has sometimes earned the dubious diagnosis, "Your ileocecal valve is stuck open (or closed)" Be that as it may, it can be found about two finger-widths to the right and two finger-widths down from the navel (Netter plate 265).

***The anus:*** The other end of the alimentary canal is an unfairly maligned, good and faithful servant—until our voluntary control keeps it up tight. Actually a double sphincter—one as part of the pelvic floor, one out beyond—both parts can be felt and separately controlled by the discerning (Netter plate 370).

### Right Side: Your Gut as a Kitchen

***The gut as a kitchen:*** In evolutionary terms, the 27-foot-long muscular tube of your digestive tract has been around a lot longer than you—your brainy self—have. Even though it does much of its work involuntarily, that does not mean it is without intelligence. It is surrounded with a network of nerves—the sub-mucosal plexus—whose wide-ranging functions and connections we are just beginning to discover. For one thing, it produces a substance quite similar to valium.

***Home shopping network:*** The oral cavity is where we decide what we are bringing to the alimentary kitchen. "Garbage in—garbage out" is an old computer term, but it applies here. The gut does the best it can, and can work wonders with a few raw materials, but in the long run, quality tells.

Letting your eyes do the choosing instead of your nose and taste buds can be problematic.

***Putting the groceries away:*** The pharynx—the opening behind your tongue, is about the oldest part of you, and its sensors in the tongue, tonsils and elsewhere start informing your brain, gut and body right away about what is on its way down. The esophagus, the first involuntary part of the tube, contracts in back of the moistened and chewed food and relaxes in front of it to move the food in a pretty straight shot to the stomach (Netter plates 57-62).

***The pantry:*** The stomach is wrinkled, so that it can expand a lot to take in a meal. It is a little unfair to call it a pantry, for it is not passive. In fact, the peristalsis of the stomach is so active that it has been called a second "chewing." At the same time, hydrochloric acid and certain peptic enzymes begin the process of breaking down food (Netter plates 258-260).

***The cutting board:*** The duodenum is the stiffest part of the small intestine, held firmly in place under the liver. Here multiple enzymes and bile pour into the tract from the liver, gall bladder and pancreas, all designed to cut and chop the proteins, fats and carbohydrates down to a size that can be assimilated (Netter plates 261 & 262)

***The oven:*** The ileum is where the breakdown takes place (Netter plates 252 & 263). (These divisions are being made too sharply—some assimllation begins in the stomach and continues in the ileum, and some digestive breakdown and assimilation is still occurring in the large intestine, but the general run of the process is accurate.) This process of breaking down the chemistry of the food produces a lot of heat, which further aids the breakdown and also provides a furnace that heats the rest of your body. There is an apron (omentum) of fat that hangs from the transverse colon in front of the small intestine, which insulates the belly and keeps that heat from being lost from the abdominal balloon (Netter plate 252).

***The dinner table:*** The jejunum is the master of assimilation. Molecules of basic foodstuffs are selected from the very liquid mass passing through and are brought aboard the body proper through the lining of the jejunum. On the other side of the lining are capillaries and lymphatic ducts that snap up the nourishment and begin circulating it, up through the mesentery to the liver for sorting, and then on to the rest of the hungry cells in the body.

**The compost bucket:** The colon in general gets what is left over, the garbage; but the functions of the different segments differ slightly. The colon removes water from the waste that is dumped from the jejunum, enough so that you do not lose too much water from your system, but not so much that you get constipated by hard stools. If the wrong bacteria are in the waste, the body passes it through the colon so quickly that a lot of water gets lost from the body (infantile diarrhea is the leading cause of death on the planet). There are two processes involved: fermentation and putrefaction. The ascending colon, the compost bucket in our metaphor, is where the fermentation takes place (Netter plates 263 & 264). Non-smelly gas generally comes from this part.

**The garbage bin:** Having risen up the ascending colon, what is left is pushed across the transverse colon and down the descending colon. The descending colon is the garbage bin of our digestive kitchen, and here putrefaction takes place (Netter plates 267 & 268). Smelly gas comes from overputrefaction. What is left is passed out the other end of the body. ■

---

**Footnote:**

1. I love words, and I have had more fun and confusion with the phrase "the whole nine yards" than with any other. If you had asked me what this phrase meant before I became an anatomy teacher, I would have replied vaguely, "I think it has something to do with football, like it's fourth and nine and you have one chance to go the whole nine yards. "Then, when I discovered that the digestive system was 27 feet long, I realized that this must be what "the whole nine yards" meant—as in "when I eat something that doesn't agree with me I just vomit it back out again, but once my wife eats something, she's stuck with it for the whole nine yards." I started sharing this in my physiology classes at the Rolf Institute, and an older fellow objected: "No, no, no, you don't understand. The old cloth ammo belts for the World War II machine guns came in metal boxes and were nine yards long. You fed the leading edge into the gun, and if there were lots of Germans coming up the hill, you gave 'em the whole nine yards." Thus edified, I went on to my next class, explaining all the above. "Unh-unh", said a young man from the South. "Those big cement makers you see turning on the back of trucks as they roll toward a job? They make cement in nine-yard batches. If you're pouring a large slab for a cellar, you need the whole nine yards." Believe it or not, I finally found the real answer in *Ripley's Believe it or Not*: The phrase originates from Medieval times, when monks were issued a bolt of cloth to make their habits. If you were fat like Friar Tuck, it took the whole nine yards. Truth.   —Thomas Myers

# Chapter 7:
# The River of Life – Breath and the Rib Basket, Part One

**B**reathing is the river of life we cannot live without. The standard truism is that we can live 30 days without food, three days without water and three minutes without air. It is our most pressing and immediate need.

"When you can't breathe," drawls the American Lung Association, with classic understatement, "nothing else matters."

The pulse of the breath—reaching out and expanding to take in something from outside of us and then contracting in to expel some of "us" out into the world of "not us"—has been part of our history since the first cells started populating the archaic sea over three billion years ago. Breathing the atmosphere has been around since we crawled out onto the land some 1.2 billion years ago. Breathing has a long and noble history; no wonder it winds itself into every part of our being.

For these reasons, the rise and fall of our breath sits right on the fulcrum between the voluntary and the involuntary. By taking control of the breath, we are able, for better or worse, to affect the functioning of the whole organism. For better, meditation adepts have for millennia been taking voluntary control of the breath in order to quite the mind and send the spirit soaring. Whole books have been written about it, and religious sects have built themselves around it. In fact, one of the first known books in the East is from around 1350 A.D., and is called the *Hatha Yoga Pradipika of Svatmarama*, a handbook on pranayama the science of breathing.

In his modern rendering of the ancient techniques called *Light on Pranayama*, yoga adept B.K.S. Iyengar urges us to take conscious and very intricate control of our breath wave in order to fill out the breath, quite the body for meditation, strengthen the mind for yoga, and prepare the somatic self for greater things to come.

For worse, voluntary control of the breath in the service of suppressing some emotion

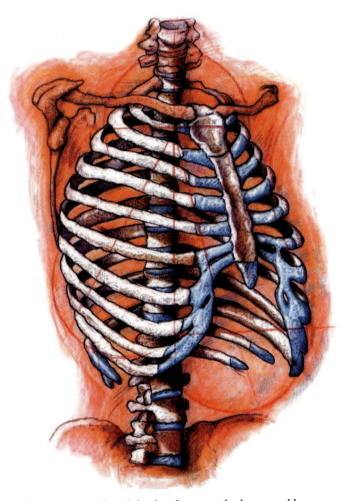

**Figure 1:** *The rib basket, home to the heart and lungs, allows us sinnous movement by summing up the small movements in more than 100 tiny joints.*

**The River of Life, Part 1**

can negatively affect the whole physiology, leading at least to diminished function, if not disease. Interruptions to natural breathing can begin with the very first breath, especially in hospitals where invasive interruptions to newly-born, novice breathers are commonplace.

So while the line of breathing in all living beings may be unbroken, it surely can be bent: by the gasps and fears of childhood, the oh, so dramatic sighs of adolescence, and the longer-term sniffs and moans of maturity.

Like dietary advice, advice about how to breathe is ubiquitous and contradictory. The spiritual teacher and rascal George Gurdjieff, in *Meetings with Remarkable Men*, takes the opposite tack to the yogis, urging us to leave the breath alone and let it take care of itself. He argues that the pattern and amount of our breathing are part of a complex physiological recipe about which we know very little, involving our particular and individual manner of eating exercising and metabolizing.

To muck about with it, even with the best of pranayamic intentions, he says, is to risk unbalancing the organism, possibly making us sick or crazy.

My own teacher, Ida Rolf, seemed to be of this school. She made radical changes in people's structure, and gave them detailed homework between sessions, but seldom, if ever, mentioned breathing or urged changes in breathing pattern on her clients, even though she herself had practiced yoga, including pranayama, for many years in her youth. She would watch the client's breathing closely, mind you, and speak about the client's breathing pattern to us, her students, but I cannot remember her urging a client to voluntarily change the flow of course of his or her breathing river. Breathing, she felt, changed naturally as a result of the structural manipulations.

Human beings in general, and frequent public speakers in particular, often take strong voluntary control over the breath to talk. Speaking employs a quick inhale followed by a much longer and precisely controlled exhale over the vocal cords. This voluntary and unnatural form of breathing can be maintained for many hours with no more harm than the minor disease of boredom to either the speaker or his listeners.

Whatever our approach to breathing, as soon as our voluntary control stops and our attention wanders somewhere else, as in sleeping for example, the involuntary control of breathing takes over to ensure our continued survival.

But the concept of the natural breath as something we have lost and might find again is a very tantalizing one. How do we find a natural breath if we do not experiment, since our breathing has so likely been altered by emotional suppression or other factors? How can we evoke a natural breath if we do experiment, since by definition an experiment is a conscious intervention? A current book that addresses this conundrum, and is recommended as being a little more user-friendly than either of those mentioned above is, *The Breathing Book*, by Donna Farhi (Henry Holt, 1996).

**O**ur Body³ chapters have been working their way up our physical structure, looking at the anatomy of each successive section in search of clues to deeper healing and integrated understanding. This simple and universal act of breathing is so rich with meaning and so connected to every other action we do; how shall we limit our discussion and still convey the marvelous complexity of this central area?

Body³ chooses not to venture into the sticky area of the how you "should" breathe, sticking instead to a tour of the structures that allow us, nay encourage us, to breathe. To keep this chapter under control, we will have a go at inspiring you about the movements of breathing and the structure of what we prefer to call the "rib basket" rather than the "rib cage," without going on so long that you expire of boredom. But first, let us look at what the basket holds.

### The heart and lungs

The rapid exchange of oxygen and carbon dioxide so necessary for our nerve and muscle metabolism requires a strange superstructure to accomplish. Of the three major body segments—head, thorax and pelvis, the thorax is the most moveable. The skull is pretty stable, though it moves slightly in its sutures, and the pelvis also allows only slight internal movement at its joints (see Chapter 4). But the chest (thorax, rib cage—we will be using all these terms pretty interchangeably here) is able to twist, bend and lean within itself, while still leaving space for and protecting the heart and lungs. These movements depend on the coordinated summing up of dozens of tiny joints.

*Figure 2:* *The pleura around the lungs is a double bag, just like the peritoneum we looked at in the abdomen (See Chapter 6.) Between the visceral pleura (which goes right around each lobe of the lung) and the parietal pleura (which is adherent to the ribs) is a very thin layer of lubricating fluid. The parietal pleura is attached to the diaphragm, the ribs, and the inner scalene fascia.*

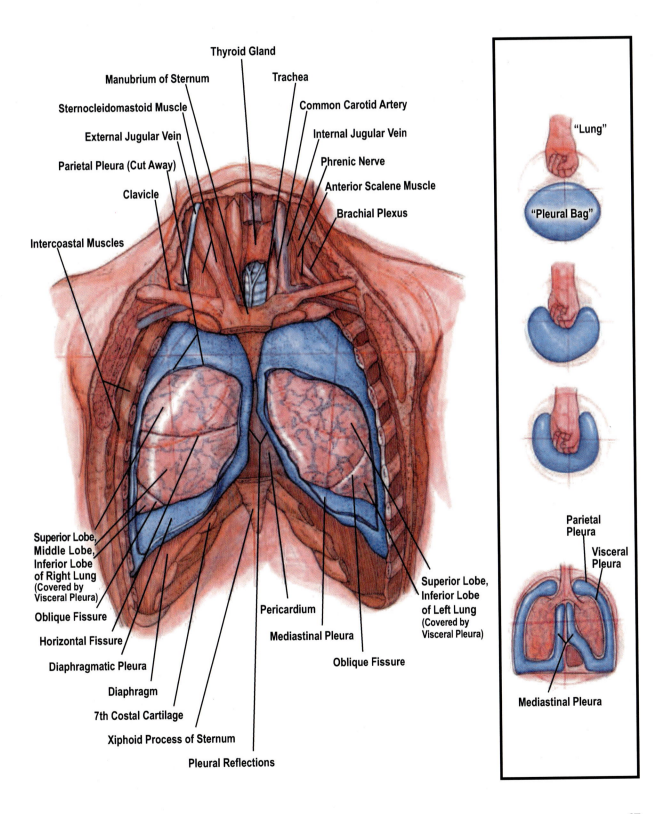

**The River of Life, Part 1**

67

The thorax is a box. We need to remember that it is shaped more or less like a section of a cone—narrower at the top than at the bottom. Our cultural ideal of wide shoulders and a narrow waist sometimes leaves the uninitiated with the idea that the rib cage is wide at the top and narrow at the bottom, but that is an illusion created by the shoulders. Strip off this superstructure—the scapula collarbone and the arm—and take the shoulder muscles with it—including the trapezius, latissimus, pectoralis, serratus anterior, the rhomboids and the rest—and you are left with the fish-like body, with the rib cage clearly smaller than the neck at the top, and about as big as the waist at the bottom.

We have already discussed the abdominal balloon in previous chapters, and the thorax is the next section up in the ventral cavity. But unlike a balloon, which always has a positive pressure, the thorax is a box that always has a negative pressure—it is always trying to collapse, and the sturdy rings of the rib prevent it from doing so.

The lungs are the engines of this suction. The spongy tissue of the lungs is surrounded with a connective tissue bag called the visceral pleura. This bag is surrounded by another called the parietal pleura, and this bag is attached to the inside of the rib cage. The suction between the two bags keeps the lung pulled out against the rib cage, even though it wants to collapse (and will, if the suction is broken by disease or injury) (see Figure 2).

Even when you take in the very biggest breath you can, the elastic connective tissue of the lungs still wants to collapse. This tension is what pulls the diaphragm up into a dome. In the pressure systems of the body, the abdomen always has a positive pressure—even when you are very hungry—and the chest has a negative pressure, even when you are holding your fullest breath.

"Science Never Sucks," says my friend Kathleen's T-shirt—meaning that fluid substances are pushed from areas of high pressure toward areas of low pressure, so it is always a blow, never a suck. For a breath to happen, the chest has to create an area of lower pressure inside the chest cavity, so that the air pressures from outside actually pushes the air into us (we are definitely "bottom feeders" in the ocean of the atmosphere). We do this by making the chest cavity bigger; the bones of the chest are stuck to the parietal pleura, which is suctioned onto the visceral pleura, and the visceral pleura is tied to the spongy tissues of the lungs.

The main way that we create this low pressure is to pull down the dome of the diaphragm, which is attached directly to the pleura from underneath. The diaphragm is far and away the primary muscle of breathing. A few years ago I was on the back of a 17-hand horse with my 5-year-old daughter, on for a little ride as the horse was led to pasture by its halter. Suddenly something happened, perhaps Gus was stung by a bee; in any case she reared up, and without saddle or reins I knew we were headed for the ground, which seemed quite far away at the time. During the fall, I twisted myself around so that I was under Misty when we landed. The force of the fall winded me more than I have ever been winded. But what "winded" means, I remember trying to think as I struggled to breathe with my intercostals and pectorals, is that the phrenic nerve has been shocked and cannot operate the diaphragm. "Winded" means trying to breathe with anything else you can find, but without the diaphragm. In those moments, it is easy to appreciate just how far ahead of the pack the diaphragm is as a breathing muscle (see Figure 3).

Between the stretched sponges of the lungs, the heart and a lot of tubing (a lot!—the aorta and vena cava, the pulmonary vessels and the bronchae, for starters) are suspended in the walls of the connective tissue complex called the mediastinum. The mediastinum (usually pronounced so that it sounds like Gloria's sister, Media) stretches between the back side of the sternum to the front of the thoracic vertebral bodies. Because you cannot touch this tissue directly (unless you are a werewolf), we will just give a little nod to its genius.

Who designed the human body? If you are a creationist and think that God did it all in one day, what a job She did! If you are an evolutionist and give it a billion years or so, it is still amazing how intricately interconnected yet independent the body functions are. The design difficulty here is that the lungs must be in a constant negative pressure while bellowing up and down as we have described, and yet the heart simultaneously needs protection from both the movement and the pressure variations. The heart also sits in a double bag, just like the lungs, consisting of the endocardium, a fairly delicate bag bound right to the heart muscle tissue, and the outer bag, the pericardium. It is a "fist in a balloon" arrangement, very similar to what we saw with the lungs (see Figure 2).

The pericardium is a much stronger bag, separated from the endocardium by a lubricated space wherein the heart can beat. The pericardium also provides the attachments to the rest of the mediastinum and the surrounding tissues, making a kind of tent around the heart to protect it from the pressure changes. The tent is pulled down, front and back, left and right, by its attachments to the central tendon of the diaphragm, up and forward onto the back side of the sternum, and up and back to the bodies of the upper thoracic vertebrae. Thus the heart can beat in peace, suspended placidly amidst the noise and haste of the lungs, the esophagus and the stomach.

Understanding how the heart is suspended between the bellows of the lungs gave me a new appreciation for this simple ancient pump, holding down the drumbeat of the circle of the sea in our bodies.

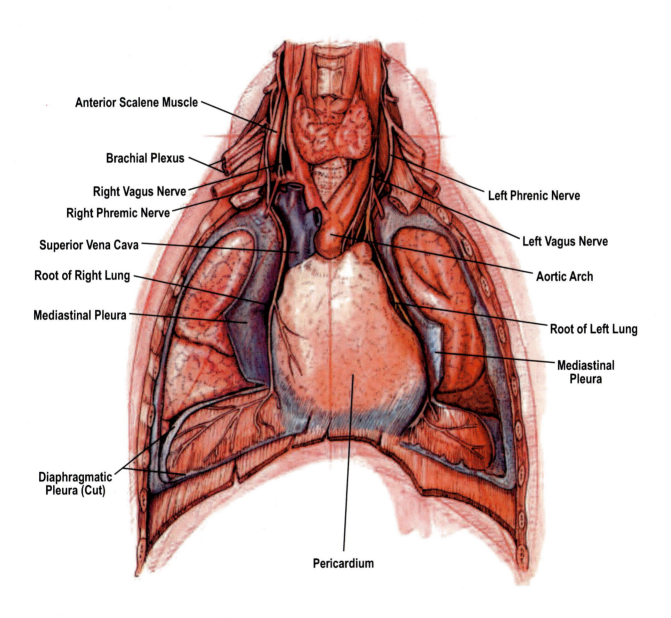

*Figure 3:* The pericardium and the pleura of the lungs form a connective tissue wall, the mediastinum, which connects the back side of the sternum to the front side of the thoracic vertebrae, providing essential scaffolding for the pulmonary vessels, the trachea and the esophagus.

**The River of Life, Part 1**

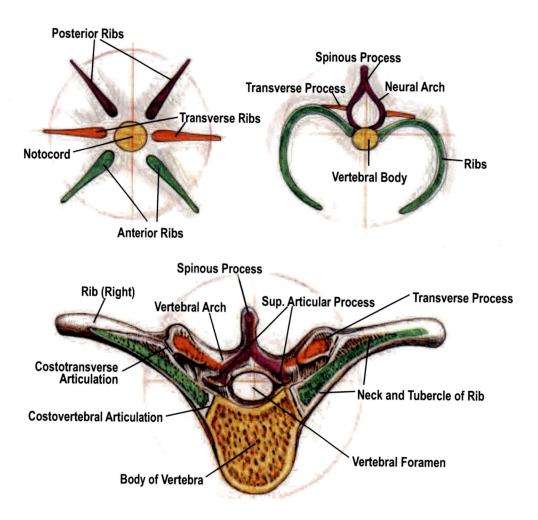

*Figure 4: The symmetrical arrangement of the cartilage ribs around the ancient backbone (notochord) altered over eons to produce the protective neural arch and transverse processes. What we call our ribs were the anterior ribs, and they still tuck in front of the transverse processes to attach to the vertebral bodies.*

## The rib basket

One of the hoped-for effects of this book is that readers get to fill in their body image where it might not be complete. What I noticed with most of my clients and even some of my *compadres* is that the rib cage seems to fade out somewhere behind the sides: how the ribs fit into the back is a bit of a mystery. It is awfully hard to treat something successfully if you do not have a fairly detailed 3-D picture of how it fits.

Let us look at the evolutionary origin of the rib cage, which gives us a great handle on this back side of the rib basket. In the original fishes, there were three sets of ribs grouped around the notochord (the proto-back bone): one about 45 degrees forward, one straight out at 90 degrees and a third set headed 45 degrees toward the back. These ribs and the notochord as well, were all made out of cartilage like most fish bones. As development progressed, the 90-degree ribs attached themselves to the notochord and became—tah-dah!—the transverse processes of the vertebrae. The backward-facing ribs performed a clever evolutionary trick: they bent around toward each other until they joined, forming the neural arch and spinous processes of the vertebrae, which protect the neural tube of the central nervous system. You can still see the leftovers of the two ribs in the bifurcated end to the spinous process of C2 or other cervical vertebrae (see Figure4).

The third, forward-facing set of ribs became

our ribs, curling around front to protect the organs and join at the sternum. But the origin story helps us see what happens to the ribs in back: they tuck in under (or deep to, or anterior to, take your pick) the transverse processes to connect with the notochord (vertebral bodies and discs). To do this, they have to pass in front of the whole back apparatus: the deep back muscles so beautifully trussed to the neural arch and all those transverse and spinous processes.

### The back of the ribs and lengthening the spine

The precise details of how the ribs attach to the spine are tremendously important to breathing, to the health of the thoracic discs, and to subtle movement in the body, so listen up: As the ribs sweep around from the front, they come to a spot called the angle of the ribs. This spot is hard to see on the skeleton, but is very easy to feel on a person (other than yourself). Walk your fingers around the ribs toward the back—it is easiest at a level of the inferior angle of the scapula—and you will notice that the ribs quite suddenly "turn a corner," heading under the lateral edge of the erector spinae, never to be felt again. What in fact happens is that not only do they go deep to the back muscles; they also go deep to the thoracic transverse processes, which are angled back a bit from their original 90-degree position. There is a small joint between the back of the rib and the front of the transverse process, the costo-transverse joint, which is one that your skilled chiropractor or osteopath can reset, to the great relief of your ability to breathe.

The real trick comes when the rib head meets the body of the vertebra. The following arrangement is true only of ribs 2-9, the first and 10th-12th do not join in this way. So let us say that we are talking here about the 6th rib, for convenience, but this applies to the rest of the middle ribs also. The 6th rib comes around back, has a costo-transverse joint with the transverse process of the sixth thoracic vertebra. OK so far, but it is what the rib head does that is really cool, an unexpected design feature that only works if you use it, and so many people do not (see Figure 5).

The rib head is a little bit pointed, like a dull arrowhead, and thus has three articular surfaces: 1) a small synovial joint with the upper edge of the body of the same vertebra, the upper corner of the 6th vertebra, in this case; 2) a similar joint with the lower edge of the vertebra body above it, the 5th in this case; and 3) a fibrous joint with the annulus (outer covering) of the disc itself, in this case, the disc between bodies of T5 and T6. The radical

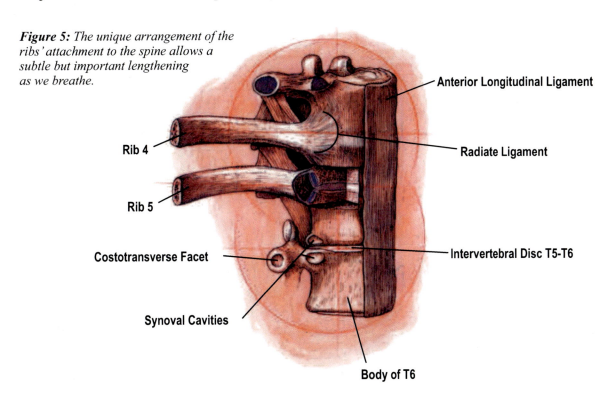

*Figure 5:* The unique arrangement of the ribs' attachment to the spine allows a subtle but important lengthening as we breathe.

### The River of Life, Part 1

coolosity comes when you breathe: As the ribs lift on the inhale, the "arrowhead" of the rib head, wedged in between the two vertebrae, spreads the two vertebrae apart from each other. This happens only if 1) the ribs move sufficiently in breathing to make it happen; and 2) the myofascial tissues deep in the back are relaxed enough to let it happen. It could happen to you.

If it is happening, it has two very health-giving effects: 1) the thoracic spine lengthens, simulating many stretch receptors deep in the spine and; 2) even more startling but logical once you look at it, this action opens up the disc, thus drawing fluid into the disc material, hydrating and fluffing it.

Great stuff, all right, but how do you know if it is happening? Seat your client on her sitz bones on a stool, the front of a chair, or even your table, with her spine erect and relaxed as possible. Stand beside her, and put one hand gently against her lumbar area, and rest the other ever so lightly on top of her head. Have her breathe in and out with the back relaxed and ask yourself two questions: 1) is my lower hand moving backward? And 2) is my upper hand moving upward?

The lower hand should (with all the usual provisos on that word) be able to feel a spinal wave in breathing such that the lumbars move slightly posteriorly on the inhale and anteriorly on the exhale. If this is not happening, the balance between the erectors and the psoas is not happening, and the tightness in either one or both will prevent the subtle thoracic movement we are seeking. Likewise, do not look for this movement in someone who has a strong forward head posture, for the muscles required to keep the head from falling off will likewise stifle the subtle lengthening in the thoracic.

But if the lumbers' have the breath wave, and the head is more or less on the body without a lot of effort, feel into the upper hand lightly poised on the client's head. Can you feel your hand being moved toward the ceiling on each inhale, and settling slowly and gently, as if on a fluid cushion, back down on the exhale. Do not cue your client about this movement, or you risk having them force it to happen, which is not the same at all (see Figure 6).

Of such subtle relative movements—in the cranium, in the interosseous membranes, in the spine, and in the organs, is deep structural health made.

In the next chapter we will turn to the front of the rib basket, parsing it into its different sections and showing how they work, separately and together, to produce trunk stability, rotation and breathing all at once. ∎

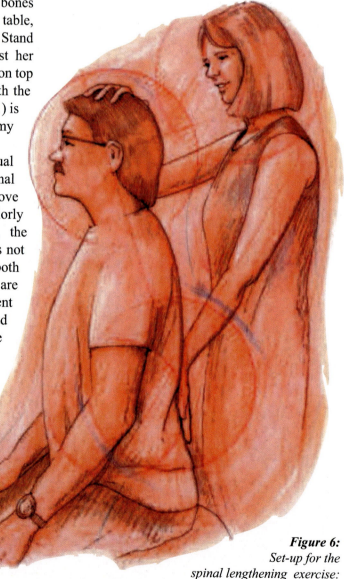

*Figure 6:*
*Set-up for the spinal lengthening exercise:*
*Your upper hand should move toward the ceiling on the inhale.*

# Chapter 8:
# The River of Life – A Front View of the Ribs, Part Two

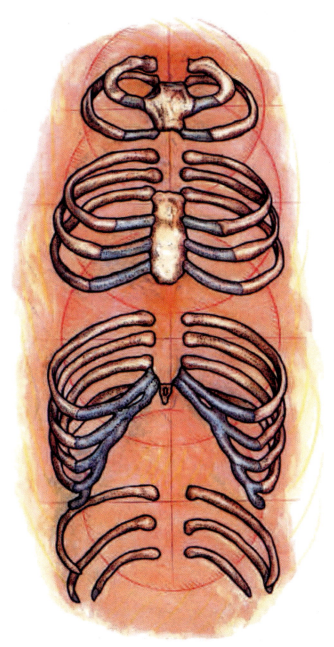

*Figure 1:* There are many ways of dividing the rib cage into functional units. Try our scheme and see if it works for you.

**Last chapter looked at the thorax in general. and how the ribs act on the spine and discs in the back. In this chapter we look at how the ribs attach in the front to the "sternebrae" instead of the vertebrae. This view from the front will allow us to divide up the rib cage into functionally useful sections and to discuss the movements of breathing in a little more depth. (To assist you in getting a more complete picture than we can provide here, we include references to Frank Netter's Atlas of Human Anatomy, published by CIBA Geigy, although you can follow along with any good anatomy atlas.)**

So, from the attachments to the vertebrae in back, let us loop around the ribs to the front of the rib cage, where we can make some sense out of the ribs' connections to the breastbone. The sternum is a wonderful and unique bone, a balance point for many forces like the sphenoid in the head or the sacrum in the pelvis. "Sternum" means "chest," but it looks like a dagger (which is the original meaning of "xiphoid"). The upper part is the manubrium, or handle; the body is the blade; and the xiphoid is the point. Each of these sections develops separately and joins in the course of embryological development; each (as we shall see) is connected to a different section of the rib basket, and each is also connected with a different chakra. At the very top of the manubrium is the sternoclavicular joint, the only place where the shoulder girdle has a skeletal joint to the axial skeleton (Netter plate 171).

We will leave this shallow saddle joint

**The River of Life, Part 2**

until Body³ discusses the shoulder, in order to concentrate on the ribs for now. None of the bony ribs joins directly with the sternum; there is always some cartilage in between. Anatomists have thought about this in two ways, and you can, too. One way to look at it is that there is one sternocostal joint, a cartilaginous joint that is shorter in the case of the first couple of ribs and very long indeed in the 8th and 9th ribs. Or there are two joints, a sternochondral joint right at the lateral edge of the sternum, and a costo-chondral joint where the rib joins with the cartilage ("chondro" always refers to cartilage). Because I look for differentiated motion at both of these joints, I prefer the second option.

The rib basket is like your Mum's old wicker laundry basket turned upside down. The most moveable part is at the top of the basket (the bottom of the rib cage) and the most stable part is the bottom of the basket (top of the rib cage). The design of the rib basket is such that the whole thing can be pulled, pushed and even rotated, somewhat like an old wicker basket, though hopefully with less complaining and squeaking. It is an odd fact that most of the rotation in the torso must be accommodated in the rib cage, but this is not known or appreciated by most rib cage owners. The rib basket accommodates these many movements while still maintaining a fairly sturdy box around the lungs and heart, and also provides support to the neck, an anchor for the shoulder and versatile connections to the pelvis.

### The neck ribs

To parse the rib basket into sections structurally and functionally, let us break the whole down into structurally logical parts. The first two ribs form a unit. They both tie into the manubrium of the sternum, the handle of the dagger. Feel the top of your sternum, running your fingers down from the sterna notch. Feel that bump on the sternum about two inches down from the top, around where a pendant would lie? Most will, and that change in angle is called the Angle of Louis, and it forms the joint between the manubrium and the body of the sternum. Now move your fingers out to the side of that lump and you will find a rib attaches at that level: that is very reliably rib #2. Rib #1 is generally not able to be felt as easily, as the collar bones cover it in front and everything else covers it in back, but the second rib is very easily identified at the Angle of Louis. And you can count down from there to figure out which rib you are on; even if you get lost figuring out the others (see Figure 2).

These ribs are connected structurally to the neck. The main muscles that take off from these ribs are the scalenes, very strong and steel-band-like muscles that anchor the lower five cervical vertebrae to these two upper ribs. You can think of them as the guy wires that secure the mobile "antenna" of the neck to the very stable upper part of the rib cage. The posterior scalene goes to the 2nd rib; the middle scalene goes to the 1st rib, with a fascial connection down to the 2nd. These two generally control lateral flexion, acting a bit like "the quadratus lumborum of the neck" (Netter plate 25).

The anterior scalene goes down only to the 1st rib, and slants a bit more forward in doing so. Because of this slant, it can pull the lower cervical vertebrae forward (acting a bit like a "psoas of the neck," but do not carry this metaphor too far). By closing the angle between the neck and rib basket, the anterior scalene can contribute to either an anterior head posture or an anteriorly held posture of the lower ribs (see Figure 3).

Sensitive and careful work with the anterior scalenes (I don't need to tell you it is right in front of the brachial plexus and vasculature, do I?) can open the angle between the ribs and the cervical spine.

If your method does not work, it may not be a problem resolvable in the usual muscular fashion.

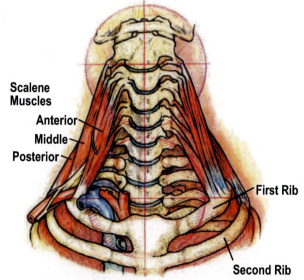

**Figure 2:** *The first two ribs form a structural unit, relating the stability of the neck, the thoracic inlet, and our voice.*

Body³: **A Therapist's Anatomy Reader**

*Figure 3: Tightened scalenes can contribute to the head being carried forward or the ribs being slanted back. Only if the scalenes lengthen can the angle open into easy alignment.*

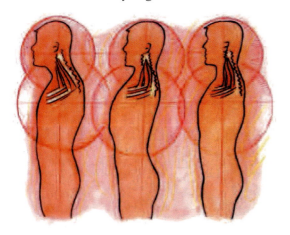

Underneath the scalenes is the scalenus minimus (which has muscular fibers), or the suspensory ligament of the lung (which doesn't), which pulls the parietal pleura (and thus the lung itself) right to the top of the thoracic cavity. If repeated gentle assaults upon the anterior scalene are not effective, you might consider referring the client to an osteopath or someone who does visceral manipulation, who may be more easily able to release the deeper tissues in the dome of the lung.

The back side of the manubrium has the insertion of several muscles, most notably the sternohyoid, that reach up toward (you guessed it) the hyoid bone (Netter plate 24). Thus this ribs 1-&-2-and-manubrium complex provides: 1) stability for the segmented tent-pole of the neck; 2) the opening for the thoracic inlet/outlet; and 3) the structural staging, front and back, for the throat chakra, your creative voice (see Figure 4).

### The heart ribs

The next section down on the ribs encompasses ribs 3, 4 and 5. In the front, at least, this section of the rib basket provides support for the shoulder and an underlying stable connection between the shoulder girdle and the pelvis. While the pectoralis major provides a connection for the humerus to the first five or so ribs, beneath it lies the elusive but essential pectoralis minor and its associated clavipectoral fascia (Netter plate 403). The pectoralis minor arises from the coracoids process, that little "crow's beak" of a bone that sticks forward from the shoulder blade under the lateral part of the clavicle. This muscle connects to the short head of the biceps and the coracobrachialis in the arm, which does not seem like a very valid connection until you imagine all those years we spent swinging from trees.

Whether going from branch to branch or merely doing a modern chin-up, the pectoralis minor anchors the deep shoulder flexors onto the front of the rib cage.

Going in the other direction from the 5$^{th}$ rib, the rectus abdominis goes down to the pubic bone. Continuing the stability of the shoulder via the pectoralis minor and the rectus, through the ribs down to the pelvis. This whole complex of myofascia needs to be opened to allow the chest to rise and the shoulder to go back when they have fallen into protraction and anterior tilt (see Figure 5).

Ribs 3 to 5 attach themselves via their cartilage to the body of the sternum (the middle part), and are thus associated with the heart and the sun of the heart chakra.

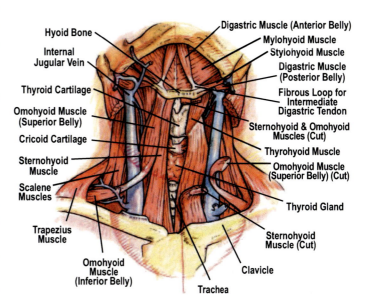

*Figure 4: The muscles that help with swallowing and modulate our voice attach from the hyoid bone down to the back side of the sternum.*

**The River of Life, Part 2**

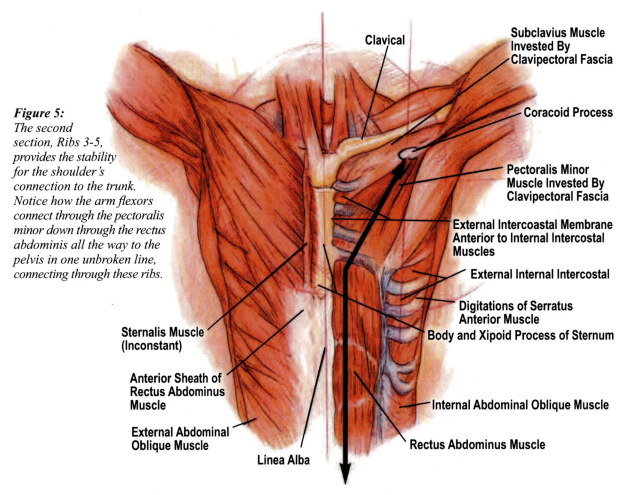

*Figure 5:*
*The second section, Ribs 3-5, provides the stability for the shoulder's connection to the trunk. Notice how the arm flexors connect through the pectoralis minor down through the rectus abdominis all the way to the pelvis in one unbroken line, connecting through these ribs.*

## The gut ribs

The next coherent section of the rib basket includes ribs 6 to 9. These ribs are a bit looser (their corresponding spinal section is more able to rotate), and they are largely controlled in the front by the three large abdominal sheer muscles of the obliques and transversus, which create trunk rotation as well as flexion. These ribs are all also connected to the sternum via a complex of cartilage that looks pretty flimsy but accommodates very well to breathing, and is better than bone when you slam forward onto a steering column in an accident. These costal cartilages form the sub-costal arch, and all join to the sternum at one point, low down the body right near the xiphoid process. If you press in strongly with the heel of your hand just beside the lower part of the sternum on either side, you will feel how flexible this "trampoline" of cartilage is.

These ribs cover the liver, the stomach and the solar plexus, and are thus connected to the solar plexus chakra—our source of animal power, the seat of fear and the mediator of our bodily needs (see Figure 6).

## The pelvic ribs

One could argue that the 10th rib is part of this complex, but Body3 chooses to put it in the floating, or "pelvic ribs" group: ribs 10 to 12. Although rib 10 is sometimes joined to the sternum by the same cartilage as ribs 6 to 9, just as often it is free and floating or nearly so. You can feel the end of the 10th rib by walking your fingers down the inferior edge of the sub-costal arch until you encounter its free end. It will probably be about straight north from your anterior superior iliac spine (ASIS), a bit anterior of your midline, and may be a bit sore to the touch. All these ribs are somewhat variable, so these are just guidelines.

The free end of the 11th rib is usually right on the lateral line, and is often quite sensitive. The 12th rib is variable in length, and you may or may not be able to feel its free end somewhere to the rear of

*Figure 6:* Ribs 6-9 handle a lot of trunk rotation, create lateral expansion in breathing, and house the assimilative organs of our solar plexus, or "animal brain": the liver, the stomach, the spleen and the pancreas.

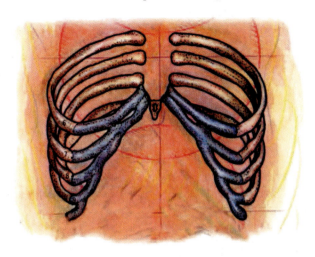

and under the 11th in any case, these ribs form the lower, most moveable edge of the rib basket. The parts of the abdominal obliques, plus the quadratus lumborum, which take off from these ribs go straight to the iliac crest, and help to anchor the rib cage and the diaphragm itself (see Figure 7; Netter plates 231, 232, 233, 234).

If your client lies on his side and you walk your fingers up the inside edge of the iliac crest from the front, you will find, at about the midline or a little behind it, the lateral edge of the quadratus lumborum fascia. You can walk your fingers from here up the lateral edge of the quadratus and perhaps find the outer edge of the 12th rib from there (Netter plate 246).

This lowest section of the ribs is associated with the kidneys and the pelvic organs of elimination and sexuality. The response to fear and the adaptive strength of the fluid system can be read in these lower ribs.

### The movements of breathing

Let us go straight to the movements of the muscles and rib basket in breathing. The first and most important motion is in the diaphragm. The diaphragm in humans is in a unique situation. For most animals, the diaphragm waves backward and forward, obliquely to gravity, so the motion is unimpeded by that pull. In humans, the diaphragm goes up and down right in the line of the gravitational pull, but that force is cleverly negated by the positive pressure in the abdomen, which pushes the diaphragm up, and the negative pressure in the thorax, which pulls it up. Between the two, the diaphragm floats at nearly neutral, same as it did and does in our four-legged friends.

Teachers have gone on ad nauseam about the diaphragm, so let us see if we can find something you do not know about it. How far does the middle of the diaphragm move down on a good inhale, for instance?

The diaphragm is a muscle shaped like an umbrella, attached all around the bottom end of the rib cage and onto the front of the lumbar spine. These crura ("legs") of the diaphragm that reach down the anterior side of the lumbars and blend with the anterior longitudinal ligament could be thought of as the stem and handle of the umbrella. The

*Figure 7:* Ribs 10-12, the "pelvic ribs," are the lowest section and anchor the rib basket to the pelvic rim. These ribs balance between breathing and walking, and are associated with the kidneys and the pelvic organs of elimination.

**The River of Life, Part 2**

77

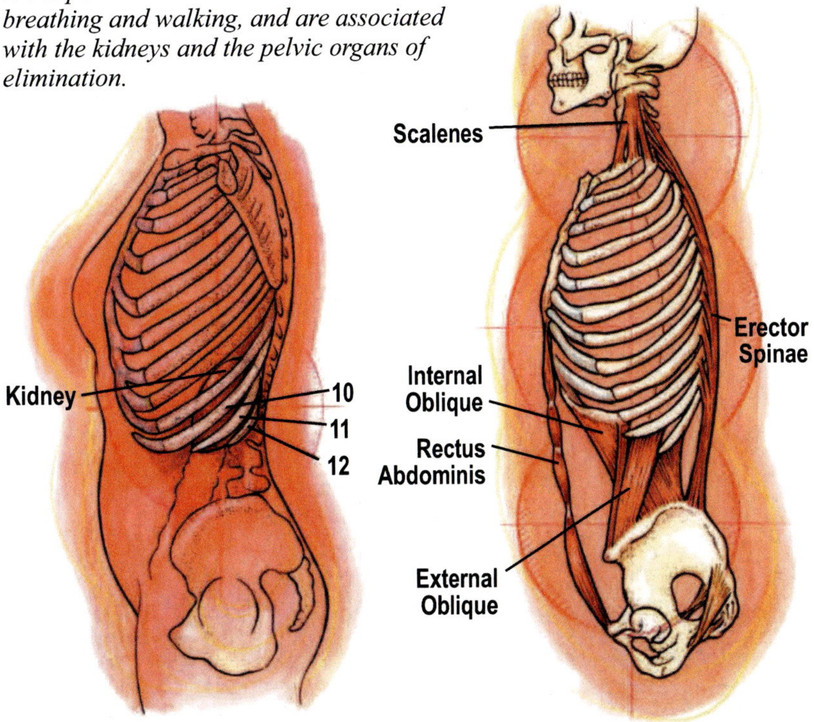

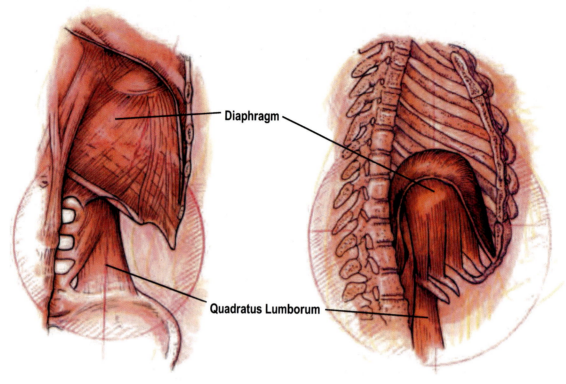

**Figure 8:** *The 12th rib is suspended between the upward pull of the diaphragm and the downward pull of the quadratus lumborum. The quadratus often wins the tug-of-war, to the detriment of full, responsive movement.*

rest of the umbrella domes up into the rib basket. Its central part is a large tendinous sheet, and the muscle is arranged out to the sides, such that most of the muscle fibers are nearer vertical than horizontal. So, how far does the middle of the central tendon get pulled down in a strong inhale? Three inches? Do I hear six? The answer is one-half inch. The pericardium of the heart is attached to the middle of the diaphragm from above (this was covered in our last chapter). If the diaphragm moved down as a whole for any significant distance, the pericardium would tighten around and squeeze the heart. Yikes! Instead, the diaphragm needs to be seen as two domes, one on either side of the heart, which is cool, because that way each dome is under a lung and can pull down on the pleura to create the necessary suction (OK, OK, pressure differential).

If you see the muscle fibers of the diaphragm as being mostly vertical, as the wall on the side of a dome would be, can you see how the 12th rib is pulled in opposite directions by the diaphragm and the QL? (see Figure 8).

(So what happens to a movie star's breathing when she asks the docs to take out her 12th rib? Does the QL snap down and the diaphragm snap up? Answer: Nope, they take out the rib but they leave periosteum, so the two muscles stay connected through this piece of fascia. It may be great for an hourglass figure, though it can't be the best thing for her breathing.)

**The most complete breathing includes a slight backwards and upwards spreading of the floating ribs on the inhale, a bit like a condor spreading its wings.**

Although Body³ does not want to get into how you should breathe, we are tempted to ask you to put your hand in back on the area of your 11th and 12th ribs, as you sit reading this. Take a deep breath in. Do you feel your floating ribs moving with the breath? If so, how? We find that the most complete breathing includes a slight backwards and upwards spreading of the floating ribs on the inhale, a bit like a condor spreading its wings. If there is no motion in your floating ribs, breathing is probably somewhat restricted (see Figure 9).

In an average breath (the average resting breath involves the exchange of only half a liter of air, little more than a pint), the diaphragm tightens and the double domes move down, using the lumbars and the lower edge of the ribs as the origin of the

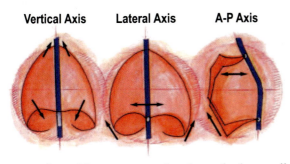

*Figure 9: Opening the "box" of the rib cage to the breath involves movement in all three cardinal planes.*

contractions. If you put your hands on the lower ribs (not your tummy) as you start to breathe in, they will not move much at first because they are what the diaphragm muscle fibers are holding onto to pull the ribs down.

In the second stage of breathing, the diaphragm comes to rest on the organs. The diaphragm continues to contract, but now the central tendon, resting on the abdominal pressure, becomes the origin, and the insertions, around the bottom of the ribs, start pulling the ribs up. The intercostals and scalenes get into the act at this point, pulling the upper ribs up to open the box in that manner. Let's see how they do it.

As the ribs are pulled up, they make the thoracic box wider. Each rib is angled down at the sides, like a bucket handle. At the beginning of the inhale, the handle lays against the bucket. As the ribs lift, they move laterally away from the middle as the bucket handle moves away from the center of the bucket—as least it would move away from the center until it was horizontal. The ribs never get beyond horizontal, so as the ribs move up they also move out, pulling on the parietal pleura which is suctioned onto the lungs, and more air is pulled (OK, pushed) in.

The third way a box can get bigger is from front to back, and if the breath is full enough and the tissues free enough, the sternum will move anteriorly relative to the thoracic spine and draw in still more air. This happens because all the ribs, at the beginning of the inhale, are angled down as they come forward from the back. As the ribs lift, the sternum is lifted up, the ribs get more horizontal front-to-back, and the chest is deepened.

So, unencumbered breathing proceeds in three stages: 1) the two domes of the diaphragm drop down until they are engaged on the organs, the liver and the stomach particularly; 2) the lower ribs are lifted, widening the thorax; and 3) the upper ribs are lifted, pushing the sternum forward and deepening the chest.

In very quiet tidal breathing, only the first stage is used. In deeper breathing, the second stage engages. In our experience, some clients do not have the third movement available to them—the mediastinal connective tissues are so tight that the sternum is not able to move away from the spine. Gentle but persistent work on the part of the client, assisted by the practitioner, can overcome this limitation. To check on a client's ability to move through these three stages, you should have them sitting or standing; if they are lying on the table, the spine and the back of the ribs may be blocked in their movement. In any case, clients on the table tend to breathe more from the belly, like babies, and revert to their common breathing pattern when they are again standing.

Although the intercostals have been shown to be electromyographically active in inhalation, Jon Zahourek, of Zoologik Systems fame, claims that they are more walking muscles than breathing muscles—and his idea has much appeal. In normal walking, the basic pattern is contralateral; that is, my right arm is going forward as my left leg and foot go forward. This is an extension of the final stage of crawling to walking, and it works very well: the momentum of the leg is counterbalanced by the opposite arm. This means that with each step there is a rotational twist going through the torso. Now, the external and internal intercostals are angled obliquely to each other, just like the abdominal obliques, and the angle is totally unnecessary to their function of lifting the ribs. Zahourek's idea is that the obliquity of the intercostals is used to mediate and brake this rotational motion, a bit like a watch-spring. Body[3] does not wish to denigrate the importance of free intercostals to breathing, but expanding our view of their function to include walking has proven useful in practice.

We should mention one other muscle while we are talking about inhaling: the transversus thoracis (see Figure 10, Netter plate 176). This muscle lies on the inside of the breastbone, just in front of the heart. It spreads up and out from the back of the sternum like a fan, going to the back side of the costal cartilages. It is a muscle we notice when we are shivering from the cold, when our chest tightens

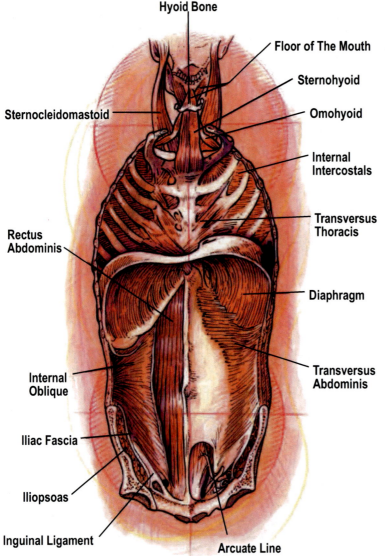

*Figure 10:* This unique view of "the back of the front" has us looking forward from the back-bone with all the viscera removed. Note the transversus thoracis muscle, which connects the lower sternum to the middle rib cartilages.

spinae muscles come into play in these situations (Netter plate 177).

On the exhale, the elasticity of the lung tissue is enough to push the air out, although many muscles, mainly the abdominals, are recruited to create more pressure, as in snorting, sneezing or blowing up a balloon (Netter plate 183). In fact, breathing is so central that a release anywhere in the body may help provide a release and relaxation of the breath.

## Smoking

While we are thinking about breath and the lungs, we ought to mention smoking, that wonderful habit that gives us a way to celebrate the Promethean gift of fire to humans.

The lungs are constructed like an upside down tree. The trachea in your throat branches out into the bronchae, which further branch out into many bronchioles that serve the various lobes of the lung. The "leaves" of this tree are more like a bunch of grapes—the alveoli of the lungs, where the gas exchange takes place, are clusters of round sacs surrounded by capillaries (Netter plates 191, 192, 193). The net result is like a sponge, with an incredible amount of surface area: if you took a jeweler's hammer and gently flattened out the lung, a healthy adult's lungs would cover an area equal to a tennis court.

The tar in tobacco slowly and steadily breaks down the walls between the alveoli, coating the surface area, and reducing the effective interface of the lungs (see Figure 11).

Lining all the bronchioles is a fur of little cilia with a layer of mucous on the top. The cilia wave in such a way as to send the mucous up away from the alveoli and toward the bottom of your throat. The mucous carries dirt and foreign bodies out of the lungs. Nicotine temporarily paralyzes the cilia, effectively stunning the mechanism that would help clear the lungs of the effect of the smoke. So when

on the inside. We often see it chronically tight on those addicted to drugs, or otherwise out in the cold. You cannot reach it directly from the outside, but it can be released through heavy breathing—such as during a rebirthing or Holotropic Breathwork session, or through the recoil techniques practiced by the European osteopaths.

Of course, other muscles can be recruited to assist inhalation, especially in asthmatics or others with breathing difficulties. Shoulder muscles such as the pectorals, the posterior serratii or the erector

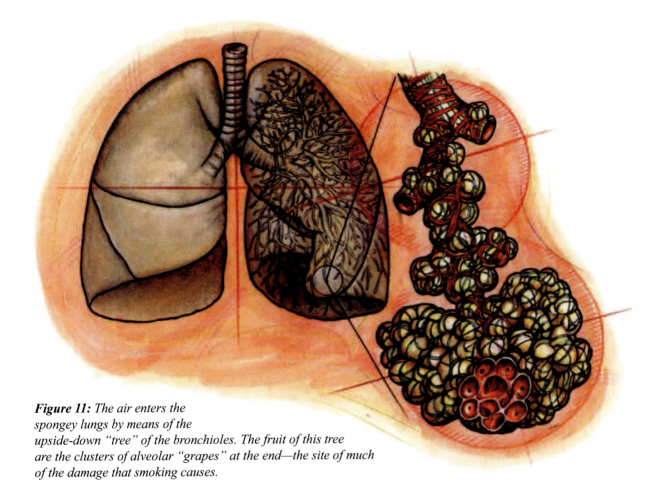

*Figure 11:* The air enters the spongey lungs by means of the upside-down "tree" of the bronchioles. The fruit of this tree are the clusters of alveolar "grapes" at the end—the site of much of the damage that smoking causes.

you finally get Uncle Charlie to quit, after a few days his cilia start working again, carrying loads of crap up the bottom of his throat, causing him to cough. Uncle Charlie waggles his finger at you and says, "See, I was healthier when I was smoking!"–and then goes on to prove it by going back to cigarettes and his cough, sure enough, disappears as the cilia go back into la-la land.

### Patterns of breathing

If Body[3] were to recommend any particular style of breathing, we would call it something like the "generous" breath, or "responsive" breath, but somebody has probably already used all these names. Not only do we not wish to see still places in the rib basket during the breath, we also like to see response all over the body. I once watched as my Taiwanese tai chi teacher "breathed" his palms in and out: his palm moved visibly in time with his breathing. I cannot do that, and none of my clients do it either, but a body-wide response to the breath is palpable with the knowing hand, and is a mark of structural integration. At the very least, we want to see and feel a breath wave moving responsively up from the pelvic floor and through the floating ribs to the upper ribs and into the neck. Though breathing styles, activity levels and body structures vary, the responsive breath can only help bring health and adaptability.

Different styles of breathing produce different psychophysiological effects. Diaphragmatic breathing—belly breathing, "down" breathing—tends to stimulate the parasympathetic system through the vagus nerve and send the body into a quiet, reflective, restorative state. For this reason, this type of breathing is favored by meditation teachers and hypnotists who want to induce a relaxed state. Although it is touted as natural breathing "like a baby," for an adult to maintain this type of breathing requires voluntary control. The mystic who lives on a mountain in a cave may be revered for his ability to maintain an even demeanor. The question is, can

**The River of Life, Part 2**

he maintain the same cool when being shoved in the bustle of the marketplace in the village below the cave? If the mystic is dependent on his breathing style, then the answer is "Probably not."

**So many of us had our breathing stepped on in some way very early in our lives, that many people evoke memories of their birth or perinatal experience when they undertake breath work.**

Breathing into the upper part of the ribs especially at a more rapid pace, tends to stimulate the sympathetic system, sending the body toward an alert, ready-for-action state. Since this state can be more associated with negative emotions, such as fear, anger or strong grief, this type of breathing, carried on for some minutes (while not otherwise exercising), can induce emotional reactions. This is an interesting phenomenon, and important to us as therapists: emotion produces physiological changes, and physiological changes can steer emotions. This forms the basis of the new drugs for depression, also calls to mind Candace Pert's work on the neuro peptides, and even harks back to William James' theories on whether the emotions produce bodily reactions, like tears or blushing—or is it the other way around?

If we go into one of these emotions, especially if we are trying to hide or deny it, we are likely to notice ourselves breathing "up" in some way, or stifling breath in general. On the other side of the same coin, if we breathe that way, we are likely to be sent into our emotions. This latter idea is the basis of such techniques as rebirthing, which use this kind of breathing to bring up abreactive material by inducing a sympathetically charged state, and then presumably discharging it, one hopes, with therapeutic effect.

Sustaining such breathing can produce a state called tetany, in which the blood loses so much carbon dioxide that certain muscles—especially those that are highly innervated (the hands, lips and feet)—tighten up involuntarily. Breathing into a paper bag for a bit can restore the blood balance and reduce the contracture, though we have seen no ill effects from tetany that was maintained even for a couple of hours. For the women of the last century who wore corsets, diaphragmatic breathing was difficult and the breathing was forced by the restriction of the corset to the upper part of the rib basket. This made women more likely to swoon in times of high emotion, and generally made these women more prone to "hysteria"—not as a result of their gender, but of fashion.

Rebirthing (it has a new incarnation as Holotropic Breathwork) might be better named "re-breathing," because it really goes into wherever we have stopped or stepped on the breath. The fact of the matter is, however, that so many of us had our breathing stepped on in some way very early in our lives that many people evoke memories of their birth or peri-natal experience when they undertake breath work. For others, the breath work may bring back memories of a childhood operation or of being tortured by a big brother. But for many, the experience or birth began the journey away from the "natural" breath.

With respect to perinatal experiences that affect natural breathing, there is a hospital based tendency to cut the umbilical cord too early, suction out the nasal passages, clean off the vernix, or the host of other things that hospital staff feel compelled to do. All of these can interrupt the first breath, or the first few minutes of breathing, when a lifetime pattern is called into being. Except in cases of medical emergency, as long as the Apgar readings are normal or better, why not let the baby and the mother (hey, and the father) alone in peace for a bit for bonding and "conspiracy"—breathing together—to take place? A baby left to nurse and gaze into its mother's eyes stands a better chance of getting a reasonable start on the lifelong habit of breathing than one who is subjected immediately to weighing, testicle counting, silver nitrate and other things that can, very simply, wait.

When we have a generation born under more natural conditions of simple respect, might we not see a natural breath? In the meantime, we therapists have plenty of tense, raw materials for our gentle experiments with the river of life that flows between the banks of the rib cage. ∎

# Chapter 9: Hanging Out With the Shoulder

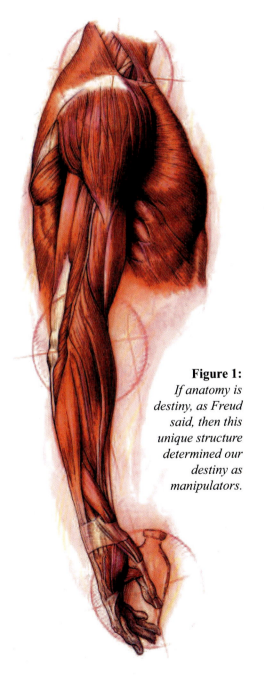

**Figure 1:**
*If anatomy is destiny, as Freud said, then this unique structure determined our destiny as manipulators.*

A number of years ago I had the opportunity to swim a few times with dolphins, I recommend the experience highly to anybody able to do it. An entire column could be filled with stories from those brief amateur encounters, but our entry point to the shoulder is going to be (surprise!) language. Smart and Well-intentioned people are trying to figure out dolphin language. But as flaky as it sounds, my experience was that dolphins communicate on some bandwidth other than sound. Those clicks and squeaks they make are, in my totally uninformed opinion, what hand gestures are to Italians: great for emphasis, color or tone, but they do not constitute the content of dolphin speech itself.

The shape of any species' speech is going to depend on its physical shape and the possibilities of its movement. Most of the attempts to understand dolphin communication have imposed the structure of our human language on dolphin noises in an attempt to find structural similarities. Good luck, because, quite simply dolphins don't have arms. Our whole language structure—subject, verb, object; someone does something to something else—is predicated on our hand and arm's unique ability to fashion the world around us. The dolphins—fast, smart and emotionally supportive as they may be—are literally not manipulators—they don't have the hands for it. The structure of their language, should we ever discover it, will reflect their radically different interactions within their surroundings. Most probably, it will partake deeply in principles of detachment and non-interference. Pray that we can learn before we manipulate ourselves right out of the surroundings the Creator gave us.

The lack of any support requirement for our shoulder girdle, the freedom of our arm to move, and the ability of our hand to perform several kinds of grips—these anatomical facts of life have shaped the very fabric of our thoughts and speech, until we can hardly conceive of thinking in any other way. Consider it—without the very specific properties of our arms, massage would be impossible, and touch therapy would still consist of licking each other for comfort, like cats and wolves (not with some of my clients, thank you!).

But seriously, folks, the unique arrangements of our shoulder and arm have made it possible for us to physically realize the tremendous creative potential of our minds. Everything we have made—from gardens to atom bombs to cathedrals to massage tables—rest on the mobility of the shoulder and arm with its agile hand at its distal end. Dolphins, with fins in place of hands, must have developed their creative potential in another direction—telepathy, perhaps.

Leaving such speculation behind, let us explore the potential of our own fascinating and unique upper girdle. The shoulder and the arm tend to get short shrift in most structurally integrating approaches to manual therapy, for two reasons: 1) they are so complicated; and 2) they do not form part of the structural column—rather, they hang off it. The course of this book is no exception: We will concentrate on a few points about the shoulder, nearly ignore the arm, and move on to somewhere else next issue.

But do not buy the not-part-of-the-structural-column argument. Sure, the shoulder does hang off the supporting column of the spine and ribs, but this is not a passive hanging around like a picture nailed to a wall. The actions of the shoulder, both habitually and at any given moment, have a strong influence on the posture of the head, rib cage and back, and need to be carefully considered in any structural analysis.

### The most versatile shoulder

To understand the shoulder girdle, we will need to look, in habitual Body³ fashion, at its evolutionary history for clues. The shoulder almost certainly started on its evolutionary journey as a stabilizing pectoral fin. As our ancestral fish moved out onto the land, the fin moved a bit anterior on the torso to allow the budding land creature to use it to push itself through the mud of ancient swamps (see Figure 2).

As we follow further evolutionary branching, as if in a film, leading to our own twig, we see the "arms" moving from stabilizing fin to belly-crawl assistants, and then differentiating into stronger limbs that are able to lift the belly off the ground

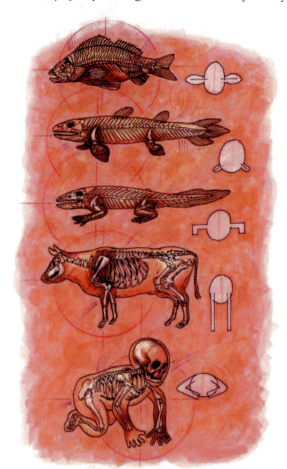

**Figure 2:** *The shoulder has been deployed and employed in a variety of ways throughout its evolutionary history.*

and stand increasingly under the body. In a horse or a dog or any number of familiar four-legged creatures, the foreleg or arm is the primary weight support under the rib cage. In most of these animals, the rib cage sits into a "sling" that runs under the torso from the inner edge of one shoulder blade to the other (see Figure 3). This sling is made from the two sides of the serratus anterior muscle and their associated fasciae.

So, in terms of our mammalian history, the first shoulder was a compressional support member, a weight bearer, just as our leg is now. It had to be straight and strong to resist the pull of gravity on the torso it supported. The trade-off for this stability was limited mobility. A horse can stand around all day and even sleep while bearing most of its weight on its forelimb. But when you wake up, you can yawn and absently scratch your left armpit with your right hand—imagine a horse trying to do the same action!

If the Darwinians are to be believed, our shoulder

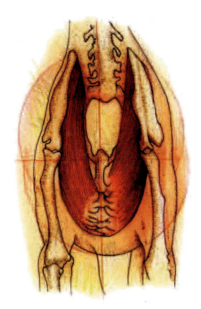
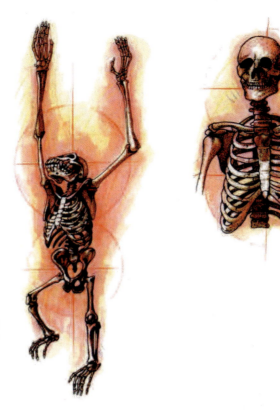

*Figure 3:* Even in our short mammalian history of 70 million years, the shoulder has supported us compressionally, then tensionally, and finally been totally supported by us.

went through another important stage between our quadrupedal friends and us: the hanging arm. In the tree-dwelling, brachiating monkeys, the body's weight is still supported by the arm, but in tension (hanging) rather than compression, as in the four-legged. Instead of being pushed toward the body, the shoulder is pulled away from it, kept intact by the myofasciae, specifically the deep muscles of the shoulder, that keep it from detaching as the primate hand holds the branch and gravity pulls the rest of the body down (see Figure 3).

Only when these brachiating primates headed back to the ground (or, if you believe Elaine Morgan, author of *The Scars of Evolution*, into the water) did they learn to stand on two feet, leaving the arms free to enjoy their seven degrees of freedom and to become the manipulative geniuses they are for us today.

Historically, then, our shoulder and arm have spent time in three very different positions: supporting most of our weight in compression from below (in horizontal flexion); supporting most of our weight in tension from above (in full flexion); and finally being supported (and about time, too) by the rest of us (see Figure 3) in what we call extension or neutral position.

To keep focus, this chapter on the shoulder throws light on three facets of the shoulder and arm only: 1) the connections of the bone-ligament core from the axial skeleton out to the hand; 2) the function of the muscular core of the shoulder; and 3) a comparison of the structures in the arm and the leg. The intricacies of the lower arm, the carpal tunnel, and even the traps, lats, pects and delts will all have to wait for another time.

To assist you in seeing these relationships, we include references to plates from Frank Netter's *Atlas of Human Anatomy*, published by CIBA-Geigy, although you can follow along with any good anatomy atlas.

### The flow of the bones

Clients tend to forget that the whole shoulder and arm skeleton is attached to the axial skeleton at only one point: the sternoclavicular joint (Netter plate 395). Take the shoulder and all its associated muscles off the body, and all you see of the torso's connection to the arm is the shiny cartilage of this joint at the top of the sternum. (I know, I know- at the end of a long day of working, it can feel as if there is a joint, a nearly arthritic one, between the scapula and the neck or ribs in the back, but there is

**Hanging Out With The Shoulder**

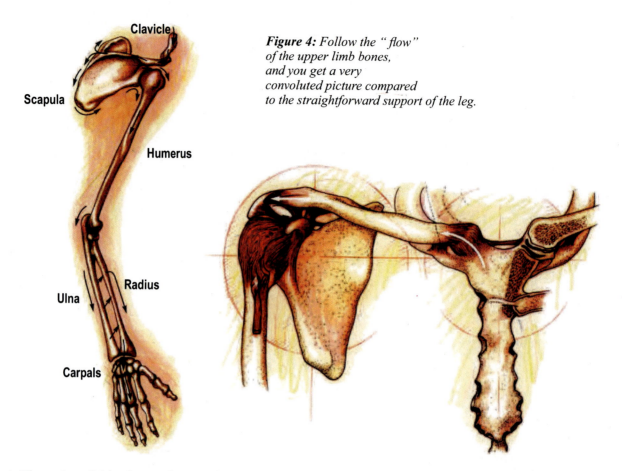

*Figure 4:* Follow the *"flow"* of the upper limb bones, and you get a very convoluted picture compared to the straightforward support of the leg.

not. The point of this chapter is to understand how you can settle that complaining musculature that's trying to act like a joint.) Besides the cut edges of the muscles, the only other opening from the torso into the shoulder would be the tubes and peripheral nerve trunks of the neurovascular bundle that exists between the scalenes in the neck (Netter plate 65).

The flow of movement in the arm is one thing, and the flow of the muscles is another that we will examine. But the flow of the bones—the progression of stabilization from one bone to the next—in the shoulder is quite unusual, and changes our usual conception of the shoulder. (I modified the following from something I got from a dancer who says she got it from Bonnie Bainbridge-Cohen. I have been unable to find it in Bonnie's writings, but freely acknowledge her as the source, with any errors being my own. For an introduction to Bainbridge's radically interesting ideas on developmental movement, pick up her book, *Sensing, Feeling & Action*, published by Contact Editions.)

Following the bones carefully, we travel from that one point of skeletal connection, from the sternum onto the clavicle, straight out to the acromioclavicular joint (acro + omo = high shoulder, or the high point of the shoulder). From here, the superficial muscles, the deltoid in particular, flow from the acromion down to the humerus, but the bones do not. The flow of the bones travels instead around the acromion to the spine of the scapula, which runs medially to the vertebral border of the scapula (Netter plate 396-7). From the point where the spine meets the medial border, the flow goes both up and down along this inner edge to the superior and inferior angle of the scapula. Here the direction turns laterally again, along the superior border at the top and the lateral border at the bottom, leading our to the glenoid fossa where the flow now goes into the humerus (Netter plate 400).

Down at the distal end of the humerus, the connection at the elbow is really between the humerus and the ulna at the trochlea (Netter plates 411-412). The relationship between the humerus and the radius is much more tenuous. The ulna passes up toward the little finger. There are two joints between the radius and the ulna, one near the elbow and one near the wrist, which allow the movements of pronation and supination in the forearm. Between these two joints is the interosseous membrane, which forms the energetic bond between these two bones (Netter plate 413).

Look at the primary direction of the fibers of this membrane (see Figure 5). Notice that, while there are fibers going in several directions, the predominant direction of fibers is going from proximal on the radius to distal on the ulna. (Make this simple; Look down at the inside of your left forearm with your palm turned up. Draw lines with your finger from close (proximal) on the thumb side toward the hand (distal) on the little finger side. This is the primary direction of the interosseous membrane fibers.)

Why should the fibers run this way? If you look at the wrist, the radius (on the thumb side) is quite large, and takes the largest part of the force from the carpals. (The wrist is sometimes called the radiocarpal joint, showing how little the tiny end of the ulna has to do with the hand.) Thus, force that is transmitted from the hand-say, catching a ball or applying pressure to a trigger point—to the arm passes from the heel of the hand to the radius, which passes it on to the ulna through the "spring" of the interosseous membrane.

The flow of the bones, then, goes from the humerus to the ulna, from the ulna to the radius via the interosseous membrane and into the first three carpal bones (Netter plate 429). These three connect with the four other carpal bones, which in turn connect with the five metacarpals and fingers. The arm, like the leg, is arranged in a 1-2-3-4-5 pattern, but along a more circuitous route than the straightforward, compressionally supporting leg (see Figure 4, the sidebar at the end of this chapter, and Chapter 1).

### The "core" of the shoulder

The long-term function of our very mobile arm depends on a very precise positional balance of the shoulder girdle relative to the rib cage and neck. This position rests in turn on the balance of tone in the underlying muscles that connect the shoulder girdle to the axial skeleton. Delineating this balance is the purpose of this section.

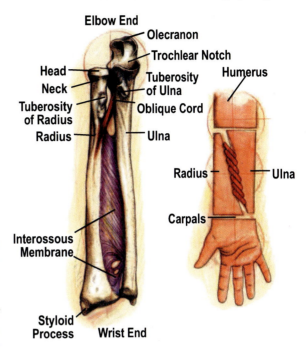

**Figure 5:** *Except for the oblique cords, the majority of the fibers of the interosseous membrane pass proximally from the ulna to the radius, enabling them to act as a shock-absorbing spring.*

Too much emphasis is placed on the traps, lats, pects and delts in exercise and rehabilitation schemes, and not enough on the underlying muscles we are calling the core of the shoulder. These deeper muscles, or myofascial structures to be precise, form the contractile straps that hold the scapula and clavicle in place.

There are only three muscles that hold the clavicle to the axial skeleton: the sternocleidomastoid (SCM), the anterosuperior aspect of the trapezius and the subclavius (Netter plates 22, 175. 219). The trapezius, which connects the distal portion of the clavicle to the skull, is great for elevating the clavicle, and can thus determine its angle. The clavicular head of the SCM attaches so close to the sternoclavicular joint that its effect on the position of the collar bone is negligible; it has much more to do with head position and rotation than with shoulder girdle position.

The subclavius is listed as a "depressor" of the clavicle, and, indeed, you can feel it do just that: Delve in under the medial part of the clavicle, past the superficial pectoralis major to where the subclavius lies, just on top of the first rib. With your fingers there, depress the tip of your shoulder, and feel the muscle bulge a bit (you have to have your fingers in

**Hanging Out With The Shoulder**

pretty deep to feel it). In daily life, however, how often do you depress your clavicle?

If you look at the muscle, it does lie under the clavicle so it can pull it down, but it mostly runs parallel to the clavicle, suggesting that it is a "puller-in" or a mediator of the clavicle. But you don't do that in daily life either, do you—or do you? When you think of our monkey friend, hanging from the tree (see Figure 3) the entire weight of the rest of the body is hanging from our one point of skeletal contact, the sternoclavicular joint. Seen in this light, the subclavius is a great muscle to have, to reinforce this joint and prevent its dislocation when subjected to this strain. Perhaps, in functional terms, we would have done better to call the subclavius the "preventus lateralis clavicularis" or something.

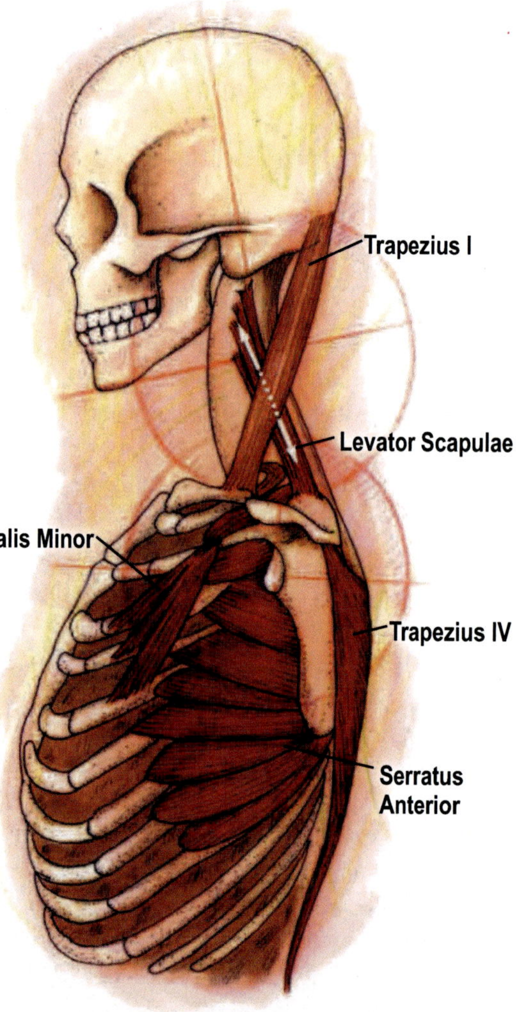

There are many more muscles that hold the very mobile scapula to the axial skeleton, and we will spend the majority of our time with them. Besides the trapezius and (sometimes) the latissimus dorsi, the muscles that connect the scapula to the axial skeleton are the levator scapulae, the rhomboids, the serratus anterior, the pectoralis minor and the omohyoid. (Those tempted to include the rotator cuff muscles are reminded that we were looking for the muscles that hold the scapula to the axial skeleton, while the cuff muscles go to the humerus, and are thus totally appendicular muscles.)

Leaving aside the tiny omohyoid (Netter plate 24), and the sometimes-attached-sometimes-not latissimus (Netter plate 160), the rest of these muscles are responsible for the postural placement of the scapula on the back of the rib cage. Although we could go through all the possible and confusing movements of the shoulder—protraction, retraction, anterior tilt, upward and downward rotation, elevation, depression, and God knows what all, suffice it to note that if you lay your client face down, you can take the scapula through a full circle on the back. What determines where in this circle the scapula will lie in postural rest? The balance of these inner muscles, pulling around the "compass" of the scapula, is the answer.

### The scapular "x"

When you start looking at it this way, the whole thing simplifies out pretty easily, because these muscles organize themselves in to an "x" around each scapula. Arrayed along the medial border of the scapula are three muscles that pull up and in on the scapula: the levator scapulae and the two rhomboid muscles.

The levator (Netter plate 160), which starts from the very apex of the scapula, the superior angle, and twists up to the transverse processes of the first four cervical vertebrae, gets unfairly blamed for a lot of shoulder problems. Nearly everyone can find a sore spot right where the levator joins the scapula, and "Oh, my shoulders are so tense, I must be holding them up" is often heard. Looked at from the side, however, you could imagine the levator like the reins of a horse, saying "Whoa!" to the tendency of the upper cervical (and thus the head) to go forward (see Figure 6). Seen this way, the progression toward

*Figure 6: In the complex of muscles which surround the scapula, the levator scapulae may have more to do with neck position than scapular position. As the head goes forward, the levator tightens to stop it, making its scapular end start slowly screaming.*

this soreness is not initiated by people lifting their shoulders in some kind of fear or stress reaction; rather, it is initiated by a forward head posture, the most common of Western alignment faults. The head goes forward, the levator contracts to try to prevent it from progressing, the shoulder is pulled passively upward, the traps and the levator, locked in a strained position, get sore. Do some work to get the head to float more over the rib cage and watch that soreness disappear more permanently?

Now, turning our attention to the rhomboids (Netter plate 178), we can see them as part of the first leg of the "x." This leg combines the rhomboids with the serratus anterior (Netter plate 177). We have already seen how important the serratus was to shoulder support in the quadruped; now we can see its postural role in the human. The serratus runs from the first nine ribs on the side, passing in front of (deep to) the scapula to attach all along the medial border, right next to the rhomboid. In fact, you could say that there is really one long muscle—the "rhombo-serratus" muscle—that runs from the spinous processes of the lower cervicals and upper thoracics out to the ribs, with the medial border of the scapula attached to the middle of it (see Figure 7).

This muscular sling determines the position of the scapula, and thus the shoulder in general along the line of these muscles. If the rhomboids are chronically tighter (as they are in many reduced thoracic curve, "flat back" postures), the shoulder will be retracted and lifted. In cases like this, some digging out of the buried vertebrae from the excessive strain of the erectors is necessary prior to stretching the rhomboid to ease the scapulae out laterally.

If the serratus overcomes the rhomboids, then the shoulder blades will sit wide and drop, as is seen in many bodybuilders or others with kyphotic thoracic curves. To work with such chronically protracted scapulae, have your client sit on a massage table or stool, his back to you. Place the flat of your relaxed fists on both sides of the body, on the belly of the serratus anterior muscle. Your hand will probably include some of latissimus and the teres major, and that is OK. Let your elbows be wide. Bring your hands slowly together, following the curve of the rib cage toward your client's mid-back, firmly bringing all this tissue medially. At the same time, encourage your client to breathe in and take his sternum upward

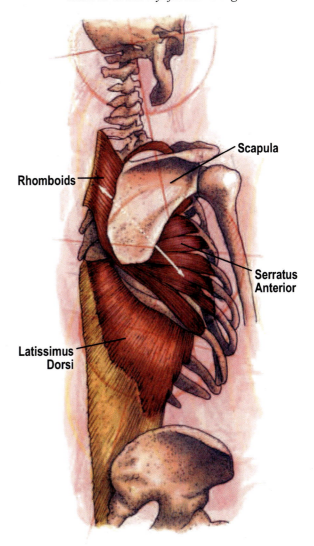

*Figure 7: The rhombo-serratus muscle. The medial border of the scapula is positioned by the relative tensions in this myofascial "sling."*

and forward as you bring his shoulder blades in. This action simultaneously reduces kyphotic curve, activates the rhomboids and repositions the protracted scapulae.

In both these patterns, a slow, mindful, daily series of repetition of the cat stretch—bringing the spine from full flexion to full hyperextension while on all fours—will help to mobilize and properly position the scapulae in this dimension.

The other leg of the scapular "x" is a little harder to see, but is equally important. To understand this leg, we must first divide the trapezius into different muscles, or at least different sections, which we will call Trap I-IV (Netter plate 160). Trap I goes from the occiput to the lateral third of the clavicle. Trap II

**Hanging Out With The Shoulder**

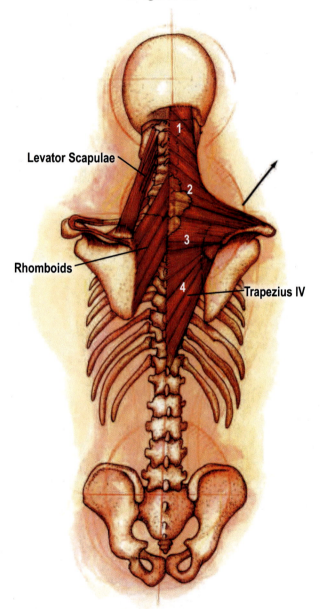

**Figure 8a:** *The other leg of the scapular 'x' involves the trapezius and the pectoralis minor muscle. 8a below shows us the trapezius muscle, divided into its components: 1) occipito-clavicular part, 2) nuchal-acromial part, 3) upper thoracic-scapular spine part, and 4) the part under discussion, the lower thoracic-medial border part. The arrow asks "What muscle counter balances Trap IV's pull on scapular position?" The answer is pictured at right in 8b.*

goes from the nuchal ligament (or cervical spinous processes) to the acromion of the scapula. Trap III goes from the upper thoracis to the middle of the spine of the scapula.

Trap IV, part of the "x" we are going to discuss now, originates of the spinous processes of about T4 or T5 to Tl2, and runs up to the medial portion of the scapular spine. This is the only muscle that pulls down and in (all right, inferiorly and medially) on the scapula.

The puzzle is, though, what muscle could pull superiorly and laterally on the scapula? Such a muscle would have to be higher than the shoulder and attached to something way lateral to the ear, would it not? The body's solution is clever: wrap the strap around the front of the body, and tie it to the front of the ribs. Viewed in this manner, we can see that the pectoralis minor (Netter plate 403), which ties the coracoid process down to ribs 3, 4 and 5, is really the antagonist of the Trap IV for this dimension of scapular position. While Trap IV is pulling the scapula down and in, the pectoralis minor, by pulling the coracoid down and medial, tends to take the back of the scapula up, out and into an anterior tilt (see Figure 8).

Although having Trap IV overcome the pectoralis minor so that the scapula is too far into posterior tilt is rare, having the pectoralis minor pull the scapula into anterior tilt is as common as, well, the overprotected hearts. To work this relationship, slip your fingers into the armpit, behind the pectoralis major, until you find the three slips of the pectoralis minor between the major and the anterior ribs. (Be mindful, especially when working with women, of not trapping lymphatic tissue between your fingers and the muscle.)

Stretch the myofascia of the pectoralis minor from its origin on the rib toward the coracoid process, while the client brings the shoulder blades together and down, military fashion. The muscle is part of a whole wall of fascia called the clavipectoral fascia, so while finding the muscle specifically is best, stretching any shortened fascia between pectoralis major and the ribs will help you achieve your goal. This work can be done with the client supine or sitting.

There are many more interesting and productive relationships here in the shoulder; this "x" is just one set. Traps I and II, for instance, which are constantly building up frequent tension points, also balance with the pectoralis minor in another functional dimension: hanging the shoulder off the body like a pub sign. The trapezius provides the upper stability, which gets transmitted to the coracoid process through the coracoacromial ligament. The pectoralis minor pulls down and in, providing another point

*Figure 8b:* *The pectoralis minor muscle counters Trap IV's pull on scapular position. By pulling down, and in, and forward on the coracoid process, it pulls the scapula into anterior tilt and protraction. If this part of the 'x' is too tight, breathing, open-heartedness, and open-handedness are all limited. Have a look at any picture of Richard Nixon to see this pattern.*

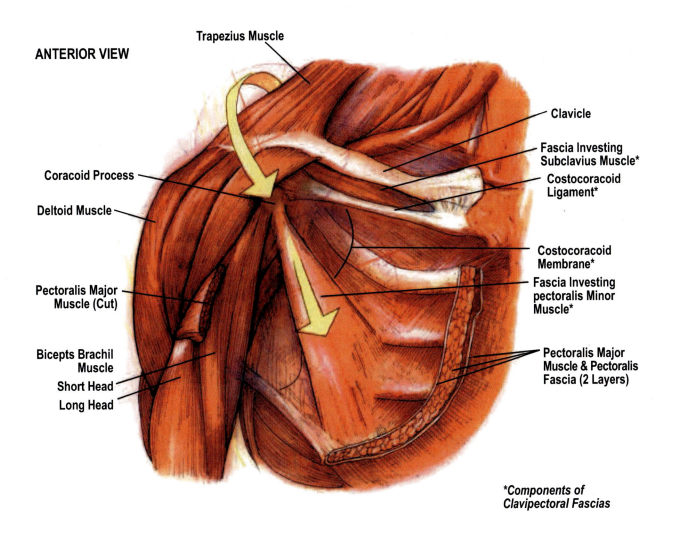

*Components of Clavipectoral Fascias

of stability, with the coracobrachialis and the biceps taking off to the arm from the coracoid process. Any given bit of anatomy, especially around the shoulder, is often called upon to perform multiple functions.

But mastery of these four muscles of the "x"—Trap IV, the rhomboids, serratus anterior and pectoralis minor—will allow you to reset most scapular problems with ease and precision. Scapular malposition is the breeding ground for some back and neck problems, and is definitely part of the solution in most recalcitrant rotator cuff problems that have trouble healing.

From here, the "flow" of the muscles goes into the rotator cuff and on into the flexors and extensors of the upper and lower arm (Netter plates 400, 403, 406, 415 -20). There are many good stories along this trail, but we will leave them for another time, in hopes that we have expanded your understanding of the shoulder with this chapter. We have put in a teaser—a comparison of the structures in the arm and the leg (see sidebar, "A Comparison of the Arm and the Leg").

Join us next time in a look at a few aspects of that unique tangle of truss work, the spine.

### A Comparison of the Arm and the Leg

In evolutionary terms, the arm and the leg developed very differently, at different times and with different functions. The shoulder girdle came first, interestingly, and was fairly well-developed when the pelvic girdle started to come along. But Nature, once she has a good idea, loves to repeat herself with variations.

The eye, for instance, so complicated as to be nearly inexplicable without a deity to just put it there, has apparently developed dozens of times independently in various parts of the animal kingdom. There is something about "eyeness," electro-magnetic sensitivity that just draws an eye into being over many generations of variation.

Is there something about "limbness" as well, that accounts for the similarity between the arm and leg, even though they have been used for many different purposes over their long histories? The bat's wing, the dolphin's fin, the horse's leg, and the human arm all have nearly the same underlying set of structures. Homology is a fascinating study. Our small foray into that subject here is mostly for fun, with an aim of clarifying your understanding of both the arm and the leg.

It was by examining the relationship between the coracobrachialis and the brachialis that I first understood the relationship between the adductor magnus and the short head of the biceps—the "fourth" hamstring. (See Chapter 2 and use Netter plate 395-505 to tease these babies out. This is a partial list, and alternative correspondences could be successfully argued).

Don't stretch these analogies too far, as they will snap under too much strain. Other different but still equally valid equivalencies could be argued. And the ability to compare breaks down as we get more distal, where the two limbs diverge more and more. But it is a useful exercise just the same, which I use as a teaching tool with my students.

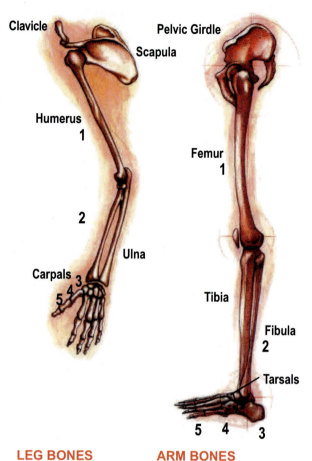

| LEG BONES | ARM BONES |
|---|---|
| Hip Bone | Scapula |
|     Iliac crest | Spine of scapula (and clavicle?) |
|     Ischial tuberosity | Supraglenoid tubercle |
|     Anterior inferior iliac spine | Infraglenoid tubercle |
|     Acetabulum | Glenoid fossa |
| Femur | Humerus |
|     Greater and lesser trochanter | Greater and lesser tubercle |
|     Popliteal fossa | Coronoid fossa |
| Patella | Olecranon |
| Tibia | Ulna |
| Fibula | Radius |
| Metatarsals and phalanges | Metacarpals and phalanges |

| LEG MUSCLES | ARM MUSCLES |
|---|---|
| Gluteals and tensor fasciae latae | Deltoid |
| Piriformis | Supraspinatus |
| Deep lateral rotators | Infraspinatus and Teres minor |
| Quadratus femoris | Teres major |
| Iliacus | Subscapularis |
| Quadriceps | Triceps |
|     Rectus femoris | Long head of triceps |
| Hamstrings | Biceps brachii |
| Adductor magnus | Coracobrachialis |
| Short head of biceps femoris | Brachialis |
| Gastrocnemius | Brachioradialis |
| Popliteus | Pronator teres |
| Deep posterior compartment | Wrist and finger flexors |
| Anterior compartment | Wrist and finger extensors |
| Peroneols | Ulnar deviators |
| Tibialis ant and post | Radial deviators |
| Plantaris | Palmaris longus |

**Footnotes**

1. Mees, L.F.C. *Secrets of the Skeleton Form in Metamorphosis*, 1984 Anthroposophic Press, Hudson, NY
2. Dawkins, Richard *Climbing Mount Improbable*, 1996, W.W. Norton & Co., Scranton, PA.

# Chapter 10:
# The Spine (Part 1): The Spring in the Spine's Step

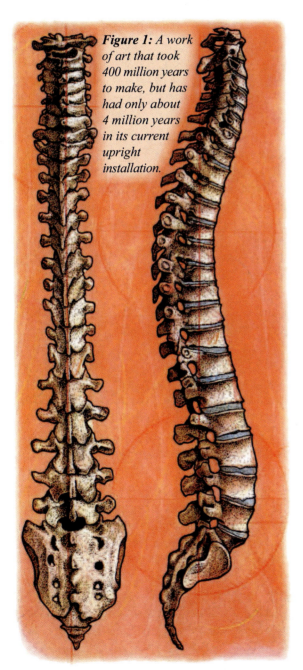

*Figure 1: A work of art that took 400 million years to make, but has had only about 4 million years in its current upright installation.*

**W**hen we want people to show more moral strength—something we often sigh for these days in our leaders, right and left—we appeal to any of three parts of their body: We ask them if they have the guts for the job, we urge them to put their heart into it, or we shake our heads sadly and say, "That bubba has more wishbone than backbone." Body³ has already looked at two out of the three: the shape and the scaffolding for the intestinal organs and the heart. Now let us take on the complexity of the spine.

Our spine is a potent image, not only its many symbolic meanings, but also its simple visual shape, instantly recognizable as human in its elegant curves and skyward orientation. Even as a piece of mechanics, the spine can be described in various ways: a column, rod, beam, strut, crane, pole, mast, stem, trunk, spring or a whip. In this chapter, we want to hover between the actuality of spinal mechanics and our common cultural images of it, in hopes of giving you another way of looking at how the spine might function, a point of view which leads directly to a soft-tissue approach to spinal health.

Besides being a rich mine of metaphors, the spine really is complicated enough to puzzle medical writers from Aristotle right through the present day. It is complicated enough to support whole branches of medicine—chiropractic, osteopathic, orthopedic—devoted almost exclusively to its study. It is complicated enough to generate many conflicting theories of how it is put together and how it works; complicated enough to fill a library with books. So how shall we deal with it in one short chapter? Suffice it to say that this is cheerfully incomplete, and focused on putting forward an appealing but totally unproven theory. And it will take us two chapters to do even that much. This chapter will focus first on the front part of the spine, the disc-vertebrae portion: then on the posterior part, the neural arch and all the processes that stick out from it. Through examining the articular facets in particular, we will learn about the kinds of movement these shapes allow in different parts of the spine. In the next chapter, we will expand our view to include the posterior muscles of the spine, and put forward a "tensegrity continuum" theory of how the spine achieves "lift"—the most effortless and resilient upright balance. (To assist you in seeing these relationships we include references to plates from Frank Netter's *Atlas of Human Anatomy*, second edition, published by CIBA-Geigy, although you can follow along with any good anatomy atlas.)

**Figure 2:** *The spine has functioned as a segmented ridgepole, and as an oblique armature. Now we are actively engaged in finding out whether and how it can function as a segmented tent pole.*

### "Lift" in a segmented tent pole

To begin, let's look at the skeletons of our quadrupedal friends and notice that the spine functions as a segmented ridgepole (see Figure 2). The four-legged horse is a bit like a four-cornered house: each of the four legs offers a pillar of support, the shoulder and pelvic girdles are like the gables at either end of the house, and the spine serves as the ridgepole. The ridgepole has to be segmented to allow movement to take place, but posturally it is slung atop the heap of bones. The head is hung—cantilevered, actually—off one end of this ridgepole and the tail is cantilevered off the other. Constant tension in the soft tissues is required to keep the head up, which is why your cat and dog both love to be rubbed on the neck behind their ears.

Look at the human: mostly the same bones, but a totally different architecture (see Figure 2). The segmented ridgepole has become a segmented tent pole. What a design problem—supporting a tent pole with 24 moving parts above the sacrum, with a 12-or-so-pound boss—the head—sitting on top of all of them, with the wind-filled sail of a rib cage billowing in and out, and with a wildly mobile shoulder hanging off on either side. It's a total wonder that we work at all!

If that were not enough, it also has to hold and protect a couple of pounds of runny custard (the brain and spinal cord) contained within it, without putting any strain in the delicate nerve strands that run out through holes between the shifting bones. But it must still allow wide freedom of movement to the vibratory and chemical sensors that are your eyes, ears and nose.

To keep some boundaries on our discussion, we are going to leave out heaps of anatomical detail to focus on two questions: How does the spine hold itself up? And how can the spine get functionally longer? This last phenomenon is what Ida Rolf, the developer of Rolfing® bodywork, called lift and what dancers call lightness. When the spine lengthens—defies gravity, so to speak—the core of the body lifts, and the whole feeling of standing and moving changes. What is this, and how can we get it for ourselves and our clients?

Part of the answer lies in pelvic balance, discussed in Chapter 4 and part lies in the ability of the spine to expand in breathing (see Chapter 7). But here we will look at the spring in the spine's own step. To get the full picture, we need to fill in some of the details of spinal construction.

### The front and back of the spine

Whether deployed as a ridgepole or a tent pole, spinal design is pretty similar: a series of bony bodies separated by discs ventrally; and a series of arches with joints between them dorsally. Look at the spine as a whole viewed from the side (see Figure 1 or Netter plate 142) and you will see the spinal cord and intervertebral foramina (the holes where the spinal nerves exit and enter) lie right between these two pieces. For analytical purposes, we are going to consider these two parts of the spine—anterior and posterior separately.

For the purposes of this chapter, we will assume that the reader is familiar with the basic nomenclature of spinal sections, primary and secondary curves, and the names of all the sticky-outy bits.

### The anterior spine: bodies and discs

First, let's look at the anterior half of the spine, the vertebral bodies and the discs. The discs are like a soft-centered candy, with a gelatinous pulp in the middle, surrounded by layer after layer of cartilage-impregnated fiber (see Netter plate 144). Each layer of collagen fiber runs in a different direction, like the grain of the various layers of plywood, so that the outer part of the disc, the annulus, is very strong and resilient. The annulus is very firmly bonded to (actually continuous with) the fiber in the bone of the bodies themselves, so no disc can "slip" (we all know that by now, don't we?). The gooey, thick-skinned water balloon of the disc can bulge, herniate, or finally even rupture, but it cannot move out of place.

A bulging disc can usually be easily returned to normal function through manual therapy and rest. Even a herniated disc, where the annulus has been overstretched, will often respond positively to skilled soft tissue or bony manipulation. A ruptured disc, where the nuclear pulp has actually broken through the skin of the disc and congealed into old bubble gum in the spinal canal, is a different matter altogether and often requires more invasive treatment.

There are several types of herniations and ruptures, but the most common tend to be posterolateral, right into the spinal nerve roots (see Netter plate 146). There is a reason for this. The anterior and posterior longitudinal ligaments reinforce the discs (sec Figure 3B), but unfortunately they do not cover two areas of the disc (about 9 o'clock to 11 o'clock and 1 o'clock to 3 o'clock as we look down on the disc from the front). The posterior longitudinal ligament protects the spinal cord, but these areas just too either side is prone to herniations that tend to press on the spinal nerve roots. This is a design flaw that we must ask God about when we get the chance.

### The vertebral bodies have much less bone, relatively speaking than the bone in your head, your arms or your pelvis.

Now, it is easy to think of the spine as a collection of bones, especially since we see it that way so often, in pictures and in the skeletons and plastic spines that hang around our massage schools. The discs are usually

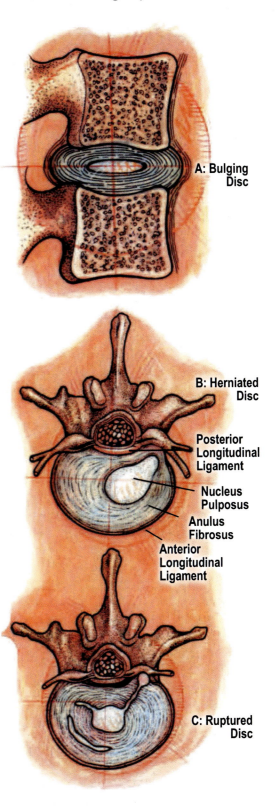

*Figure 3:* Under pressure, the outer skin of a disc can bulge, herniate, or, in extremis, rupture. In a rupture, the extruded nuclear pulp quickly congeals and must be surgically removed.

A: Bulging Disc

B: Herniated Disc
Posterior Longitudinal Ligament
Nucleus Pulposus
Anulus Fibrosus
Anterior Longitudinal Ligament

C: Ruptured Disc

**The Spine, Part 1**

represented by inert pieces of felt, or more recently plastic, stuck between the vertebrae. We are trained to look at the front of the spine as a series of vertebrae with discs in between. Historically, though, the exact opposite is the case. The original backbone (notochord) in the early pre-vertebrates was one long disc, one long tube of fibrocartilage with a fluid center. This one-long-disc-spine was whipped back and forth by the muscles to provide motive power for swimming. Shark spines, for instance, are still totally cartilaginous. Our bony vertebral bodies were later additions, modifications of the original disc material; our discs are remnants of the original spine. So the accurate way, in evolutionary terms, is to see the spine as a series of discs with vertebrae in between.

If this seems like splitting hairs to you, I have to tell you that it does not to me. The next time you cradle someone's head in your hands, or cup their sacrum, put your attention up into the spine. Instead of putting traction on the head or sacrum, as we usually do to lengthen the spine, press ever so slightly (an ounce or two) into the spinal axis, and feel the continuity of the discs, as if they were one interrelated system. Some twists and restrictions in the spine can be unwound directly from the discs, and all aberrations will have a disc component, even if they are not 'discogenic.' This realization has made very practical changes in how I approach the spine: the discs are of primary importance; ligaments are secondary: the vertebrae are decidedly tertiary.

If we just looked at this construct of the front of the spine, the bodies and the discs without any of the neural arch, we would see a basic column. But what a strange column it would be! The discs in the sacral and coccygeal spine largely have disappeared during the first year of development, leaving pretty solid, immovable bone (see Netter plate 145). For the lumbar spine, the discs are quite significant, accounting for about 30 percent of the length of the spine. In the thoracic and cervical parts of the spine, the discs are relatively thinner, accounting for about 25 percent and 17 percent, respectively, of those spinal sections.

Because of the malleability of the discs, this column would be able to move freely in any direction—flexion, extension, lateral flexion or rotation. If you pressed on the top of this simple spine, it would bounce a little because of the resilience of the discs, but you would not be able to put much of a downward load on it for two reasons: 1) a direct downward load would tend to bulge out the discs until they herniated or ruptured; and 2) the bone in the vertebral bodies is surprisingly cancellous, or spongy (see Figure 4). The vertebral bodies of women who suffer from extreme osteoporosis sometimes collapse. Most of the rest of us avoid this, but even in the healthiest person, the vertebral bodies have much less bone, relatively speaking, than the bones in your head, your arms or your pelvis.

With these two facts in mind, we might well begin to wonder whether the front of the spine is really such a good column as we thought at first, and if it really bears the load of our weight as a column would. Columns bear weight by continuous compression: One brick rests on the next brick the weight of those two bricks rests on the next, and so on, until the weight of all the bricks is given to the ground. A series of lightweight "lava rocks" interspersed with water balloons hardly seems like a good candidate for a serious weight-bearing column. And it's not just the weight of the vertebrae

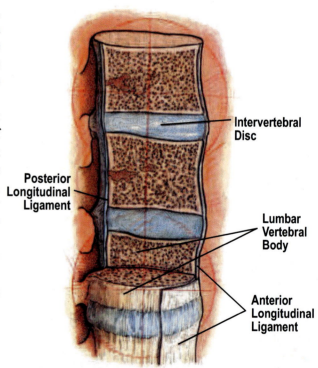

*Figure 4:* *The front of the spinal column—squishy discs alternating with spongy bone—is hardly a good candidate for a weight-bearing column.*

themselves, the rest of our body weighs in, too. Thus the weight of the head rests on the atlas, the weight of the head and neck on C7, but the weight of the head, neck, ribs, shoulders and arms all rest on L5. In engineering terms, if this were really the case, the lumbar vertebrae would have to be much bigger than they are. Something else must be going on here.

### The posterior spine: The neural arch

To see that something else, let's turn to the posterior half of the spine, the neural arch (see Figure 5). The neural arch consists of the arch around the spinal cord, which is in turn divided into the pedicle (the "foot" that stands on the vertebral body) and the lamina (which is removed in a laminectomy to give breathing room to nerve roots pressured by herniated discs). The neural arch, unlike the discs, is made from far more solid (compact) bone, suggesting a weight-bearing role. We should also note (see Figure 1) that these spinal nerves exit the spinal cord through holes that do not pass through the vertebrae themselves but rather through a foramen shaped by the lower edge of the pedicle above and the upper edge of the pedicle below (see Netter plate 147). Thus, if we lose space between the vertebrae, either through disc degeneration or excess tension in the spinal muscles, the resulting reduction in this spinal foramen could conceivably put pressure on the exiting nerves.

As you will remember from our discussion of the ribs in Chapter 7 that the neural arch was formed, millions of years later than the anterior notochord part, from a posterior-facing set of ribs that bent together to protect the spinal cord. Their ends form the spinous process. The two ends of the ribs can still be seen in the axis (C2) and sometimes some other cervical vertebrae. The bases of these ribs attach to the back of the bodies are the pedicles. Another set of ribs transformed into the transverse processes, which attach to the neural arch from the side.

In addition to these three, there are four articular processes on most vertebrae, two of which reach up and two down to link up with the vertebrae

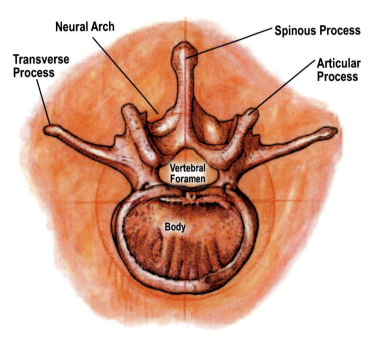

**Figure 5:** *The posterior part of the spine is formed from an old set of ribs that bent over to form a protective arch for the spinal cord. The arch bristles with processes that form the trusswork for the transversospinalis muscles.*

above and below. These articular processes form the basis for the intervertebral facet joints that are heard popping during chiropractic adjustments and morning stretches.

So most vertebrae have a total of six joints in common with their neighbors: two facet joints and a cartilaginous joint (the disc—it's a joint too) to the vertebra above; two facet joints and a cartilaginous disc to the one below (see Figure 6). While the discs-and-vertebral-bodies part of the spine would be happy to have you move in any direction at all, these facet joints in the rear restrict and allow particular movements in no uncertain terms. The orientation of these facet joints is important to know, and you can help yourself to remember their direction by learning the facet joint prayer (see sidebar, "The Facet Joint Prayer").

Look at the lumbar vertebrae on the posterior view of this chapter's opening figure. In which plane do the lumbar facets predominantly lie? Stick an imaginary piece of paper into the facets and you will see that they lie mostly in the sagittal plane— the piece of paper has to be straight up and down and come in directly from the back.

**The Spine, Part 1**

## The Facet Joint Prayer

This prayer may not propitiate the gods, but commit this to memory and you will never forget how the spinal facets are oriented.

*While the front part of the spine would allow any movement at all, the back part of the spine has a role in limiting and directing movement through what the facets allow or disallow. To remember these directions, try the facet joint prayer: Stand with your hands in front of you at pubic bone level, palms facing each other and finger tips up. Your hands are in the sagittal plane, just like the lumbar facets. It's not that easy for your wrists to do it, probably, but approximate it anyway. Start moving your hands up your body, and when you reach the level of the 12th thoracic, just above the navel, suddenly turn your thumbs out, so that your palms face your belly, still with your fingers pointing up. Keep moving your hands up, but slowly let your fingertips lean away from you, so that by the time you reach the level of your nose, they are horizontal. Memorize this and you will never forget how those facets lie, and you will always know what movements the spine allows at any given level.*

—*Thomas Myers*

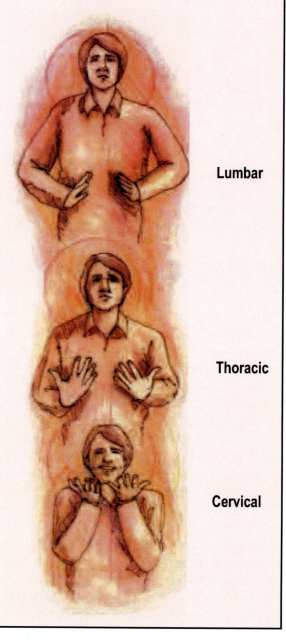

Lumbar

Thoracic

Cervical

These lumbar facets easily allow flexion, extension and hyperextension, and some lateral flexion. What is prevented by these facets, especially in standing, is rotation. This may seem counterintuitive, because when you twist your body, your waist and your lumbar area seem to twist a lot. But if you have two friends about, you can test the validity of what I am saying. Have one friend stand, and while another friend holds her hip bones steady put one index finger on the first friend's spinous process of the fifth lumbar, and the other index finger on the spinous process of the first lumbar. Have your first friend turn her whole spine to look over one shoulder then the other, while your second friend continues to hold her hips steady to keep them from participating in the twist. Watch your fingertips: See how little they move? The flesh of the waist twists, but the lumbars do not or at least not much more than five degrees total in standing.

Have your friend bend over to flex the lumbars, and then lean back into hyperextension; now watch your finger spread and grow nearer. A lot, right? The

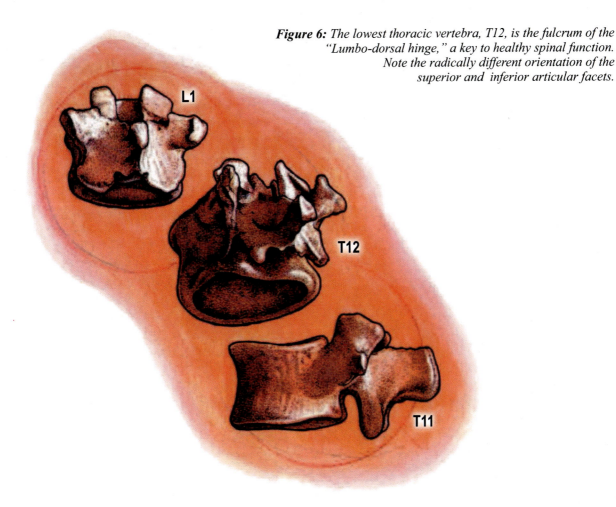

*Figure 6: The lowest thoracic vertebra, T12, is the fulcrum of the "Lumbo-dorsal hinge," a key to healthy spinal function. Note the radically different orientation of the superior and inferior articular facets.*

sagittal plane orientation of the facets allows for significant movement in the sagittal plane, but very little in the transverse plane. If you do a similar test for lateral flexion, you will find varying amounts of lateral flexion in the lumbars of different people, but it is allowed as the facets slide past each other.

If you perform a similar set of tests on the thoracic spine, putting your finger on the spinous processes of T12 and T1, again with the hips stabilized so that the legs don't get involved, you will find that a lot of rotation is available in the thoracics, but not much flexion or extension. This change comes quite suddenly at T12, where the downward-facing facets (with L1) are in the sagittal plane, but the upward-facing facets (with T11) are in the frontal plane, or very close to it (see Figure 6 or Netter plate 143). To slip a piece of paper into these and the facets superior to T12 requires holding the paper more-or-less vertical and slipping it into the joint space from the side of the body, rather than from the back as was the case for the lumbars.

This "lumbo-dorsal hinge" is a crucial place of change in the body, both for spinal mechanics and for what lies in front of it (see Chapter 5). The limitation you will find in flexion-extension in the thoracics is due to the solid sternum in the front and the long, close spinous processes in the back, but the frontal orientation of the facets doesn't help either. The thoracic spine will also have a limited range of lateral flexion, but this is more about the ribs running into each other, and less about the shapes of the facets.

Moving up from T12, the thoracic facets all lie mostly in the frontal plane (actually on the circumference of a circle about the size of the body, thus they allow trunk rotation), but as you move farther up the spine toward the neck, they slowly change toward being more horizontal (see Figure 7 or Netter plate 13). By the time you get to the top of the neck, the axial and atlantal facets are more or less horizontal, and the head swivels and nods on these flattish surfaces (see Netter plate 12).

**The Spine, Part 1**

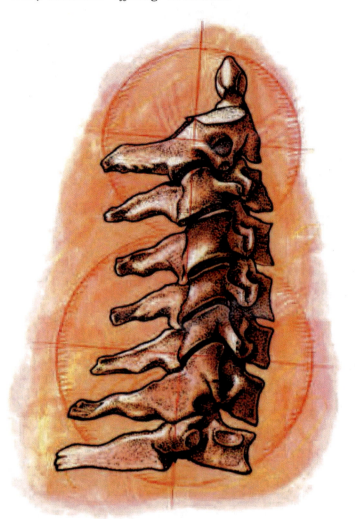

*Figure 7: The cervical articular facets move gradually from a slightly oblique angle to a nearly horizontal "offering" to the skull.*

You can perform similar tests with the neck, but you will find, as you might expect, that the neck is the most mobile of all the spinal segments, allowing significant amounts of all three motions: flexion-extension, lateral flexion and rotation.

## On to a different model

By now we have created a picture of an unlikely spine: The front is a series of lava rocks with water balloons between them, and the back is a strong arch designed to protect the spinal cord, spiky with sticky-outy bits. The articular facets and spinous processes, in particular actually overlap with each other like the redwood shingles of the California house in which I happen to be writing this chapter. If the posterior part is given weight to bear, it would seemingly shove these shingles together in a painful way. How to understand it? It is to the muscles and fasciae, and to a different model of spinal geometry, that we must go if we are to make sense of this Rube Goldberg-esque[1] machine of spinal complexity—and that is exactly where we will go in the next chapter. ∎

---

**Footnote**

1. Goldberg was a cartoonist who became well-known for his depictions of complicated mechanical contrivances for accomplishing simple tasks.

# Chapter 11:
# The Spine (Part 2):
# Tensegrity Continuum

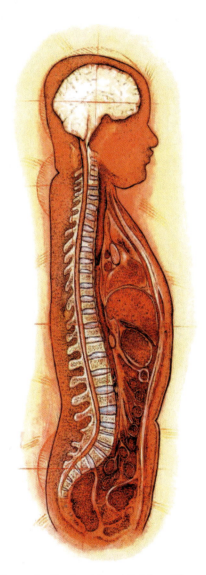

*Figure 1: Our backbone divides either side of the spinal cord, with the ancient "disc and body" column in front, the more recent neural arch in back, and the spinal cord and surrounding meninges poised right in the middle.*

In the last chapter we began thinking about support in the human backbone, exploring its "springy" nature and wondering how to bring about the "lift" we recognized in a healthy spine in Chapter 10. We looked at the front column of the spine—the discs and vertebral bodies, and compared it to the back of the spine—the neural arches and their processes. We meandered off down several side roads, so our thesis thus far, which we will complete in this chapter, can be summed up simply: The front of the spine is a poor candidate for a supporting pillar, even though it occupies the more central position in the body. This part of our "spinal column" consists of spongy bone in the vertebral bodies ("lava rocks") interspersed with squishable discs ("water balloons")—hardly a strong candidate (see Figure 1). The posterior section of the spine, the neutral arch, consists of more solid bone bristling with spinous, transverse and articular processes. Is this perhaps a better bet for a weight-bearing structure?

Any mechanical explanations of the spine, like current explanations of the brain or the universe, are always incomplete. But looking at the possibilities may spark new conceptions and open new avenues to our minds and hands. The particular possibilities we look at here speak directly to a soft-tissue approach to spinal health. And balancing the tone and energy of the soft tissue is the domain of bodyworkers everywhere, no matter what brand name appears on our business cards.

Looking briefly, as we so often do here to our four-legged friends, we see that the weight-bearing function of their spines is totally different from our own (unless we are young enough, sick enough or inebriated enough to be stuck crawling, of course). The spring of the spine, stretched like the cables of a bridge between the supporting towers of the pelvic and shoulder girdles, is kept from sagging to the ground: a little bit by the weight of the head and tail cantilevered off either end, though principally by the sling of the anterior longitudinal ligament stretched from one end of the spine to the other, supplemented by the tension of the abdominal and chest muscles, which by

**The Spine, Part 2**

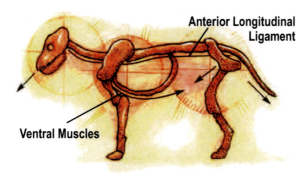

*Figure 2: The discs and muscles in the quadruped spine get nearly a free ride in terms of postural stresses.*

shortening the ventral side of the body, work to help keep the spine more or less horizontal (see Figure 2).

Gravity goes obliquely across four-legged animals' spines, not down through them, so there is very little pressure on the bodies and the discs, except as exerted by the animal's muscular effort. The spinal muscles surrounding the neural arch have little postural function, and are free to guide the movement of the spine in orientation and locomotion. Because of this arrangement, quadrupeds have need for fewer chiropractic adjustments, though failure of the system can still result: witness the swayback of the old or overweight horse, for example, and the success of equine bodywork applications.

The human spine, straight up and down in gravity, presents a different set of challenges, solved quite differently by nearly the same set of muscles and bones. Or, as with the case of the sacroiliac joint we looked at in Chapter 4, is it in fact as different as it first appears? As with so many parts of the body, the answer is multiplex and not yet fully answered, but even an attempt to make the case is worthy of exploration.

This chapter, our usual references to Netter's *Atlas of Human Anatomy*, second edition, published by CIBA-Geigy, are very few. You might find plates 146, 147, 160 and 161 useful, although you can follow along with any good anatomy atlas.

### Our models applied

Can we meld the various models of applied combinations of tension and compression together into a useful view of our spine (see sidebar, "Metaphors of Spinal Function")? Can we use the models to argue that the neural arch is really handling the weight of the axial body?

Our first problem: How could the neural arch be the main weight-bearer of the spine if it sits so far to the back of the body? A central tent pole holds the circus tent up much more easily than a tent pole off to one side. If the tent pole is off-center then you must have some strong and substantial guy-wire pulling away from the body of the tent to counter-balance it, as with the sailboat mast shown in Figure C in the sidebar (pg. 108). You can also see some wonderful examples of this in some innovative structures such as the Munich Olympic village and Denver's new airport.

In the body, therefore, there would have to be some active wires pulling down behind the neural arch to counter-balance the tendency of the rest of the body to pull the neural arch into flexion. And of course they do exist: the entire set of erector spinae and transversospinalis muscles.

*Figure 3: Jon Zahourek building layer by layer in clay, onto his teaching tool, Maniken™ Zoologik™ System: Kinesthetic Anatomy in Clay™. Zahourek has illuminated pattern after pattern in the evolution of vertebrate structure. Shown here: muscles, tendons, ligaments, cardiovascular and nervous systems.*

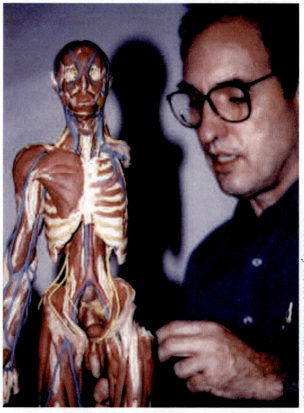

*Photo by Reneé Whitman Zahourek*

## The spinal muscles

So many massage therapists look at the welter of muscles traversing the spine and say, "Forget it! That's too complicated for me. I'll leave it to the experts and just work on whatever hurts." We do ourselves a double disservice when we think like this. For one thing, the holistic soft-tissue approach is capable of doing many good deeds for the body movable, and the developing field of bodywork is going to make this whole journey, sooner better than later. So we cannot throw up our hands, because our hands are the experts in the field of whole-body function. Experts these days, by definition, specialize. We are unique: experts in seeing, feeling and listening to the whole gestalt of everyday development and function. That means we need to know a lot and be sensitive to feeling much more. So all hail Upledger, Rolf, Rosen, Trager, Feldenkrais and a host of others: not so much for the fine techniques they leave us (though they are surely useful), but because they lead us to feel something new about the whole system.

I'll get down off my high horse to explain the second reason we should not dismiss the back muscles: Once you understand the pattern, the whole mess falls into place and is readily understandable. (Not that this makes it easy, mind you, but at least not an unclimbable wall.) I give total credit for the following schema along with many thanks for the practical help it has been to my practice—to the great clarifier, Jon Zahourek, developer of the Anatomiken and Zoologik series (see Figure 3).

The spinous and transverse processes provide a trusswork for the attachment of the many ligaments and muscles that surround the spine. These muscles form in three patterns, exemplified by the deepest, shortest and most ancient of the spinal muscles. The intertransversarii (long name for a tiny muscle) pass from transverse process to transverse process, one segment at a time, all the way from the bottom to the top of the spine (see Figure 4). They are involved in lateral flexion and in that most ancient of spinal movements, the side-to-side sweep of swimming. The interspinalis muscles run from spinous process to spinous process, also covering just one segment. These muscles act to approximate the spinous processes, thus creating spinal extension. Both of these sets run vertically, parallel to the spine (just like the longitudinal strings in Figure F in the sidebar).

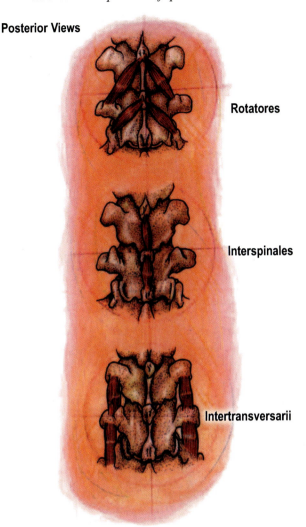

*Figure 4:* Deep in the spine, and deep in our history, lie these three patterns of spinal musculature.

Posterior Views

Rotatores

Interspinales

Intertransversarii

The third primary set of muscles, the rotators, runs from spinous processes down and out to the transverse processes, like pine tree branches. They help with spinal extension, but, true to their name, they also help to create spinal rotation. The rotatores brevis cover only one segment, but the rotatores longus cover two segments passing from the spinous process of one vertebra to the transverse process of the vertebra two segments down. Thus the rotatores longus are angled more steeply, more vertically, but still like a pine tree.

The overlying layers of spinal musculature repeat the basic patterns of interspinalis (spinous process to spinous process), intertransverse (transverse process to transverse process) and rotatores (spinous process to transverse process). As we move out toward the

**The Spine, Part 2**

surface, the muscles cover more and more segments, until at the surface we have the muscles familiar to our hands that span the entire spine.

Though a full explanation requires more space than we have here, the multifidus and the semispinalis groups continue the spinous process to transverse process pine-tree pattern, the spinalis muscle—most easily felt in the middle of the back right next to the spinous processes—continues the spinous process-to-spinous process pattern, and the longissimus and iliocostalis—the easily felt cables that run the length of the spine—create the transverse process to-transverse process pattern (see Figure 5).

We have said that for the neural arch to work as a weight bearer, these muscles would have to be pulling down in the back, and this they certainly seem to do. The muscles, of course, cannot choose which way they pull; the laws of physics determine whether the origin moves toward the insertion or the other way around. But the longissimus and iliocostalis groups are firmly anchored in the sacral fascia, and if these muscles are totally relaxed, our bodies curl forward into flexion. We see some postural patterns where these spinal muscles seem to be pulling the sacrum up toward the lower ribs, and others where the shoulders and upper back are pulled toward the head, but these feel like aberrant patterns, indicative more of pain and dysfunction rather than normalcy. The normal pattern links the downward-pulling spinal muscles to the sacrum, and from the sacrum through the sacrotuberous ligament to the hamstrings.

We can now see how this whole structure would work to 1) support weight; 2) protect the spinal cord; and 3) take pressure off, rather than put it through, the bodies and discs. The sections of the neural arch rest on each other at the facet joints. The back muscles pull down on the spinous and transverse processes behind the fulcrum of these facet joints, actually lifting the front of the vertebrae, taking pressure off the discs and spinal cord (see Figure 6b). This would work against spinal stenosis, and actually stretch the anterior and posterior longitudinal ligament. And, of course, this simultaneously prevents us from falling into flexion.

In this model, the spinal meninges, the dura and pia mater, as well as the spinal cord itself, are delicately poised in the safest, steadiest area just in front of the fulcrum of the facet joints.

These joints look suspiciously like pure tensegrity structures, with the "shingles" of each upward-facing articular facet overlapping with the downward-facing shingle from the vertebra above. The joint capsular tissues, then, could operate like the circumferential bands of a tensegrity mast, lifting the spine skyward when tension was released from the longitudinal bands (the long back muscles). These joints are also hydrostatic as well: enclosed, cushioned water balloons. Thus the neural arch—not the bodies and discs—functions as the weight bearer—or, more properly, the weight distributor (see Figure 6b).

The fact of the matter is, however, that these are not the only forces at work. Excess muscle tension in the abdominal and other flexors of the ventral surface,

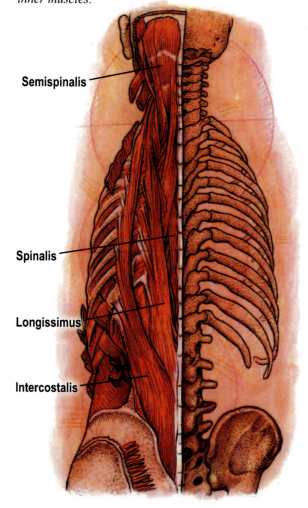

**Figure 5:** *These outer muscles reflect larger, many-segmented expressions of the deeper, inner muscles.*

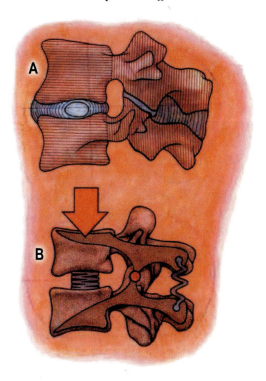

*Figure 6a and 6b: This image, based on one in Kapandji's The Physiology of the Joints, shows how the downward pull of the back muscles could take pressure off the discs.*

whether created by too much exercise, organic tension or emotional holding, can overcome this natural balance, pulling the spine into flexion patterns. Every day we see the weight-lifter's kyphotic dorsal spine; a "flat" lumbar spine due to excessive running or sit-ups; a dowager's hump; and a host of variations on this theme. Caving in to these patterns, by the light of this theory, would start to put unaccustomed pressure and weight through the bodies and discs, initiating the host of bulges, herniations and other pain-producing aberrations of the delicate balance the upright human spine requires.

Furthermore, the spinal myofasciae, trying to create their normal downward pull, and further struggling against the additional pull from the body's flexors, are put directly into strain where they go into spasm or otherwise move out of place (narrowing, widening, or twisting depending on the situation).

So, whoops!—isn't this theory getting very inconvenient? Are we not trying to relax the back muscles? But if we do, according to this theory, would it not result in pitching the spine more into flexion, or compromising the discs? Not the good result we were looking for. These are two responses to this. For one thing, we certainly do have to counter-balance any relaxation we get in the back extensors with work to relax the trunk and hip flexors: otherwise, we may get temporary relief at the cost of long-term increase of problems. Secondly, we value balance—an evenness of tone—across the complex of back muscles, rather than valuing relaxation of any single part. The back muscles, after all, must have continuous tonus to keep us from falling over. They are built for it. The key is not removing tension altogether (impossible anyway) but rather creating consistent balance of this tension—what Rolfing® instructor Jeffrey Maitland termed palintonus ("even tone")—that keeps us out of pain.

## The mysterious upright spine

In point of fact, the evidence of research and the evidence under our hands seem to say that the spine is capable of operating along this entire spectrum—the tensegrity continuum. When we ask the spine to act like a stack of bricks—which we do when we load it momentarily with a load of groceries or chronically with a beer gut or a locked-down set of abs—it can act like one, but at an eventual cost to the discs. If we ask the spine to consistently counterbalance off-center weight, it will, but at a cost of long-term held tension and immobility. The spine can act like a sailboat mast, but those cables down our back will approach the steely wires of ocean-going vessels. Our spines perhaps most commonly imitate the Otto

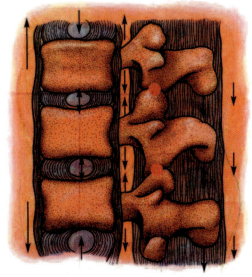

*Figure 7: The equilibrium of forces across the healthy spine allow the springs to work at maximum efficiency.*

**The Spine, Part 2**

mast (see Figure D), with rotations slipping in that cause odd pockets of tension hidden throughout the spinal musculature.

Only in our most balanced dancers, in Fred Astaire and the Cirque du Soleil acrobats, do we see a consistent demonstration of pure buoyant tensegrity in almost constant equipoise. But by working with skill, thought and economy (and with the client's engaged participation), we can release the pulls from the front of the body—in the groin, the belly and the chest, and in the pre-vertebral muscles—the psoas, quadratus lumborum and scalene muscles. Only after these are free can we delve fully into the job of freeing the spine. Not relaxing it fully—its pull is so necessary to hold us erect and alert—but smoothing it, evening out the areas of high and low myofascial tonus that create pain, discomfort and dysfunction.

All vertebrate spines are indeed miraculous, and the upright spine is both a hallmark of human form, and a continuing source of mystery. This short chapter only begins a tour of its wonders, and spinal mechanics, as evidenced by the biomechanical tomes available to chiropractors, osteopaths and physical therapists, is far more complicated than we have tried to explain.

But the spectrum of tension-dependent models we have seen here point to an expanding role for soft-tissue manipulation, whose possibilities are just beginning to be explored. The high-velocity thrust, with its popping joints, torn tissues and habit-forming application, may be receding to become a thing of the past, as gentle soft-tissue manipulation ascends in efficacy and specificity, to unwind the constraints that keep the spine from springing to new heights.

## Metaphors of Spinal Function

There are only two ways to support anything in our local universe: through tension or compression. If I wish to hold something up, I can hang it from above, or brace it from below. I can hang the picture from the wall (tension), or set it on the mantle (compression). All the other forces in the universe—shearing bending, twisting, etc.—are more-or-less complicated combinations of simple hanging and bracing.

Most supported structures exhibit a combination of hanging and bracing. A tree is braced into the ground, but the branches and leaves hang from the braced girdles. Planets are compressed balls that "hang" from the sun.

Human spines are also clearly supported through a combination of tension and compression, but how they are combined has been modeled in various ways. The bones are clearly designed to handle compression and the ligaments to handle tension, while the discs look ready to handle a bit of both. Here are six metaphors of spinal support, all of which point toward something useful, though none has cornered the market on the truth.

"Tensegrity," by the way, is the late designer and inventor Buckminster Fuller's term for structures whose integrity depends on the tensional members—the rubber bands, or, in the case of the spine, the soft tissues. In our culture, most of the manipulative work on the spine has concentrated on the bones, the compression members, which leave us "tension-member manipulators" outside the loop. Here we move gradually from the stack of bricks, which needs little or no tensional support, toward these strange and wonderful tensegrity structures that depend entirely on their "soft tissue balance" for their integrity. Tensegrity has been called "the architecture of life" (Scientific American, January 1998).

The story of the spine is not completely written yet, but if we keep exploring in this vein, the role of the soft-tissue approach to spinal health—and thus our power and effectiveness as whole-body healers—will become greater and clearer.

## Ida Rolf's stack of blocks

The simple Newtonian view depicted in Figure A is so much a part of our thinking that we can hardly think of the spine in any other way. Like any of

*Figure A:* This image, the body as a stack of blocks, gives us an image of alignment, but no sense of springness of lift, and no role for the tension members.

our simpler architecture, from a cairn of rocks to the Washington Monument, it depicts the spine as a structure of continuous compression. This means that the weight is carried down directly from compression member to compression member all the way to the ground. No tension members are necessary at all. Start from this model, and you end up with orthopedic surgery and chiropractic high-velocity thrusts as the way to achieve a sturdy balance in the spine. (Ida Rolf, a master of soft-tissue spinal manipulation, did not end up there, of course, but her modeling was nevertheless mired in the images of her time.)

Recognizing the limitations of applying this very simple model to the spine is as simple as imagining that all the soft tissue around the skeleton suddenly disappears. In even the most delicately aligned person, the skeleton would clatter to the floor, as it is not a very well-stacked set of blocks.

To evoke the image, you probably thought about the skeleton that stood in the corner of your massage classroom. Was that skeleton braced like a stack of bricks, like a continuous-compression structure? Most likely it was not braced from the floor, but rather it was hung from a stand, wired together with its feet off the ground. It is interesting and puzzling: We are steeped in the idea of the spine as a column and the skeleton as stacked up from the ground, while the evidence that does not work very well that way is easily seen in classrooms around the world.

### Todd's counterbalance

Our first admission of the some role for soft tissue (and the role of tension—physical tension, not problematic tension) comes through seeing that the blocks—we are, after all, a very tall, thin tower of blocks, like dominoes stacked end to end—need simply to be counterbalanced by centers of muscular pull.

In Figure B we see an image, derived from the work of dancer Mabel Ellsworth Todd in the 1930s, of how the centers of muscular pull counterbalance the tendency of the skeleton to collapse. The counterbalancing forces wave back and forth from the front to the back of the body: the bottom of the foot, the back of the calf, the front of the thigh, the butt and lower back, the chest and the back of the neck. Throw the system out of balance and you require excess tension in a pattern of places not designed for it: around the heel, the front of the

**Figure B:** *The tendency of our tall, jointed structure to fold up is counterbalanced by strategically placed muscle centers (MC).*

shin, the hamstrings, the groin, the mid-back and the throat/jaw, for example. Sound familiar?

Notice that this model still involves the idea of a continuous line of compression down to the ground; the tensional element merely modulates the tendency of this stack to collapse. We do not have to look very far into our experience to find another model, more dependent on tension for its integrity, which can also be applied to the body.

### Mollier's sailboat

In a sailboat, the mast—a spine-like event if ever there was—is likewise a continuous compression structure, and it carries its own weight when the boat rests at anchor. But spread some sail in a morning northerly, and the pressure on that stick of wood becomes enormous — more than good Maine pine or even Argentine aluminum—could stand. Masts therefore are reinforced with steel "stays" that help take the strain (see Figure C). Without them, a mast, to be strong enough, would have to be so thick that it would sink the boat. And we already noted in the last chapter, that if the spine were holding all our weight, L5 would have to be much bigger than it is. The same physics are at play in both cases.

The body (here we follow another anatomist of the 1930s, the German Mollier) exhibits this same

*Figure C: The delicate balance between tension and compression that serves to glide humans over the sea also exists in our bodies.*

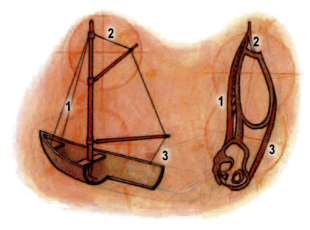

pattern. If the spine is the mast, the two cables of the longissimus complex in the erector spinae act like the stays, pulling down and back against the tendency of the rib cage, as sail, to pull the mast off-center. The scalene muscles act like the throat halyard (did some old sailor notice the comparison?), pulling up on "the gaff" of the first rib. The rectus abdominis can be seen in the same light as the sheet that ties the boom of the lower rib cage back to the hull of the pelvis. Cute, huh?

Yes, cute and interesting, but we are not done yet. The mast is still one solid piece, while our spine is segmented. Can we model some kind of segmented column that still provides stability? Yes, we can, but we will have to rely still more on tension.

### Otto's plant stem

Frei Otto, the architect who developed this structure was trying to figure out how plants hold themselves up, and specifically how sun flowers might turn themselves to face the sun, In the process, he made a singular contribution to our understanding of spinal mechanics.

This "mast" (see Figure D) is made from segments that fit loosely into each other, with a ball-and-socket type of joint. By themselves, you couldn't stack 'em up for love or money. Attached around the neck of each of these segments is a triangle of plexiglass, with a series of holes drilled toward each point, so there are three sets of 12 holes in each piece. If you have nothing better to do, help me thread these wires through the holes, making sure the outermost wire is firmly attached near the point of each triangle. As we move up the structure triangles are getting smaller, so the innermost wire runs all the way up to the top piece of plexiglass before it attaches. (Otto's original mast was 35' high.)

Hey, don't leave yet—I still need your help to wind all 36 of these cables on drums. What a complicated mess! But when it's done, we can, by pulling on the cables in different combinations, make this mast twist, turn and bend in any direction within the hemisphere defined by its radius. And by securing the cables, we can stabilize it in whatever curvy position we like.

Notice that this device is dependent on the tensional members to stand up. Cut the stays on sailboat and the mast might still stand by itself; but cut the wires on this thing, and it would collapse just as our skeleton would without its "cables."

So this design more closely approximates our spine: It is segmented, it can be fixed in position, and it can bend and twist in a variety of ways. (The movements of our own spine, as we saw in the last chapter, are actually more limited by the shapes of

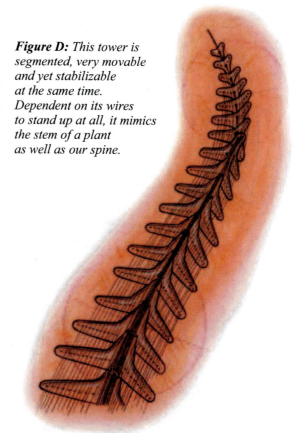

*Figure D: This tower is segmented, very movable and yet stabilizable at the same time. Dependent on its wires to stand up at all, it mimics the stem of a plant as well as our spine.*

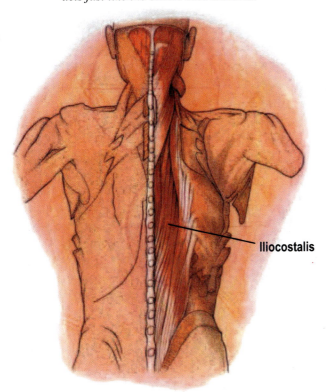

*Figure E:* *The iliocostalis portion of the erector spinae acts just like the cables on a sailboat.*

processes of the lower segment; otherwise these structures would defy physics altogether instead of just having that appearance.

Notice also that the outer edges of the processes are also strung all the way up the structure from segment to segment with longitudinal wires. If you tighten these wires, the structure will get shorter and the compressive segments will get closer to each other, ultimately touching. Conversely, the facet joints.) But does our spine have anything like these cables? Yes, it does, almost exactly: the iliocostalis group in the erector spinae (see Figure F). Look, it starts as a bunch of cables coming up from the ilium and sacral fascia, with one slip stopping on the 12th rib, the rest moving on up. There is a slip stopping on the 11th rib, and the 10th, and so on, all the way up into the neck, where it attaches to the transverse process when it runs out of ribs.

This is the muscle that allows you to lean sideways under the sink, twist to peer up at the drain, twist a piece of you the other way to get your arm in, and then fix the whole thing to be stable enough for your shoulder and arm (and a wrench) to get the nut at the trap loosened.

### Snelson's tensegrity

There is another step we could take toward the primacy of tension, to the tensegrity concept that artist Kenneth Snelson discovered, and Buckminster Fuller popularized. Tensegrity masts have compressive segments that bristle with processes, just like our neural arch (see Figure F). The strings or wires are arrayed around these segments in such a way that the "bones" are supported in space without actually touching each other. It is necessary, however, that some of the sticky-outy bits of the upper segment project down below the upper

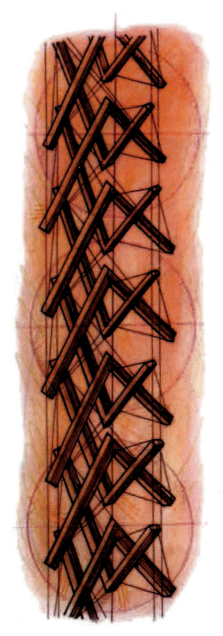

*Figure F:* *In the true tensegrity mast, the compression members float in a balanced sea of tension—just as our bones ultimately do.*

**The Spine, Part 2**

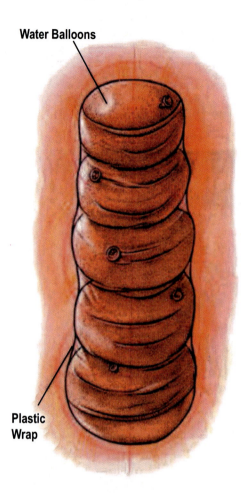

*Figure G: Water balloons can be made into a weight-supporting structure if they are wrapped in "ligaments."*

these structures have no continuous compression whatsoever, and therefore can truly demonstrate lift.

These structures have a number of properties that are very interesting in terms of their relationship to bodies. Chief among these is that strain applied to one part of the structure often causes deformation quite distant from the site of application. And is this not so often the case in structural bodywork? Where we need to work is "where it isn't," not at the site of pain itself.

### A hydrostatic model

One final model is needed to round out this picture, because all these metaphors have been dry, and our bodies are wet. A water balloon is a special type of tensegrity structure, with the surrounding skin as the tension member, and the enclosed fluid as the compression member. We could imagine each of our cells as water balloons, stacked up like rounded versions of Ida Rolf's blocks (as in Figure A) and kept in that shape by the surrounding fascial web (see Figure G).

A good example of this type of structure is an orange, with its little juicy cells wrapped in membranes, in turn surrounded by the wrappings of each section, all further wrapped by the skin. Break up the membranes by rolling the orange around on the countertop and see how much softer it gets. Water beds and blow-up furniture also fall in this category.

In the spine we find this type of structure between each vertebra in the form of the discs in front and the tiny water balloons of the facet joints in the back. ∎

if you tighten the circumferential, more horizontal fibers, the structure will get longer and the segments will move away from each other. In other words,

---

**Footnote**

1. The rotatores longus and brevis can be thought of as grouped with the levatores costorum longus and brevis (see Figure 6). Although their name implies that they are lifters of the ribs and they are often listed as accessory muscles of breathing, they are not in a very good position to do either of those things. The ribs are attached to the spine at the costo—vertebral and costotransverse joints. The levatores costorum attach just lateral to these joints, so they have very poor leverage to lift the ribs. As an analogy, imagine tying a rope near the end of a flagpole, then stepping on that end and trying to lift the flagpole. That is the position of these little muscles relative to lifting the ribs. Their function makes much more sense if you imagine that the rotatores pass down from spinous process to transverse process, and the levatores costorum keep going from transverse process to ribs: the two could function together to simultaneously extend and rotate the spine.

# Chapter 12:
# The Neck & Cranium (Part 1): Touring the Motor Cylinder

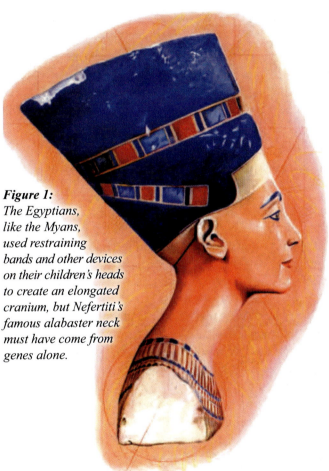

*Figure 1:*
*The Egyptians, like the Myans, used restraining bands and other devices on their children's heads to create an elongated cranium, but Nefertiti's famous alabaster neck must have come from genes alone.*

**H**ow often we hear it: "Just do my back and neck today, and really get in there, will you? It's really sore" (or tense, or achy, out-of-whack—pick your adjective). There are many reasons for our clients' focus on their necks, of course: The cervical bones are the smallest of the vertebrae and seemingly wander out of place easily. The neck is perched at the top of our upended spinal column, with a heavy and fairly solid but highly mobile head to support, and thus the neck's tissues are subject to extra mechanical force. We can round up the rest of the usual suspects: car seats, computers, leftovers from whiplashes, and the most common postural fault of all, the forward head. This posture has internal causes as well, including eyestrain, breathing difficulties, emotional attitude expressed in postural pattern, or a host of other causes usually lumped, a little misleadingly, under the heading of "stress." No wonder, then, that this area between the head and the trunk is so often, um, a pain in the neck.

Ida Rolf, founder of Rolfing® bodywork, made an interesting point about disease and the neck. There are times when you are sick and you feel that you have an illness—as in, "I have a stomach ache." Then there are times when the illness takes you over, and—even though we do not use such phrases in English—you might think, "I am my stomach ache!" and you would tend to stay home from work. In those cases, said Rolf, when the disease takes you over, you will always find a disturbance in the structure of the neck. This idea certainly bears out in my practice—you can see if it works for you.

Rolf's observation points to a central importance for the neck that goes beyond its mere mechanical position, and we can add three factors that help to account for that essential centrality. We will explore all three of these in greater detail before we are done with the neck. For one thing, all the vertical fascial planes of the body pass through the neck. The neck, being as small as it is, is the only place in the body where you can get your 10 curious fingers around that entire set of fascial planes. This makes the savvy practitioner into a puppeteer in the service of the client: Your fingers

**The Neck & Cranium, Part 1**    111

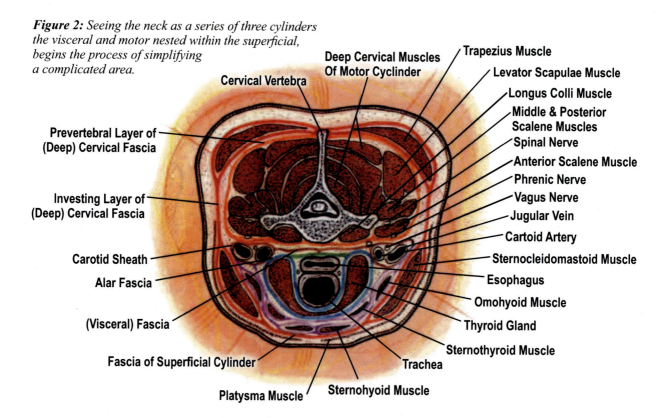

*Figure 2: Seeing the neck as a series of three cylinders the visceral and motor nested within the superficial, begins the process of simplifying a complicated area.*

can pull the strings to set almost any part of your client into motion, working just from the neck. For another thing, the front of the neck is a development center for the organs (we will explore that concept in our next chapter). And finally, the back side of the neck is the command and control center for neuromotor coordination, which will engage us this chapter.

So let us first lay out the general plan of the neck, and then concentrate on three particular areas in the neck's "motor cylinder." We will: 1) "box the compass" of the many muscles that attach to the neural arch of the neck vertebrae; 2) try to make some sense out of the posterior suboccipital group; and 3) add just a few comments about the design of the neurocranium. Next chapter, we will move our camera around to the front of the neck and head, taking on the visceral connections and implications of the throat, jaw and facial bones. As usual, we offer references to helpful corresponding plates in Frank Netter's *Atlas of Human Anatomy*, second edition published by CIBA-Geigy, although you can follow along with any good anatomy atlas.

### The superficial cylinder

The overall plan of the neck can be seen in Figure 2. It is a series of three cylinders: one front, one back, and a superficial cylinder encasing both of those (Netter plate 30). Taking the superficial cylinder first, we can see that its laminae are invested with two muscles: the sternocleidomastoid (SCM) and the trapezius (see Figure 3 or Netter plate 22-23). These muscles nearly wrap around the whole neck, but they leave a couple of interesting triangular holes that give us access to the deeper structures.

The trapezius insertion grabs onto the spine of the scapula out to its end at the acromion, and on around the front to the lateral third of the clavicle. The SCM attaches to the sternum, with its other head attaching to the medial third of the clavicle. This leaves only the middle third of the clavicle without a superficial muscle covering. It is almost as if the trapezius and SCM were one large muscle that is split into two by the primate clavicle, growing out extra long to push our shoulders to the side of our rib cage. Through the hole created by this split, we can see the muscles of the motor cylinder that we will soon be exploring (see Figure 3).

These two outer muscles share three elements: 1) they are in the same fascial plane (this superficial cylinder); 2) they are powered by a cranial nerve (C XI), which indicates their importance; and 3) they are, by embryological derivation, linked to the old "gills," or primary breathing apparatus. This last element perhaps explains their connection with held emotion and trauma, and the frequency and stubbornness of their trigger points. Beneath this protective wrapping are two fairly separate sets of structures—the visceral cylinder in front and the motor cylinder in back. You can easily feel the difference: Take the front of your throat gently but firmly in your hand, and move it back and forth. Feel how easily it moves? Now reach around and take the back of your neck between your thumb and fingers and try to wiggle that in the same way. Feel the difference? These two structures essentially divide the neck.

### The motor cylinder

The motor cylinder consists of all the muscles and fascia that surround the cervical vertebrae. Because there are around 13 (depends on where you count and how you count) muscles attaching to the transverse and spinous processes of the cervical vertebrae, it can be pretty daunting to figure them all out (see Figure 4). Once you see the logic of it, however, it gets manageable. We are going to work our way around from the front. The first thing we need to notice is that the transverse processes of the neck have two bits—the anterior tubercle and the posterior tubercle. The anterior tubercle is actually more like a short rib, but we can leave that idea alone and just think of the transverse process as being rather large.

Imagining that we start at the 4th cervical as an example (we will leave the special case muscles at the top two vertebrae for later on in this chapter), the most anterior muscles, the ones that line the very front of the neck, are the longus colli and longus capitis (see Figure 5 or Netter plate 25).

The longus colli and longus capitis are very important, because they are the postural flexors of the neck, and as such are antagonists to the many extensors and hyperextensors that pull on the back of the neck. The tendency of the erector spinae and suboccipital muscles to chronically contract and create hyperextension in the upper cervical joints can only be counteracted by proper tonus of these deep and powerful muscles. It takes some talent (and more precision than I want to attempt in this

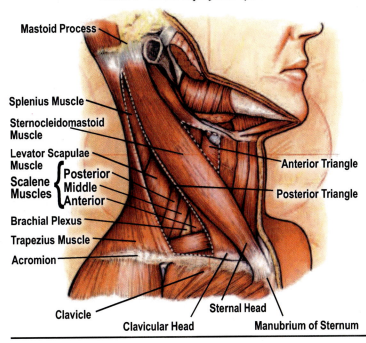

**Figure 3:** *Here we can see some crucial muscles of the motor cylinder, which we can access through a triangular "window" in the superficial cylinder.*

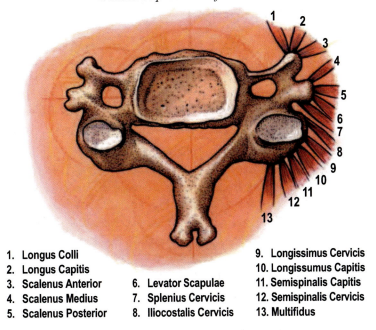

**Figure 4:** *Many myofacial guy-wires vie for space on the transverse processes of the neck.*

1. Longus Colli
2. Longus Capitis
3. Scalenus Anterior
4. Scalenus Medius
5. Scalenus Posterior
6. Levator Scapulae
7. Splenius Cervicis
8. Iliocostalis Cervicis
9. Longissimus Cervicis
10. Longissumus Capitis
11. Semispinalis Capitis
12. Semispinalis Cervicis
13. Multifidus

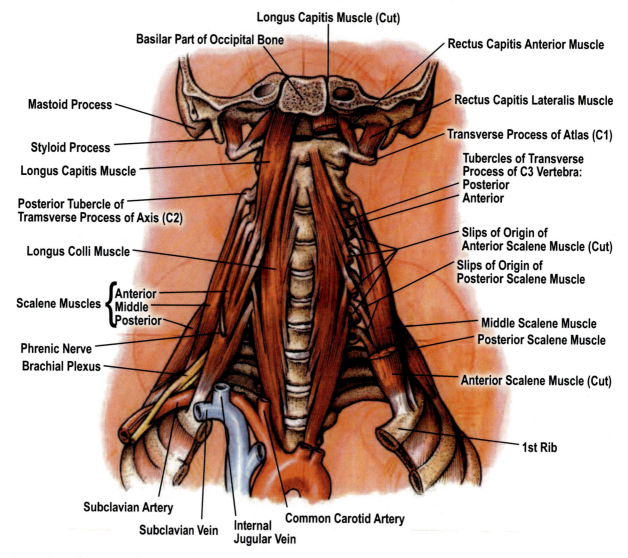

*Figure 5:* *The motor cylinder from the front, with the surrounding deep fascia removed. These muscles are essential territory if we are to bring structural health to the neck and head.*

chapter) to slide posterior to the SCM and anterior to the scalenes and cervical transverse processes to get directly to these muscles (without, oh, by the way, occluding the carotid artery). Indirectly, however, you call on these muscles to work when you slip your fingers under the occiput and ask your client to flatten her neck against the table as you gently traction the head away from the back. This sends a flood of messages from these muscles up to the brain, even when you are not working them directly. In the case of the military neck, an over-straight cervical spine, these muscles are generally too tight and need direct or indirect loosening.

Moving out and around the front of the transverse process to its side, we encounter the first of the three scalenes, the anterior scalene (see Figures 3 and 5). This band, about a half-inch wide and readily palpable under the SCM, passes down and forward to attach to the first rib. Thus it can help pull the lower cervicals into flexion while the suboccipitals pull the upper cervicals into hyperextension, resulting in the familiar forward-head posture. The design, as we indicated in the last chapter on spinal tensegrity, is for the scalene to support the first rib up. The unfortunate reality is that all too often it ends up pulling the cervicals down and forward instead. Seen in this way, the anterior scalene could be said to be the "psoas of the neck," but don't invest too much in that metaphor. If the anterior scalene goes down and forward like a psoas, the next two scalenes, the middle and posterior, go down and to the side, more like a quadratus lumborum of the neck. They attach to the first two ribs at the bottom, and to the posterior tubercle of the transverse process at the top (see Figure 4).

Between the anterior and posterior transverse processes is a "gutter" for the cervical nerve roots, and sure enough, you can see the brachial plexus emerging from the neck behind the anterior scalene and in front of the other two (see Figure 5). So when you work on these muscles and the client starts to feel tingling in the fingers, it is not a sign of imminent enlightenment, it is a divine message that you need to move off the brachial plexus. On the other hand, to avoid this area altogether is to miss structures rich in connections and postural significance. It is beyond the scope of this series to give specific instruction in this type of work, but getting well-trained in this deeper cervical work is highly recommended over dismissing the area entirely as an endangerment site.

We have worked our way around five important muscles of the 13 that surround the vertebrae. Their lower attachments also make a journey around the bottom of the neck. The SCM attaches to the sternum in front, the longus colli and capitis attach down to the neck itself to the thoracic bodies, and the scalenes start the march around the upper ribs. To what else can we attach to steady the neck? Why, the scapula, of course. Our next muscle back, still palpable between the SCM and the trapezius, is the levator scapulae, sweeping down from the first four transverse processes to the upper apex of the scapula (Netter plate 178).

We already discussed this muscle's role in forward head posture in Chapter 9, so we will limit ourselves here to palpating it with surety. The scalenes and the levator are pretty skinny there in the neck, and hard to distinguish sometimes (see Figure 3). The middle scalene is pretty easy to feel, because it is the most lateral muscle of the motor cylinder at the bottom of the neck. If you run your fingers along the side of your supine client's lower neck, a bit like gently strumming a guitar, the most prominent string you "pluck" is the middle scalene. The posterior scalene tucks in behind it, but so does the levator. How to separate them? With your client supine and you seated up by her head, find the middle scalene and feel your way behind it. Reach across your client with the opposite hand, hold her shoulder down, and ask her to lift the shoulder to her ear against your

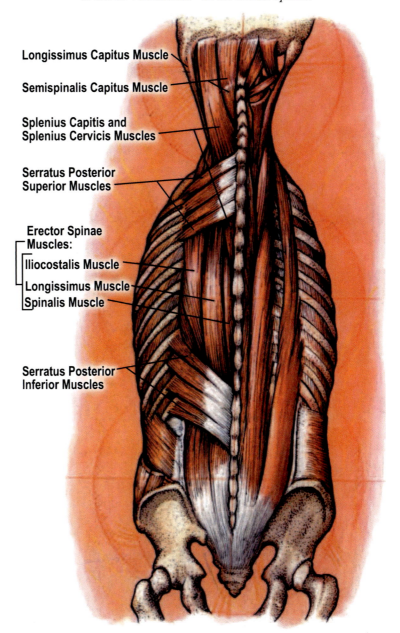

**Figure 6:** *The posterior serrati join with the splenius muscles to act as "retinaculae" on the erector spinae.*

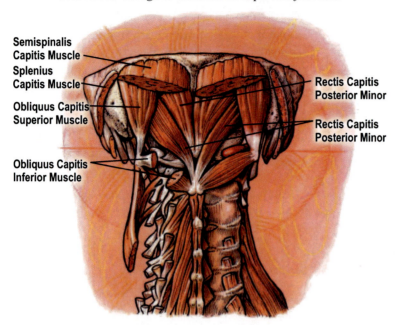

*Figure 7: The traditional view offered of the suboccipital triangle does not do enough to elucidate its important function.*

resisting hand. The levator should pop into your hand, and the scalenes should not. If you do not feel it, move your feeling fingertips around a little and repeat the test. It is in there, I guarantee it.

From here the rest of the muscles of the neck take on a sensible pattern, even if there are a lot of them. The splenius muscles (same root as "splint") wrap like bandages around the cervical and upper thoracic portion of the erector spinae (see Figure 6 and Netter plates 160 & 161). They can be seen almost as retinaculae for the erectors in the neck, in the same way that the serratus posterior muscles act as retinaculae for the erectors further down the torso. The posterior serrati have a second function. They assist in breathing. The splenii have a second function also: They act to rotate the head to the same side as the contraction (ipsilateral).

Underneath and medial to the splenii, the erectors maintain the same set of relationships they had in the spine (see Chapter 11). The iliocostalis, being the most lateral, would be next on our journey (see Figures 4 and 6). The longissimus, the upper end of the long back cables, are next in, heading for the "transverse process" of the mastoid. The semispinalis lies close in to the midline, nudging up against the nuchal ligament with the little multifidus and rotatores underneath.

## The suboccipitals

It is to the very top of these short, deep muscles that we must go to find our next subject of discussion—the suboccipital muscles. These muscles are so deep that they are very hard to palpate, but they are tremendously important, so we must understand them. Unfortunately, they are also badly presented in most of the popular anatomy books (see Figure 7 or Netter plate 161), so let's see if we can make a little more sense out of them.

First we must set ourselves up with a bit of background about the bones and joints involved: the occiput, the atlas (C1) and the axis (C2) (Netter plates 12-15). The occiput sits on the atlas on two condyles just forward of the foramen magnum. Although some other movements are allowed—a limited amount of rotation and lateral flexion—this occipito-atlanteal (O-A) joint mostly allows flexion and extension (a "yes" motion) of the skull on the neck. The atlas sits on a "tooth" of the axis, and is able to rotate (a "no" motion) around that tooth in the atlantoaxial (A-A) joint. There's a reciprocity of "yes" and "no" in the joints, and a reciprocity of transverse processes and spinous processes in the bones. The axis has very small transverse processes, but a large spinous process, which you can readily feel below your skull in back; it is the topmost spinous process you can feel. This is because the atlas has nearly no spinous process; what little there is lies too deep to be felt (so if you are counting cervical vertebrae down from the skull, remember that the first one you find is #2).

The atlas has large transverse processes, however which can be easily palpated and simultaneously assessed for any postural lateral translation and rotation. Have your client supine again, and sit at her head with your hands around the skull such that the second joint of both your index fingers lies against the mastoid processes, leaving the first joint free. Your wrist should be closer to or on the table, so that your index finger follows roughly the direction of the SCM. Now gentle flex the distal part of your index fingers into the flesh just

*Figure 8: Only when you see them from the side do the differing functions of these muscles make "under your hand" sense: The two shorter ones pull the occiput forward on the atlas; the longer middle one creates true hyperextension.*

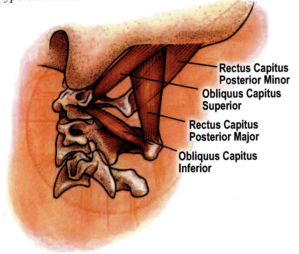

inferior to the mastoid.

If your wrists are too high and your fingers point downward, you will miss the atlas. If your wrists are too low or your index finger is in front of the mastoid, you will go into the space between the jaw and the mastoid, which is definitely a no-no. But if you are right on top of the mastoid, the tips of your fingers will be able to feel the large transverse processes of the atlas, either directly or by implication, just inferior and interior to the mastoid. With a little practice you will be able to accurately feel whether one transverse process is more prominent than the other (indicating a lateral translation to the prominent side) or forward of the other (indicating a rotation of the O-A joint), or closer to the skull than the other (indicating a lateral flexion).

We are going to look at four muscles, the posterior suboccipital group which is strung from the occiput to the large transverse processes of the atlas, and the spinous processes of the atlas and axis. Three of them run down from the occiput, deep underneath the occipital shelf, so let us take them on, going from medial to lateral (see Figure 9).

The rectus capitis posterior minor (RCPM) runs from the occiput to the spinous process of the atlas, crossing only the O-A joint. But we already said that the atlas does not have much of a spinous process, so what few anatomy books seem to show clearly is that this muscle runs down and very much forward to do this (compare Figure 7 to Figure 8).

Additionally, the RCPM has recently been discovered to have connections through the posterior atlanto-occipital membrane to the dura mater, and this, coupled with new finding that the RCPM can be permanently damaged by whiplash and other trauma, is opening exciting new avenues of assessment and treatment.

The next muscle lateral, the rectus capitis posterior major (RCPMaj) runs down to the spinous process of the axis, but since that bone has such a huge spinous process, this muscle runs pretty much straight up and down. This points to a difference in function between these two muscles: the RCPM, the little guy, is going to tend to pull the occiput forward on the atlas (occipital protraction, sometimes called axial flexion), while the RCPMaj, the big guy, is going to create pure hyperextension in both the A-A and the O-A joints. Whew! Complicated, but important in treating this area.

The third muscle out, the obliquus capitis superior (OCS), runs down and forward again, this time to the large transverse processes of the atlas. This muscle, which runs parallel to the RCPM, will have the same effect—pulling the occiput forward on the atlas (as well as helping to create a postural rotation if it is tighter on one side than the other).

The fourth muscle of the series is the obliquus capitis inferior (OCI), which is badly named, since it does not attach to the head, but runs from the large transverse processes of the atlas to the large spinous process of the axis. This muscle parallels the splenius capitis we talked of before, providing the deepest and smallest muscle of ipsilateral rotation, creating that "no" motion, the rotation of the atlas and occiput together on the axis. You can find this muscle by locating the transverse processes of the atlas and the spinous process of the axis, positioning your fingertips right between the two, fixing the skull with your thumbs, and calling for head rotation against the resistance.

Why are we getting so excited and derailed about tiny little muscles buried so deeply in the back of the neck? For several reasons, but space allows us to discuss only one: Very simply, these muscles are the command and control center for the rest of spinal movement. They overflow with muscle spindles and fascial stretch receptors. They are the link between our eyes and the rest of the body's musculature. To

**The Neck & Cranium, Part 1**

feel this for yourself, put your palms over your ears with your fingers spread so that your thumbs come to rest under your occiput. Press your thumbs in deeply enough to feel not just the superficial muscles but those deep little guys way under the occipital shelf. Close your eyes (not necessary, it is just easier to feel kinesthetically that way) and look strongly left and right with your eyes. Use your fingers against the side of your skull to keep your head from moving; just your eyes move. With your thumbs, can you feel all that muscle tonus change deep in your neck? Look up and down, and feel another set of muscles working, without the head moving a millimeter. The fact of the matter is, you cannot move your eyes without changing the tonus of your suboccipitals, and they, in turn, affect the standing tonus of the rest of your back. It's hard-wired in.

Now, the rest of your back muscles listen to these little guys to see how they should move. Toss your cat lightly into the air, for instance, and watch it in slow motion as it does its famous cat-trick of always landing neatly on all fours. The cat uses its eyes (and presumably its inner ear) to orient its head in gravity, and then the spine (very quickly) unwinds in a spiral from these muscles at the top of the neck down to the tail so that the whole cat is now ready to land. Though we are upright, our head-neck-upper back relationship functions in much the same way. Thus, how you use your eyes, and more particularly, how you use your neck, determine the tonus pattern for the rest of your back musculature. This was first identified as the 'primary control' mechanism by F.M. Alexander, and plays into myriad postural patterns we see every day in our practice. Loosening the neck is often key to intransigent problems between the shoulder blades, in the lower back, and even in the hips.

Though treatment of these muscles can be complex for the above reasons, we can pause here long enough to facilitate palpation. Once again, your supine client's head rests in your hands, but this time the occiput is in your palms, so your fingers are free. Curl your fingers up under the occiput, "swimming" in to the deeper layers past the trapezius and semispinalis to these little guys, and put your ring fingers together at the midline, so that six fingertips are arrayed along the bottom of the occiput. With adjustments for differently-sized hands and heads, your ring finger will be in contact with the RCPM, your middle fingers on the RCPMaj, and your index fingers on the OCS (see Figure 9).

This means that to reverse the common postural problem of the occiput being held forward on the atlas, you need to create length and release in the muscles under your index and ring fingers. To combat postural hyperextension of the neck, you need to release the slightly more prominent RCPMaj under your middle fingers (while getting your client to engage the longus muscles in the front of the neck).

This chapter is only a basic primer in the beautiful complexity of the human neck. Your feeling study of its structure will be rewarded by increased confidence in applying yourself to the many problems the neck presents, which, in turn, will show gratifying results in the increasing well-being of your clients.

**Figure 9:** *With a little practice, these important links between the eyes and the spine can be located and assessed with ease and certainty.*

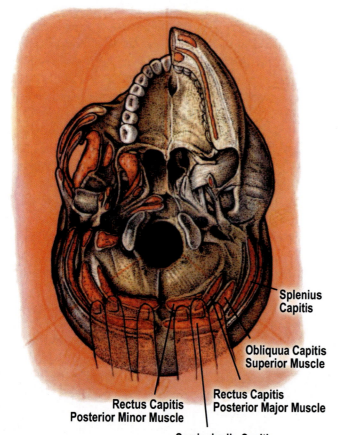

Splenius Capitis
Obliquua Capitis Superior Muscle
Rectus Capitis Posterior Minor Muscle
Rectus Capitis Posterior Major Muscle
Semispinalis Capitis

## Two Notes Sounded on the Cranial Drum

The cranium can be divided into two: the neurocranium, consisting of the bones that surround the brain; and the viscerocranium, the bones that make up the face. Since the neurocranium is really the top of the motor cylinder, we add just a couple of interesting points about it. Although the following is not "embryologically correct," it is still a clinically useful metaphor: The neurocranium can be thought of as four more "vertebrae" sitting in a primary curve on top of the neck. The occiput, obviously, is the next one above the atlas. Then we get the "temporal-parietal" vertebra. In front of this is the "frontal-ethmoid" vertebra. The final, topmost vertebra of this series is the sphenoid, though it is in fact folded under the rest. The sphenoid manages to connect with all the other bones of the neurocranium, including a large and strong synchondrosis with the body of the occiput. Together, these "vertebrae" surround and protect the brain, and move with it in the primary waves of the craniosacral pulse.

Another clinically useful metaphor to use when looking at the skull is that of a tennis ball or baseball. The paired bones (the two temporal and parietals) for the side-to-side part of the tennis ball, going from petrous process around the top of the skull to the petrous process on the other side, almost but not quite joining. The singular bones (the frontal, ethmoid, sphenoid, and occiput) form the other, front-to-back part of the tennis ball, going from the front of the top of the head (the coronal suture) around under the brain pan to the top of the back of the head (the lambdoidal suture),

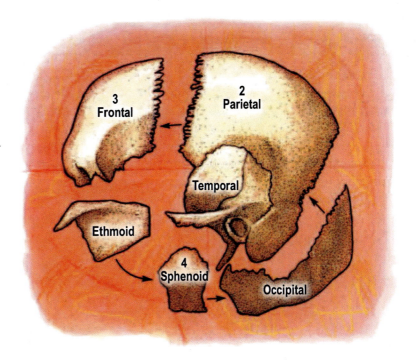

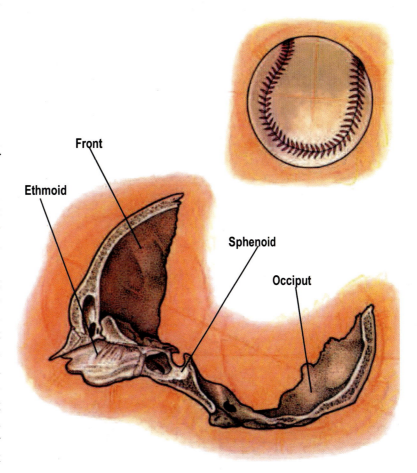

**The Neck & Cranium, Part 1**

almost but not quite joining.

Together, these two from a strong interlocked structure. For me, the clinical interest lies in connecting the cranial and structural work: The side-to-side bones are often involved in issues of lateral differences in the body, and the front-to-back bones reflect the sagittal issues in the body below. It is a useful diagnostic tool, and the cranial and structural work together often have a stronger effect than either alone. Interestingly, each part of the tennis ball is completed into a circle: the temporal-parietal part is completed by the mandible-the jaw is slung under the skull from temporal to temporal, completing the circle. And the front-to-back part is completed by the falx cerebri, the strong dural connective tissue which runs from the sphenoid and ethmoid all the way around the top, bridging the gap and attaching firmly to the occiput at the other end.

These two tiny ideas are all we will offer in this series pertaining to the strange and wonderful "winged question mark" –the falx, the tentorium, and the dural tube—which surrounds our central nervous system. It has been explored so brilliantly and delicately by all the pioneers of craniosacral work, from William Sutherland to John Upledger to Hugh Milne and others, and I urge you to expand your skills in this direction. ■

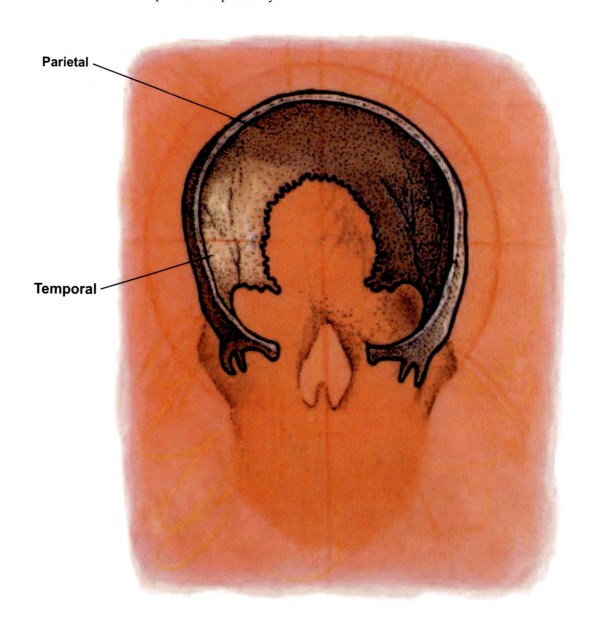

# Chapter 13: The Neck (Part 2): The Visceral Voice

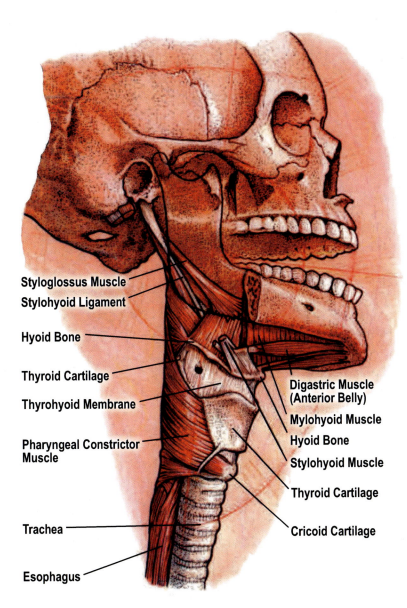

*Figure 1: Hanging from the skull and the jaw, the voice box is a uniquely human trait.*

**I**f this were a PBS science special instead of a written chapter in a book, it would begin with the sweet, sad, swelling tones of Maria Callas filling La Scala with the aria from *La Bohéme*. Then I would step in front of the camera in some breathtaking location, and in beautifully clipped English announce, "This month we will explore the magic of the human face and throat." Ah, well, we can dream, can't we? But hey, with a slightly smaller budget and a decidedly American accent, that's what we are going to do anyway.

What is it that is so unique about the human voice? Anthropologists have long pondered what makes humans unique, different from the rest of the animals (usually trying to place us, by subtle or not-so-subtle means at the top of the heap). One by one ideas have been proposed, and then fallen: *homo habilis*, human as toolmaker, fell before the chimps and other animals who fashion natural objects into tools; *homo ludens*, human as player, fell before our playful cats and wolves. Even *homo loquens*, human as speaker, was summarily dismissed when a group of chimpanzees, who do not

The Neck, Part 2     121

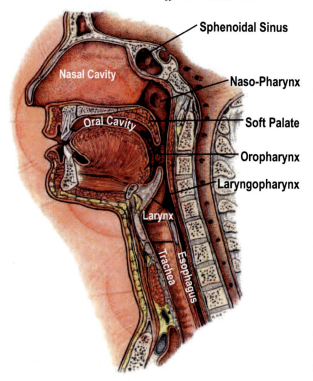

*Figure 2A: Our upper respiratory passages can be divided into several different chambers.*

have the apparatus to speak as we do, were taught American Sign Language. They creatively used the language in new ways, including combining the signs for "water-candy-fruit" when presented with watermelon, and for "you" and "shit" displayed angrily at a keeper who had displeased the primate "speaker."

Even if we proposed homo cantans, human as singer, we would have to bow before the creative and lyrical birds that grace the salt marsh outside my window, or the long and haunting arias of the humpback whales out in the Gulf of Maine beyond. Even our current name for our own species, *homo sapiens*, "the one who knows he knows"—human as aware creature, tends to wilt a little before the sad, knowing eye of the gorilla in the zoo, or the infinite depth of the whale's seemingly timeless gaze.

But still, there is something special about what comes out of our mouths. It is not merely our phonation (making sounds with the vocal cords): my cats do that eloquently every morning. It is not based on syntax, for the chimps, cetaceans and birds display a definite syntax in their "language." What separates our voice from any animal's utterances, as beautiful and intelligent as they may be, is that our voice is for us an integrated sense, almost like seeing. We not only speak language, we feel it—and we feel through it.

Movement and speech develop together. First in our lives comes non-verbal communication, the relation between moving and hearing, between our parents' voices and the feel of their hands on our body, guiding it, and our movement in response. Think of how differently this moving-hearing relation could be perceived: the parents cooing at the baby, making eye contact as they gently play with the baby's hands, or a parent snarling "Stop that!" as he or she yanks the child away from something interesting but breakable. The child's movement and speech then develop together in response to the rhythms they hear and feel around them. Movement of the body provides a large part of the underlying syntax of speech. Then the ear and the voice keep informing each other in this process we call language. Breathing, swallowing and sucking movements also contribute to speech development, but the overriding influence is how the child perceives and responds in movement to what he or she hears. Thus, bodywork can affect the whole communicating process in a very fundamental way.

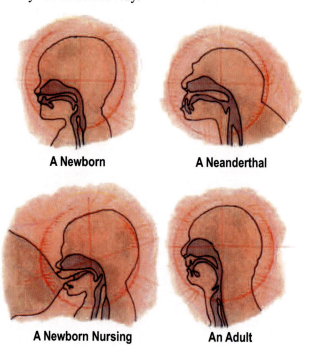

*Figure 2B: The proximity of the uvula and the epiglottis of a newborn human, a chimp and a Neanderthal allows them all to nurse (or drink) and breathe at the same time. When our larynx descends, we give up this tremendous advantage in favor of the ability to speak.*

A child is born with the possibility to learn any language. By the age of one, however, vocal-chord movement is already tied into the rhythms of family and culture. By two or three years old, these patterns are clearly established, expressing themselves most clearly as the habitual pattern of movement we call an accent, which becomes so ingrained in our muscular habit of phonating that we may not lose it even after many years of speaking another dialect.

The human throat is structured in a unique way (see Figure 2A), and seemingly, the only advantage to this structure is the ability to speak the way we do. All mammals, including human infants, can suck and swallow while breathing. This is because the throat is short, and by raising the larynx they can keep the air passage separate from the food passage, allowing the milk to pass behind the larynx into the esophagus without having to interrupt breathing—an obvious advantage to the human infant's survival. (A short throat gives an obvious evolutionary advantage to other animals—the ability to continue to sniff for danger while feeding).

As we grow, we lose the ability to suck and swallow while breathing, as our throat drops and gets longer and the front of the occiput changes angle (see Figure 2B). Some have speculated that the relatively narrow developmental window in which we are prone to Sudden Infant Death Syndrome corresponds to the time when the larynx is only partially descended.

We are also more prone to choking we cannot use the two passages simultaneously, so we have to alternate, which sometimes leads to problems, especially for people like me who love to talk while they eat. But the longer throat and bigger chambers greatly increase our ability to make vowel and consonant sounds; neither the chimps nor a baby's throat chambers are open enough to make anything like the full range of sounds we use every day.

Language underlies many of our most striking accomplishments ("I have a dream"); and exposes our most embarrassing pettiness ("Did somebody say McDonald's?"). There are various theories of how speaking evolved. There is the "boo-hoo" theory—that language proceeded out of the expression of strong emotion; the "woof-woof" theory—that we were imitating animal noises; and the "yo heave ho" theory that language grew as a way of organizing group activities like hunting. Personally, I imagine it grew out of the deep human need to gossip. Or perhaps the children, who seem to have such a facility with language, taught the adults to talk. But whatever the source, it must have provided a decisive evolutionary advantage, for we gave up the ability to separate the air and the water/food passage in favor of a throat that can speak and sing out the many vowels and consonants so distinctly.

Most of our current schools of hands-on healing do not tend to include the area of the throat in their work, so we might conclude that we have little effect on it. But our voice is not just air sawing over the vocal folds; it is intimately tied up with our

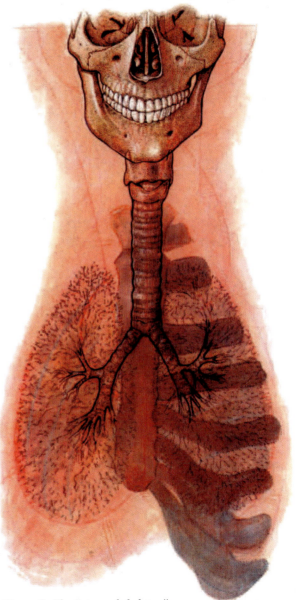

*Figure 3:* The "visceral skeleton" *includes the bones of the face from the eyes down, the hyoid, respiratory cartilage, the costal cartilage and the sternum.*

**The Neck, Part 2**

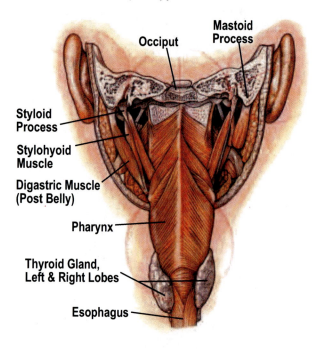

*Figure 4a: This is the posterior side of the visceral cylinder, the back of the throat which hangs from the skull behind the cartilage of the visceral skeleton. We are looking forward, as if from the bodies of the cervical vertebrae, with the intervening layers of fascia removed.*

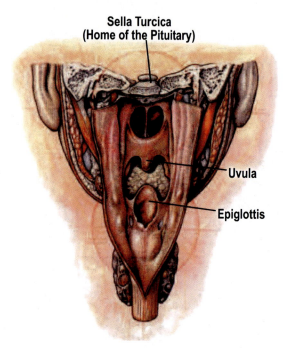

*Figure 4b: Open it up and you can see the strange trap-door arrangement to which we have resorted to reduce the confusion between the respiratory and alimentary passages. Swallow and the epiglottis cleverly folds backwards to shut off the air tube.*

movement and our feelings, as we have seen. If our voice is not separate from our patterns of behavior, then all of our work on human structure and movement will have an effect, sometimes subtle, sometimes very telling, on the voices of our clients.

In the last chapter we explored the wiry command and control center in the back of the neck, and let it give a nod to the bones that surround the brain. In this chapter we turn our attention to the front of the neck and head, to the structures that make up and surround our voice—what some have called the "visceral skeleton." As is our custom, you will find references to Frank Netter's *Atlas of Human Anatomy*, second edition, published by ClBA-Geigy, to supplement the illustration we have included (although you can follow along with any good anatomy atlas).

### Equal rights for all cartilage!

The skeleton hanging in your classroom contains a number of ideas in the way it is put together. One idea, which could almost be called a prejudice, concerns which cartilage is included as part of the skeletal system, and which is not. Traditionally, the intervertebral discs are included, formerly made from felt, now more often from plastic. The cushioning hyaline cartilage between the ends of bones in synovial joints is routinely left out, though in some plastic skeletons the menisci of the knee are sometimes included on one side. The costal cartilage, which joins the bony ribs to the sternum, is so universally included that many of our clients are surprised to learn that the entire rib cage is not bone, that every rib has a cartilage extension between the end of the rib and the sternum. But the laryngeal, tracheal and bronchial cartilage that hang from the hyoid bone are always left out.

Most bones start as cartilage; the two tissues are certainly related, so why include some and not others? Join my Unfair to Cartilage grass-roots movement! To get oriented, let's take a tour of the visceral skeleton, which will include the bones of the face from the eyes down, plus the jaw, the hyoid bone, all the cartilage that reaches down into the lungs from the pharynx, and finally the "breastplate" of the sternum and the costal cartilage. Although the bones we include are usually grouped with the axial skeleton, our contention is that with this added cartilage they form a designation separate from

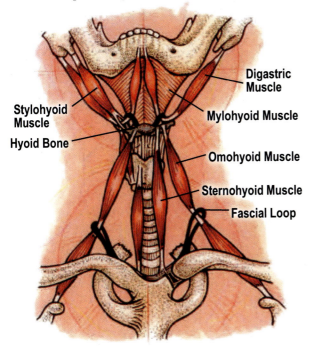

*Figure 5: The hyoid sits precisely balanced in a complex of muscles that participate in swallowing, speaking, and protecting our head's blood supply.*

hyoid bone, another "C" that is in turn suspended from the skull and jaw (see Figures I and 4). Since this is an under-served area in most massage school education, let's examine this a little more closely. The hyoid can be felt by putting your fingers right under the jaw above your larynx, squeezing gently, and wiggling your hand back and forth.

The hyoid is poised within a balance of muscles which go in three directions: down the front of the neck toward the sternum, up and forward to the inside of the jaw, and up and back to the skull (see Figure 5 and Netter plate 24). So it stays in place through the balance of this three-way pull, and lifts up for swallowing when the two upper sets of either axial or appendicular: the visceral skeleton (see Figure 3).

Let's start at the bottom of this "visceral-skeleton" complex, with the upside-down tree of the lung's bronchioles. This beautiful fractal shape branches off again and again, serving air to the vast surface area the lungs' alveoli present (about a tennis court's worth in the healthy adult—only a fractal shape could manage that task) (Netter plates 187-193). From all the lungs' five lobes, the bronchioles gather into the two bronchi, joining at about the level of the sternal angle, and passing up behind the heart into the trachea (see Figures 1 and 3, and Netter plates 68 and 74). Feel your own trachea down by the sternal notch where it emerges from the rib cage, and you will feel how movable the whole structure is. If you move your finger up and down, you will feel the ridges separating the various segments of the trachea. Each of these segments is shaped like the letter "C," with the ends toward the back (Netter plate 71 and 190). If you work up some spit and swallow, you will feel the whole throat assembly jump up toward your mouth, which it must do to shut the door of your windpipe so that the fluid passes over the top of it into the esophagus behind (see Figure 4 and Netter plate 60).

This set of structures is suspended from the

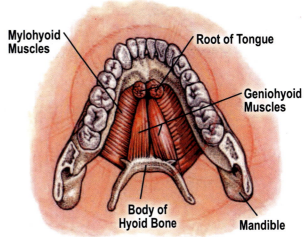

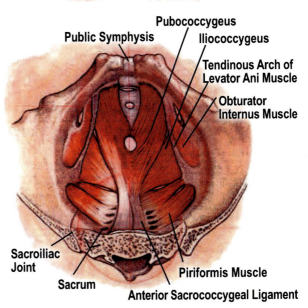

*Figure 6: The floor of the mouth and the floor of the pelvis, show a parallel muscle structure. Coincidence or conspiracy? You decide.*

**The Neck, Part 2**

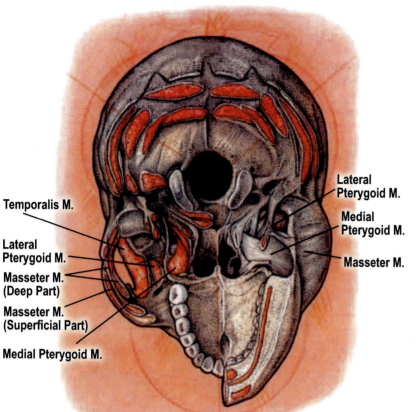

*Figure 7: Looking at the jaw from below shows us how much the sling formed by the masseters and the medial pterygoids have to do with jaw position.*

Temporalis M.
Lateral Pterygoid M.
Masseter M. (Deep Part)
Masseter M. (Superficial Part)
Medial Pterygoid M.
Lateral Pterygoid M.
Medial Pterygoid M.
Masseter M.

muscles contract.

Looking at the downward-pulling muscles first, we see two major muscles: the sternohyoid and the omohyoid. The sternohyoid is pretty straightforward, and has several smaller muscles under it that traverse the same territory in smaller jumps. The omohyoid goes down toward the sternum in the same way, but then loops through a little fascial sling, and swings out sideways to the scapula. Why the hyoid bone would need a connection to the shoulder, either for us humans or even as part of our four-legged history, is a mystery to me, but I am open to being enlightened about it. One purpose for its strange pathway is clear, however: The sling is right in front of the vascular bundle going from heart to head, the carotid artery and jugular vein. The omohyoid makes a little tent around these structures, protecting them from any occlusion when the neck muscles contract (Netter plate 24).

The muscle that goes back and up from the hyoid is the stylohyoid (see Figures 1, 4 and 5), which pulls up and back, just like the reins on a horse, on the ends of the hyoid, joining the skull at the little "pencil lead" of the styloid process on the temporal bone. If you can find a way of toning or shortening this muscle, your fortune is made, for you could improve everyone's double and triple chins by pulling the hyoid up and back (but no fair pressing in between the jaw and the mastoid process—you might damage the styloid process).

There are two muscles pulling up and forward on the hyoid, and these form the floor of the mouth under the tongue (see Figure 6). One, the geniohyoid, goes straight from the front of the hyoid to the back of the chin. The other, the mylohyoid, sweeps in from the sides of the jaw to also attach to the front of the hyoid (Netter plate 47). You can feel these two if you put one finger down in beside and under your tongue and one under the jaw and gently press them in between.

These muscles show an interesting parallel to the floor of the pelvis (see Figure 6), suggesting a connection which Michel Odent, the famous French obstetrician/gynecologist who pioneered water birth, makes good use of: A major part of his birth preparation process is getting the pregnant women to sing regularly. "If you can open ze throat and ze mouth." he says, "it is easier to open for ze birth."

One last muscle of this series, the digastric, runs a peculiar course. It starts under the chin, running back over the hyoid, which reaches up to grasp it in the middle via two little fascial loops (see Figure 5 and Netter plate 47). The second belly of the muscle then passes up around the stylohyoid to the inner aspect of the mastoid process. When this muscle contracts, these loops pull the hyoid (and the rest of the visceral skeleton) straight up.

The jaw is the next "C" up in this series of arches, which is of course also tied to the temporal bone at the temporo-mandibular joint (TMJ) (Netter plate 49). Deane Juhan has aptly called the jaw the "drawstring of the organism." We can certainly get into trouble over not closing this drawstring, and allowing too much food in or too many words out. On the other hand, any massage therapist with any experience knows how chronically and resistantly tight the muscles of the jaw can be, as if nothing was ever going to get in or out.

The four muscles that move the mandible—three to close and one to open, which should tell you something—can best be understood by viewing them from below (see Figure 7). The temporalis is hard to see from below, but that is the most straightforward one, pulling right up on the coronoid process of the mandible (Netter plate 48). The other three are the masseters and the medial and lateral pterygoids (Netter plates 48 and 49). The masseters are very visible working on the outside of Christopher Lambert's or Sean Connery's jaw when they contemplate mayhem. You can feel yours right under your cheekbone when you bite, coming right down to the outer corner of the jaw.

The medial pterygoids come from the sphenoid bone, that butterfly-shaped "pelvis of the head," right down to the inside corner of the jaw, where they form a "sling" with the masseters. This bilateral sling can close the jaw in a circular way to "mill" your food, for if you watch you will see that you do not chew straight up and down. Working the masseters without balancing it out with the pterygoids can lead to imbalance in the jaw and the cranium. It is beyond the scope of this column to give that kind of technique in written form, but you can find the fairly large medial pterygoids, if your gag reflex is not too sensitive, right behind and medial to your lower teeth.

The lateral pterygoid is very difficult to reach, but it actively opens the jaw by reaching back from the sphenoid to the inside of the head of the mandible, pulling it forward to open the jaw (see Figures 7 and 8). This muscle actually has two heads, one to pull the bone forward and one to pull the cartilage disc in the TMJ forward.

The last two arches of our series are the maxillary bones that hold our upper teeth, and the zygomatic bones which form our cheekbones. Thus the frontal and ethmoid bones are part of the "neuro-cranium," but the facial bones—including the ones we have not named—could be thought of as the "viscero-

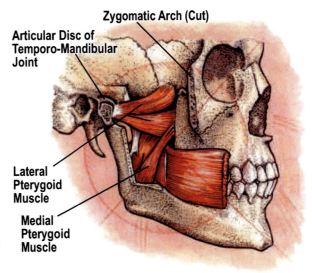

*Figure 8: The lateral pterygoid heads reach back from the sphenoid to open the jaw by pulling forward on the head of the mandible and (we hope) its associated cartilage.*

cranium," or as part of the visceral skeleton (Netter plates 1-3).

All of these arches, by the way, start in embryological development as part of the throat, which makes sense if they were originally part of the gills, and migrate up to the face during fetal development. The softer parts of our "gills" migrate downward (pulling the Xth cranial vagus nerve with them) to contribute to the heart, lungs and diaphragm (Netter plate 214). This again ties these facial bones to our viscera.

So let us turn now to the human face, which is certainly a world unto itself, with its intense familiarity amid an infinite variety of expressions. Objectively, to visiting Martians for instance, our face may seem ugly. Look at noses, or ears, for example. You could look at ears as beautiful and "shell-like," as the Cockneys say, or see them as a microcosm for the whole body, as the auricular acupuncturists do, or you could say, as a Martian might. "What ugly antennae these humans have on the side of their heads!"

The muscles of the face, some of the most superficial, sensitive and fascia-free muscles of your entire body, are stretched across these arches from ear to ear, centered around a spot called the modiolus, on either side of your mouth (Netter plates 20 and 21). Pinch your cheek from the inside and outside by the side of your mouth with thumb and forefinger, and you will feel the bump of this area distinctly (see Figure 9).

The face is perhaps a small part of the body—but to your brain, it is huge. You have several representations of your body in your brain, the most common being relative to the sensory and motor cortex, as shown in Figure 10. Notice how large the face is in relation to the rest of the body, the mouth, tongue and lips in particular. This is because of the intense amount of sensory endings in and around your mouth—put a pencil in your mouth and see how big it feels—and the need for such fine motor control over chewing, talking, and, of course, kissing. The conclusion we can draw for our profession is that work on the face, and around the mouth in particular, has a disproportionately relaxing effect on the person as a whole. For another possible reason for this effect, see "The Face as Microcosm," this chapter, page 129.

The throat is a development center for the organs of the chest and belly, the voice resonates with our whole structure and movement history, and the face is a microcosm of the whole—not small arguments for the power of gentle, thorough and sensitive exploration of this very human area by all who use their hands to heal.

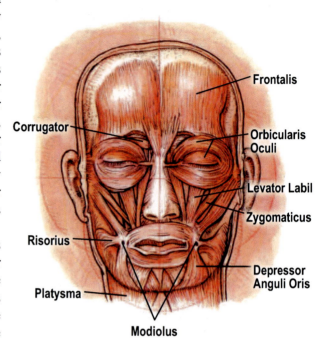

*Figure 9:* The facial muscles—and we have far more than any animal—are stretched over the skeleton like a mask and are mostly centered around our mouths.

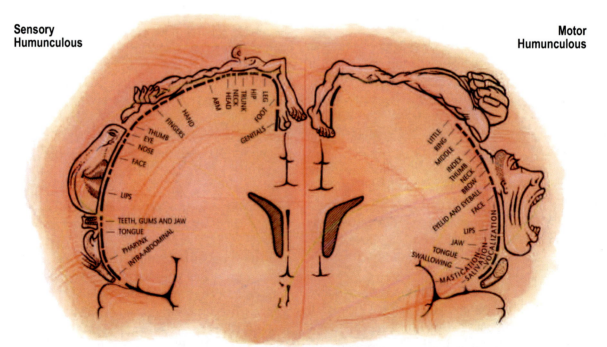

*Figure 10:* The "body image" mapped onto the sensory (left) and motor (right) cortex, called a homunculus, shows how large the lips, mouth and throat area loom in our picture of ourselves. Note also how big the hand is, and how small the torso and legs are in comparison.

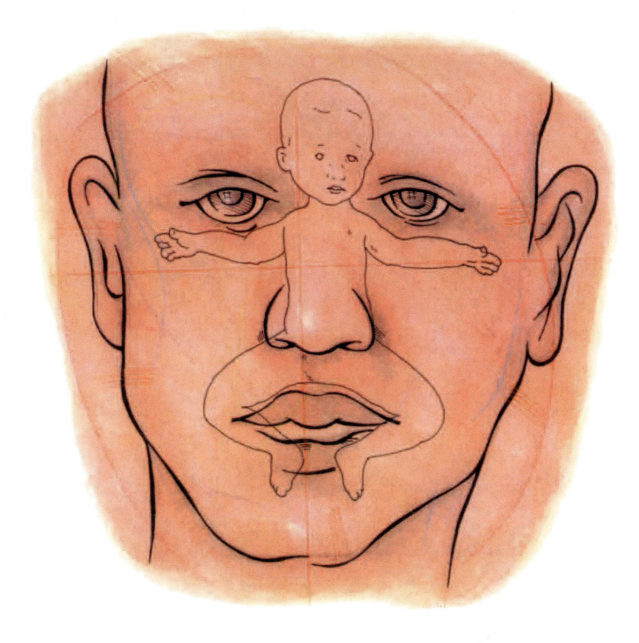

### The Face as Microcosm

The idea that there are microcosmic representations of the body within pieces of the body is a familiar one to most therapists. Many practice, or at least have learned, foot reflexology or its sister, hand reflexology. Others are familiar with the theory of iridology founder Bernard Jensen, N.D., that the body is mapped around the iris of the eye.

Acupuncturists have added the ear: they see it as an upside-down fetus, with the head in the lobe and the "tail" where the ear joins the head at the top. This is the source of sailors having earrings in their ear: when they stopped in ports in the Far East, the acupuncturists would give them an earring right through their eye point in the lobe, so they would have a sharp lookout in the crow's nest. And maybe you remember the dieting craze of a few years back when people were rubbing little darts taped onto their ear when they got hungry. The little darts were put over the stomach points.

Other parts of the body are probably also, by the law of holography, little echoes of the whole. I have even seen a chart of the sexual organs with a similar map of reflexes to the body on them, but for obvious reasons I'll leave the publishing of it to the specialists in that field.

**The Neck, Part 2**

The face is also a microcosm of the whole, with a similar chart, a summary of which is set out here. Like hand and foot reflexology, the side of the face corresponds to the same side of the body, with the head up near the eyes, the chest around the nose, and the pelvis and legs referring to the mouth and chin area. We have already spoken of the relation between the floor of the mouth and pelvic floor, and other practitioners, particularly the craniosacral group, have noted the ties between the jaw and the pelvis.

Unlike foot reflexology, which works for sure but whose mechanism is a mystery, the reflexes in the face have an embryological basis. In the very earliest stages of development, the embryo shows three layers: the ectoderm, the mesoderm, and the endoderm, one on top of the other. An amazing series of folds—the most complicated origami in the world—will turn these three layers into a human being. Basically, the ectoderm will form the skin and the nervous system, the mesoderm will form the bone, muscles and joints, and the endoderm will form the alimentary canal and its accessory organs. The face, however, retains this original order: the eyes are an extension of the nervous system, the nose an extension of the muscular heart and the connective tissue-y lungs, and the mouth the leading end of the alimentary tube.

Thus, you can use a basic reading of the face to measure health, vitality, and the person's physiological "emphasis" in these three fundamental systems. ∎

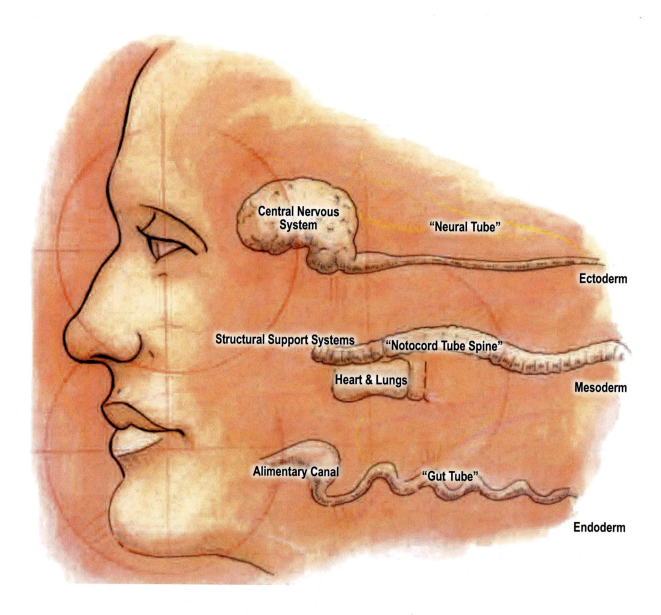

# Chapter 14:
# Moving In The World

**To understand the movement of life on this planet, we can return to the fundamentals: the four original Greek elements of Heraclitus: earth, water, air and fire. Heraclitis was a kind of early Zen master who first realized that "you cannot step in the same river twice," and who anticipated both Taoism and modern physics in 500 B.C. when he wrote that "everything flows and nothing stays."**

**T**hroughout this book we have slowly worked our way up the body, looking with awe at the intricacy of even its most simple system—the musculoskeletal "chassis"' for movement. From the architecture of the arches to the facets of the face, we have searched out some remarkable connections between human inner experience and our structural anatomy. Without reference to specific technique, we explored how hands-on practitioners of any persuasion can gain access to these many anatomical niches which carry such rich meaning for our clients and ourselves.

Now we launch ourselves into the next dimension. Body to the 4th power is the body in context; our 3D body with its never-ending additional dimension: moving in the world. The subject of movement is huge—worthy of another entire series—and even cutting it down to "training people in movement" will not help very much. But the truth is that every session we do, no matter how passive the client is training in movement. Whether it be straight-forward range of motion, or the interior movement of a suppressed e-motion, or just the simple elusive movement we call relaxing, each session we do evokes—or tries to, at least—a change of movement in the client. Somatic recognition of

**Moving in The World**  131

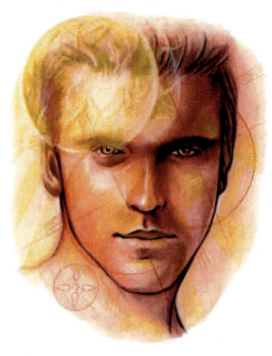

**Apollo, Greek God of the Sun**
*The element of fire reminds us of the solar primacy of energy in motion.*

this fact of life can have a profound effect on our daily practice.

Moreover, since all behavior is, in the end, made up of movements, anyone in the business of teaching movement is in the business of changing behavior. We could say that the science of behavior modification is really as old as parenting. The overt science, though, began with Freud and the other "alienists" about 150 years ago, and that makes it very young. Most "professional behavioral change agents" for adults—we call them psychotherapists—still sit in a room with people, talking them carefully through to behavioral change. This method has had some wonderful successes, and some spectacular failures. More recently we have become enamored with biochemistry, with drugs like Prozac used as behavioral change agents. But are these the only or the best way to evoke behavioral change? For some behaviors, surely, but for some others, a direct approach to the pattern of movement itself (rather than the thought or motivation behind it) is quicker, easier and even sometimes more profound. Consciously or not, this is what the hands-on therapist does every day.

A new activity—any novel movement at any level—"needs to occur before it can be perceived," according to Bonnie Bainbridge-Cohen, movement explorer and founder of the school of Body-Mind Centering. Leading a client to a new kind of movement leads him to perceive it, and leading him to perceive it can lead to his ability to reproduce and control it. This is the fundamental strength of our direct movement approach to behavioral change.

Talk therapy, on the other hand, can lead to what I call the "Woody Allen syndrome" (named not for the man but for his movie persona) in which you understand more and more about why you do not change. Thirty years of psychotherapy and all his characters are still obsessing over the same issues. The point is actually to change how one responds, is it not?

Of course, our hands-on therapeutic approach to behavior modification—teaching movement—is also in its infancy, and its power is just barely being envisioned, let alone tapped. But in another 50 years, a lot of behavior that now leads to a recommendation for a psychotherapist may instead lead to a referral to a skilled bodywork or movement therapist, who will simply search for resolution of the structural or movement pattern, without a lot of digging into the psychological story that goes with it. On a small scale, this is already happening.

## Fire

There are so many kinds of movement in the body. It is tempting to make movement synonymous with life, as Moshe Feldenkrais and many others have, except that everything we usually define as not-living is moving too. When Albert Einstein was asked if there was anything he knew for sure, he hesitated, and then answered, "Something's moving." (Emilie Conrad, creator of Continuum movement, has modified that statement to echo Heraclitus: "Everything's moving.")

Something has been moving around us and through us for 15 billion years or more, flying out from God's original sneeze, also known as the Big Bang. Our local remnant of this primary flaring-forth, the Sun, is the source for all our local movement; without it we would be frozen into no movement. The sun's enormous radiant energy powers all the little things that run and grow over the Earth, changing the surface of this planet much more quickly than the other planets in the solar system that have no life. You could say that all the plants and animals are the playthings of the sun.

Thus, although we could hardly power a flashlight with the amount of electrical energy stored within us, without our body's battery output—powered ultimately by the sun—we would still run down. With it we create the intricate patterns of movement that lead to love and art and war and betrayal and simple appreciation and glum depression that characterize the human experience. But movement and changing movement is unthinkable without the basic available energy. When you consider whether a client can make a structural or a behavioral change, the first question you have to ask is, "Does she have the energy for it?" If the answer is not a ready "Yes," then the first order of business is to either explore another goal, or help the client get more energy.

### Earth

Earth herself has such love for all these things that run upon her surface that she keeps them bound close with the power of gravity. (Or is it another mother's cloying inability to let go of her children? You decide.) Such is the power of her love that all beings, especially those above the surface of the ocean, must reckon with gravity's power in limiting their shape, a subject we have explored again and again in these columns. The plant's desire to grow toward the light and the animal's desire to move across the land, can only be fulfilled by a successful and sustained response to the earth's gravitational embrace.

Of course, it is the "earthy" part of us that is moved by the fire of energy within us. If we reduce a human body to its constituent parts, we would have a stew of proteins, fats and sugars of various kinds. Elementally, my dear Watson, we would find carbon, hydrogen, oxygen and nitrogen head the list, though there are significant amounts of calcium, phosphorus, potassium and sulfur, and trace amounts of all of the 92 standard chemical elements. Altogether, if a body were rendered down to its constituent parts, it might add up to $20 worth of chemicals by today's prices, no more. The value in any organism comes in the arrangement of those parts, and the movement that intricate arrangement produces, not in the substance itself.

A very significant part of that arrangement is how it hangs in the strong gravitational field of its mother planet. So, the second question you need

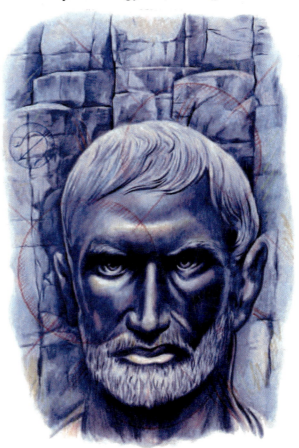

***Hades, Greek God of the Earth's Underworld***
*The element of earth reminds us of the saturnian limitations that gravity and substance impose upon all living forms, including us.*

to ask yourself when looking at the possibility of change in a client is: What is the client's relationship to gravity? Can they get aligned with the change they want to make? Are they grounded enough to make the new movement required? Are they spending so much energy just staying upright that there is little left over for life or for the change they seek? Once you have the available energy resources, the next task is to help clients achieve the easy upright alignment that facilitates change.

### Water

So if energy radiant (electromagnetic) and energy attractive (gravity) are fundamental to an understanding of life's movement on this planet, fluidity comes in a close third. It is nearly impossible to even conceive of life without a fluid medium within it somewhere. On our planet, this fluid is water, the "strangest stuff around" according

**Poseidon, Greek God of the Sea**
*The element of water, the wizard of changes, reminds us of the awesome power that lies in the fluid interplay between accommodation and persistence.*

to Marilyn Ferguson, author of *The Aquarian Conspiracy*. Nearly all forms of terran life contain a large percentage of it—about two-thirds to three-quarters in humans. Those forms of life that contain only a small amount of water are likely to be slow movers, slow growers, not exactly the life of the party. As the old Islamic proverb has it: "Water in motion—life; water when still—poison."

This equation of water with life becomes all the more interesting when we consider how small the band of temperature is where water exists in its liquid form. From 0° Celsius (freezing) all the way down to the absolute zero of deep space, -273.15°C, when molecular movement ceases, water exists only in its solid form, ice. From 100°C (boiling) all the way to, say, the temperature of the sun's corona—2 million degrees Celsius—water exists only in its gaseous form as steam, ultimately ceasing to exist at all. Only in this narrow band between freezing and boiling, about 1/10,000th of the range we know about in our local universe, can life as we know it exist. What a miracle that the planet has kept that temperature range on much of its surface (actually even more narrow than freezing to boiling—the ambient temperature has rarely gone above 50°C or 120°F) for several billions of years, supporting the myriad growth of life nearly everywhere.

How thin and fragile that life is! Most life on this planet exists within two miles either way of sea-level; in other words, as a ridiculously thin skin on the surface of the planet. If you reduced the earth to the size of a globe and compared the two, the ink on the globe would go deeper into the paper it's printed on than the oceans go into the surface of the earth. The Rockies and Himalayas would be barely discernible to even our knowing fingertips. The space shuttle and all those satellites that handle our phone calls and spy on us and tell us our position at sea would be flying around the surface of the planet no farther away than the width of a wooden match. These comparisons give some idea of how thin an envelope our precious and unique atmosphere is. The confines of our livable world, which seemed so generous a few short centuries ago, are now seen to be perishingly narrow. And at what peril we humans hurtle around, changing the surface and the air willy-nilly, turning the sunlight stored in the trees into carbon soot in the air, threatening the maintenance of that skinny margin of temperature necessary to keep life as fluid as we have come to love it.

Whew, take a breath, Tom, and return to the personal, and make it relevant to the bodyworker's daily fare. Oh, but it is, and it leads directly to the third question you must ask yourself when considering change in your clients: Where is fluidity missing? Is the tissue hydrated enough? Are they drinking enough water, and is that water reaching the relevant tissues? The original osteopathy of Dr. A.T. Still was based on the "Law of the Artery": Are the arteries free enough, unimpeded enough, to allow blood to reach every nook and cranny of the body? Every place that is out of the fluid loop in the body is ripe for the development of malfunction or disease.

This is, of course, true for the planet as well, and drinkable water for all of us little cells is likely to be the most pressing political and environmental issue of the next century or two.

## Air

The fourth of the Greek elements, air, figures into our movement equation also. On our personal hierarchy of needs, nothing is as pressing as the need for air. For all land vertebrates, the diaphragm is in almost constant motion, bringing a tide of air in and out of the body. The heart has a nonstop job of setting the pace for pumping the air—now attached to the red blood cells—around the body to the cells that crave it.

The wave of the diaphragm and the beat of the heart symbolize life for us they are the first things we look for in an accident victim as signs of life. Although the heart rate goes up and down with our excitement and exercise level, we go into a panic if it misses even a beat or two, or if it races without an obvious reason. And our posture will totally rearrange itself to ease our daily breath, such is its primacy.

So this becomes our fourth "elemental" question: Does the client have the breathing capacity to make the change they want to make? Enhancing respiratory function, as Bob King has termed it, is the surest and simplest way to increase the adaptive capacity in the organism. Increase the adaptive capacity and you ensure the reserves necessary to make and sustain the change your work will open up for the client. Put the other way 'round, trying to sustain a new posture or a new psychological attitude (and is there any difference between these two?) without an improvement in the adaptive capacity of the breath is often a doomed enterprise. This becomes a recipe for disappointment, for temporary gain followed by discouraging failure.

And the positive side of that coin is equally true—open the breath and many other changes become possible. Ida Rolf's series of structural bodywork sessions begins with freeing the superficial restrictions to the breath, freeing the rib cage from any fascial anchors that restrict its easy excursion, preparing the body's adaptive capacity for the changes to follow.

## A taxonomy of movement

Fire, earth, water and air—available energy, grounding, fluidity, adaptive capacity—all of these four elements are moving around within us, setting us in motion, limiting that motion, allowing and disallowing in Heraclitus' constant interactive flux. The musculoskeletal system we have been studying is our main way of moving through the environment, but there are many kinds of movement in the body, all of them ultimately the play of the sun, however much we may think of our actions as freely ordained.

At the basis of all these movements would be the energetic motions explored by the physicists—quantum movement, the spin of electrons and quarks—but we will leave to Deepak Chopra and Fritjof Capra to explain the daily relevance of such movements. The Brownian motion and internal chemical motion of changing bonds and electrolytic valences we will likewise leave aside here for the chemists to explain. The following list simply contains all the different kinds of movements that we all see on our tables every day.

In assembling this list, I am indebted to conversations with Deborah Raoult, a true polymath of movement. Deborah is a deeply grounded and vitally humorous student and teacher of Zen's stillness, of yoga's formality, of Continuum's utter biologic freedom, and of Body-Mind Centering's organic genius. Not to mention the ultimate test of inner movement and adaptability: raising three extraordinarily bright and active children. Our categories are not categoric, but rather flow into each other, all interweaving together to make up both our everyday and extraordinary movements.

There are three major domains of movement that we consider. This chapter we will explore the inherent movements of all our cells and tissues, and

*Hermes, air-borne messenger to the gods*
*The element of air reminds us of the possibility and potential of spirit, the mercurial reach of the mind's hand.*

**Moving in The World**

*Each successive level of biological organization builds its movement as a synergy of movements from the level below it (above it, in this diagram).*

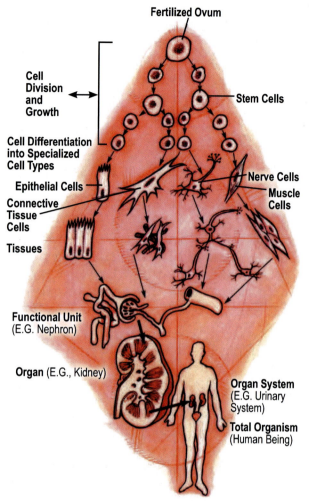

the smooth muscle movements stimulated by our autonomic nervous system. Next chapter we will complete the story with a tour of the more familiar movements modulated by our somatic nervous system through striated muscle cells.

We present this list of inherent movements in hopes that it enriches what you see in your clients:

## 1. Cellular motion

Cells are in constant motion, both within themselves and creating motion in their surroundings as well. They are all exchanging food and oxygen and waste through their membranes, conducting messages along the membranes, flailing their cilia and other antennae, contracting and expanding in a ceaseless pulse, secreting enzymes and other chemicals, and dividing themselves in reproduction. (Deb says that we should include dying here, that dying is a special movement. I remain to be convinced that dying is not simply a cessation of movement.) The summation of all that cellular humming is what we call metabolism.

All cells do all of these activities to some degree, but specialized cells do certain of these movements better than others. For instance, all cells have conducting membranes—nerves just got very good at it (at a cost to some of their other functions). And all cells have contractile myosin and actin in them—muscle cells just have a preponderance of these molecules, so that they are the contraction "stars" in the body.

Obviously, all the motions of the body are ultimately cellular motions, just as we could say that all the motions in the world are ultimately molecular or atomic motions. But we can be a little more specific and interesting than that. When colonies of cells get together, their combined motions are worth looking at.

## 2. Embryologic motion

Coordinated but still purely cellular movement is most evident in the new films of the early embryo, in which we can see the tiny but mighty movements produced by the divisions, migrations and contractions of these stem cells. The effect is roughly like that of putting a straw into a bottle of soap bubble solution and blowing vigorously. The bubbles foam up out of the bottle and spiral down over your hand. The bursts of embryological cell growth are something like this, but more controlled, of course, by the genes, the laws of fluid dynamics, electrical auric fields, or whatever else it is that governs the growth of a human being. The German embryologist Erich Blechschmidt theorized that these early cellular movements underlie our later voluntary movements. Whether that is true or not, our adult movement is still the summation of thousands of individual neuronal conductions and muscle cell contractions.

## 3. Physiologic motion

Individual cell pulsations tune into each other and combine, even in the adult, to make physiologic motions of organs. The heart would continue to beat, albeit more slowly, even if you cut all the nerves from the brain to the heart. Heart cells just have that inherent impulsiveness (don't they just?) and even a few of them put together in a petri dish will start to beat together. The nerve control from the brain is a later refinement, but the heart itself still has the capability of its own physiologic motion.

The cranio-sacral pulse comes to mind as a possible example of physiologic motion, as well as the similar inspir and expir motions of the organs posited by the French visceral osteopath Jean-Pierre Barral. The two-hour cycles of organic activity put forward by the traditional acupuncturists may also fall in this category. Those of us who have been in this business for a long time suspect that there are other physiologic motions and rhythms which healers are tuned into, even though they have yet to be identified, measured and understood by consensus science.

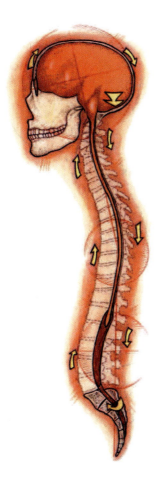

*The craniosacral pulse is clearly not a muscular movement; it marches to the beat of an inner physiologic drummer.*

### 4. Autonomic movements

Smooth muscle cells appeared earlier in our animal history than striated muscle, and are generally stimulated into contraction by the autonomic branches of the peripheral nervous system.

Although this phrase is proper in terms of consensus nomenclature, I personally find it demeaning to the venerable autonomic nervous system. In light of our evolutionary history, it would be more proper to see the central and somatic peripheral systems as Johnny-come-latelys, add-ons to or eruptions from the older, and, to my mind, wiser autonomic system. It is true that both this later nervous system and its accompanying striated muscle are more efficient at producing faster and stronger contractions; but as the Western world is finally finding out, efficiency isn't everything.

The autonomic nervous system (ANS) and its fellow traveler, the endocrine system, effect many movements across the entire body, but the largest are concentrated in the ventral cavity. You can start to swallow voluntarily with the pharyngeal constrictors behind your tongue, but very quickly the motion is taken over by the smooth muscle of the esophagus. From then on, for the whole nine yards of the digestive system, the motions of peristalsis are controlled by the part of you that is largely out of your control. Once it gathers at the other end, you assist it on out with voluntary muscles again. But all the motions of breaking up the food and moving it along from throat to rectum are only dimly felt, and, unless you are an accomplished yogi or hooked up to a biofeedback machine, can hardly be controlled by conscious will. Somewhere in our lives we have all had the experience, amusing only in retrospect, of fighting with our voluntary anus the desire of the involuntary peristalsis to expel a gas bubble at an inopportune moment.

We have already mentioned cardiac motion as a fundamentally cellular one, but in our day-to-day world, the heartbeat is controlled by the ANS. Additionally, the entire arterial system is surrounded by walls of smooth muscle, which contract or relax under the direction of the ANS to raise or lower blood pressure, or to direct the arterial blood into or out of various compartments of the body, such as toward the skin when you are hot, and away from it when you get cold.

Along with the digestive system and the

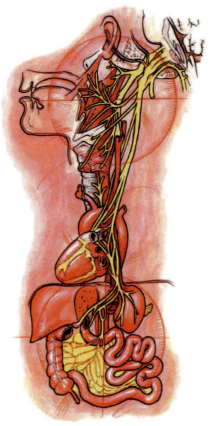

*The Xth cranial nerve is a "wanderer" (vagus) that affects smooth muscle throughout the visceral cavity.*

circulatory system, a third large system helps fill the ventral space: the respiratory system. Like the arterial system, we find that the bronchi and bronchioles are surrounded with circumferential bands of smooth muscle tissue, which relax to open our air passages during exercise, and close to ease our relaxed breathing (or close even more, making it frighteningly hard to breathe during an asthmatic attack).

But the greatest motion of all in the ventral cavity is reserved for the diaphragm, that all-important muscle that straddles the fulcrum between autonomic and voluntary. You can control the diaphragm with your will, but once your will turns its attention to other things, the autonomic function takes over smoothly, automatically regulating your diaphragmatic motion to your present needs. Thereby hangs a long tale, because it responds to your *perception* of your present needs, which may or may not be the needs of the real world. Humans are particularly susceptible to changing our breathing according to internal perceptions of fears or long-gone actions that still run us.

Besides these grand and universal themes of the ventral cavity, there are smaller and more occasional autonomic movements throughout your body and throughout your life. The contractions of the uterus during menstruation and childbirth are ANS-controlled—otherwise you would be able to stop them and rest for a while, which some women have been known to pray for fervently. The flooding of sexual arousal and the spasms of orgasm are also autonomic, though some would pray as fervently that they could go on forever.

The contraction of my pupil as I move from inside the house to the outdoor light of this Maine morning; the adjustment of the tensor tympani muscle within my ear as I switch my listening from my sneakers on the porch to the crows out on the marsh; the raising of goose flesh as my bike picks up speed in the chilly air; the dilation of bronchioles as my need for oxygen increases; the valving of arteries to my leg muscles to deliver that oxygen to where the rubber meets the road—all this runs without my conscious intervention. Indeed, my conscious intervention would probably only screw it up; I am quite content to let that part of me which does not participate in my reason operate most reasonably to keep me going.

Coordinated motions of the autonomic system are also very involved in the expression of e-motions, which sometimes spill over, either temporarily or more chronically, into the level of skeletal muscle tension. For this reason, and because our work can affect the ANS and smooth muscle indirectly, we need to be able to watch it at work within our clients. We see it in the changing color of our clients' faces, the rumble of their guts, the flutter of their eyelids—a thousand signs we take in and react to every day, whether we are conscious of it or not. While these signs are reflecting the inner movement of the smooth musculature, the therapist's ministrations are usually directed to the voluntary, striated muscles—and it is to these movements that we will turn our attention in the next chapter.

In the pause between the two parts, let us once again remind ourselves that all these divisions among movements and among parts of the neuro-muscular system are but man-made categories imposed on a God-and-mother-made seamless whole. To quote Deane Juhan from *Job's Body*: "The skin is no more separated from the brain than the surface of a lake is from its depths; the two are different locations in a continuous medium... To touch the surface is to stir the depths." ∎

# Chapter 15: Moving On

Last chapter, we began a discussion of different kinds of motion in the body, and worked our way through inherent cellular motions and their more organized but still ancient cousins, autonomically-driven motions of the smooth muscle fibers. In this chapter, we continue the survey with an overview of the different types of voluntary motion at play in the striated muscles, sometimes called the voluntary muscles.

## Voluntary movement

Right away we have a terminology problem, because not all movement of the voluntary system is "voluntary" in the sense of "consciously willed." In fact, only a small amount of the movement we make through the somatic nervous system (SNS) the part of the peripheral nervous system that goes to our musculoskeletal system is consciously controlled by us. The vast majority—more than 90 percent—is subconsciously controlled to support our conscious intent. We will explore this in a moment, but first let's look at the lowest, most primitive level of so-called voluntary movement.

## Reflexive movement

Reflexes are those automatic movements governed by simple spinal cord loops, such as the patellar tendon reflex, the one your doctor tests with the rubber hammer; or the irresistible urge to blink when something comes near your eye. These two- or three-neuron chains cannot be unlearned, and are hard-wired into the system, though they pass through the voluntary motor nerves. Your brain hears about the movement only after it has already been initiated by the spinal cord, so when the hammer hits the sub-patellar tendon, you can inhibit your knee's movement a bit, but you cannot stop it altogether.

A baby is hard-wired with more of these reflexes—the sucking reflex, for instance; the Babinski reflex, which causes the foot to dorsiflex when the plantar surface is stimulated: or the STNR and ATNR (symmetric and asymmetric tonic neck reflexes), which control arm motions in relation

to head movements. Or remember the tendency of a baby's fingers to grip quite strongly, which is probably left over from grabbing a mother monkey's hair to keep from falling. These protective automatic reflexes all fade or blend with more sophisticated responses over time until only a few are left.

### Conditioned movement

Far more common to our everyday work are the conditioned reflexes that underlie our intended motions. These are the stuff of life for a movement or manual therapist, because these subtle but pervasive movements, which take place just below our conscious threshold (but nevertheless run through our voluntary system), are subject to learning and can therefore be learned badly or well. It is these conditioned movements often end up causing postural or pain problems that develop without our knowledge.

Let's take a simple example: We will set this up as an exercise for two, but you can do it by yourself nearly as well. Stand facing a friend's side with her outstretched arm resting on your shoulder. Press your hands firmly into her belly or waist and lower back so that you can feel if those muscles contract. Now have her simply press her arm down on your shoulder. Feel the contraction in the belly or lower back? Think a second: what muscles are the prime movers or agonists for what she did? Most likely the pectoralis major and latissimus, right? So why did the belly muscles contract? Well, the agonists are attached to the rib cage, so when she pressed the arm into your shoulder, your shoulder couldn't be moved, so her rib cage would have moved up toward the arm, moving the origin to the insertion. Your friend automatically contracted her belly muscles to stabilize the rib cage onto the pelvis.

Notice that this action is not a hardwired reflex, or absolutely necessary. It assumes that the person wanted to keep the rib cage stable, on the basis of past experience. Tell your friend to perform the same exercise without contracting those muscles and it's dollars to doughnuts she will not be able to do it without some minutes of concentrated effort. When she achieves it, you will feel the pressure on your shoulder, and when her rib cage will move toward you and her arm. It's a silly-looking movement, but just as valid as any other. We just don't tend to move that way, so we automatically contract those voluntary muscles to make the movement we think we want.

Using the same position, put your hands below her belt and have her press down on your shoulder again. You will feel a similar contraction in the pants-pocket area between the iliac crest and the greater trochanter, which stabilizes the pelvis onto the hips. And so on, and so on—you could trace it all the way to the ground. So while your friend willed the contraction or the pectoralis and latissimus in response to your request to press down on your shoulder, she voluntarily contracted many more of the muscles of her body without thinking. And in fact, finds it hard to "think-move" in any other way. Thus are habits born, and thus are they so hard to break, for the will is sabotaged by the underlying voluntary movement—a great deal of which is our learned response to how gravity works, and how we work in gravity.

You may have noticed that we started out talking about conditioned movement, and we ended up talking, essentially, about fixation muscles. Although there are a great many types of conditioned movements, much of the long-term postural pain our clients bring to us is occasioned by the overuse or misuse of subconsciously employed fixation patterns, not in the prime movers or their antagonists.

### Functional movement

Functional movements are our everyday, purposeful movements: getting out of bed, getting in and out of the bathtub, getting our clothes on, driving, sitting, walking, picking up the mail from the floor, or picking up the e-mail from the computer—all these are our functional movements. We tend to take them for granted, but they are, of course, based on an initial infantile year of not being able to do them at all, and several years of learning them on top of that. And we can look at our senior friends and parents and realize that even these simple movements might not all be easy forever. (One of my favorite stories involves an English writer, newly disabled by multiple sclerosis, at a cocktail parry in London. He was parked next to a painter who had long been in a wheelchair. "You know what I call them?" the painter barked, gesturing with his drink to the rest of the guests, who were standing and talking, "The temporarily-abled!")

Even now, as fully able adults, the way we go about our ADL's (that's Activities of Daily Life, for those of you lucky enough not to have to fill out insurance reports) can lead, through misuse, to pain or predisposition to injury.

## Habitual movement can lead to strain, pain and lessened function.

Functional movement is packed with layer upon layer of habit. We have a habit of driving, which can be transferred from car to car with little change. We have habits of sitting, and characteristic ways of getting up, perhaps by pushing with our arms on our legs. Most of this habitual way of movement quickly drops below the radar of our conscious attention, and provides breeding ground for compensatory tensions that can lead ultimately to strain, pain and lessened function.

To participate fully with our felt sense of movement, and avoid becoming trapped by our own habits in functional movement, we have to do one of two things: either participate very consciously with our everyday movement, or participate in un-ordinary movements to make a counterpoint to our very necessary, but pedestrian and habituated, daily movements.

Practitioners of the Alexander Technique, Charlotte Selver and others in the Sensory Awareness movement, Moshe Feldenkrais and his followers in the Awareness Through Movement lessons, Laban Movement Analysts, and Judith Aston and her heirs in Rolfing® Movement Integration and Aston Patterning—these current groups, and many others I'm sure—work with making ordinary functional motions more efficient, less habitual, more full of the rich feeling of life.

Many other movement teachers work with movement outside the everyday. Here are several categories people explore:

## Corrective movement:

From physical and occupational therapy to t'ai chi and yoga, many movements are used to correct the problem; that come from conditioned movement, from injury, from idleness, or to restore health. This category is huge—books abound in this area—but as it is well-known to our readers, we will leave it here to consider the other categories more fully.

## Athletic movement:

Athletic performance takes us beyond the realm of everyday movement into the extremes of endurance, coordination, strength and drive. The body responds to demand, and the demands of a sport or other athletic endeavor strengthen muscle, connective tissue and physiologic systems, at the same time they tighten the sinews of the mind. Whether one competes for a team, against oneself, or just for the sheer joy of it, athletic movement improves health on many levels, from circulation to soul, but, again , they are so well discussed in other places that we need not dwell on them here.

The role of hands-on therapies in recovery from athletic effort and in improving athletic performance has also been documented elsewhere, but we can note that most performance-related athletic injury, in our experience, comes from over-using one part of the body while we under-use another. An outside eye and hand, provided by the

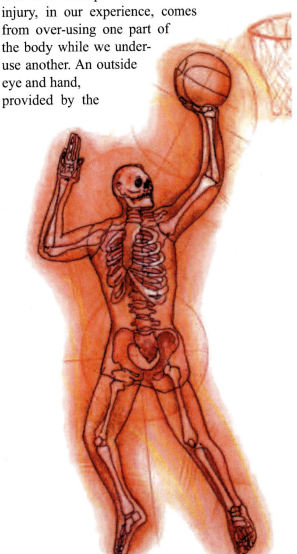

**Moving On**

massage therapist, can assist an athlete in finding all parts of the body needed to participate in any given action.

### Artistic movement

While athletic movement is most often held to a performance standard the guy who pole-vaults beautifully over a 14-foot bar does not win over the fellow who makes it awkwardly over a 15-foot bar—artistic movement, such as dance, is held to an aesthetic standard. Carriage, grace, poise, strength, lightness and integration all go into our appreciation of artistic movement.

Whether producing a dance, a sustained soft note on a cello, a spinning pot from a lump of clay, or a mind-bending spin on the point or a skate, artistic movement thrills the sense of beauty within us. Of course, any given culture's aesthetic standards may or may not conform to kinesiological good sense, and therefore many manual therapists make a living off the dissonance between what dancers think they ought to look like and what their bodies are really capable of sustaining.

### Expressive movement

Related to artistic, but worthy of another category, is expressive movement: movement that carries an emotion or a prayer to the divine. Religious dance may be athletic, like some practiced by Native Americans, or aesthetic, like the Hindu dance tradition, but the standard used to judge it should be neither athletic nor aesthetic: it is the spiritual connection that matters, not the look or the performance.

The spontaneous whoop and arms-up jump as the summit is finally reached or the game finally won could fall into this category, as could the autonomically-induced release of tears or tearing of hair and rending of garments that accompanies grief. These movements are like a momentary ritual that restores our balance, letting off the steam that life's dissonance, positive or negative, creates within us.

### Spontaneous movement

Related to expressive, but qualitatively different to those who have experienced it, is spontaneous movement that arises from within. This is inner, informal movement as meditation. Though I have heard of similar forms from Japan and other cultures, Continuum movement is the American form to which I have been exposed. In Continuum, you are encouraged to look within yourself and to watch for the movement that is already within you, and then bring it to the fore, explore it. This kind of practice, which is hard to explain but simple to achieve, is an antidote to our society's insistence on functional, linear, purposeful movement. Most of us are so imbued with the movements we have to do, or

*We share most of our DNA with our ancestral life forms, so their movement potential lies within us as well. Giving yourself time for utter intuitional freedom in your movement (as opposed to movement directed at any particular goal) allows this "bio-morphic" movement to emerge.*

are supposed to do, or are accustomed to doing, that we never get the opportunity to listen to the inner part of our being and let up on whatever is in there that might want to come out. We share DNA with all sorts of animals; likewise, these animalistic, or "biomorphic" movements, as Emilie Conrad calls them, are waiting in us for spontaneous expression. Giving our inner self a day in the sun is not quite the same as dance or prayer, but it has elements of both.

Obviously any single set of movements can contain elements of several categories. Ashtanga yoga, for instance, is inspiring as athletic achievement, as aesthetic performance, or as a form of expressive prayer—with elements of corrective movement in there also, of course. And if it is less than spontaneous or functional, understand that no movement fills all categories.

## Maturational movement

The human eye is designed to see things within a certain range of timing. While most movements are easy to see in real time, others pass us by unnoticed, or even unnoticeable. The hour hand of a clock moves too slowly, and an airplane propeller moves too fast for us to see it.

There is another movement we must recognize, in our long-term clients, our lovers, and our children, even though it is far too slow to be seen on our table: the long, slow wave of movement called maturation. We can recognize maturity when we see it, and even define some of its characteristics: tolerant vision and patient passion among them. English physician and writer Sir Thomas Browne (1605-1682) almost defined maturity when he wrote, "Those who undertake great public schemes must be prepared for fatiguing delays, mortifying disappointments, and, worst of all, the presumptuous judgment of the ignorant upon their design." Rudyard Kipling's poem "If"—with allowances for his Victorian macho attitude—also can be seen as a definition of maturity.

This movement is subtle. A college professor came to my practice recently. He had a large head, small limbs, a rounded body. It took awhile, but suddenly I realized what I was looking at: a big baby. He had married a maternal woman, cocooned himself in the womb of his university department, and, brilliant though he was, his emotional responses were pretty infantile. Could he go through the movements of growing up? I believe, even at this late date in his life, that with skilled work the answer is yes.

Other times you will see shoulders or pelves or legs that simply do not look as grown-up as the rest of the person, sometimes due to some trauma, other times due to some long-held emotional attitude. Recognizing these patterns is important to successful release of these areas.

Taken altogether, the task before us is not easy. Building a group of mature, "normal" (as opposed to "average"), embodied adults requires all our skill, all our talents. The huge population of pseudo-adult consumers, fueled by corporate competitive greed, is creating our current dire ecological situation; only a committed group of truly adult citizens can turn it around toward responsible planetary stewardship. It is to this task and the practitioners who undertake it that these columns are gratefully dedicated. ∎

The photos below show Reginald before any work (left), directly after 10 sessions of structural bodywork under the direction of Dr. Ida Rolf (middle). and one year later without any further work (right). The photos have been altered only to keep them the same size. Between the beginning and the end of the work, Reginald gets 'straighter' in his legs, pelvis and ribs, but in the second photo he still looks unsure of where he is. You could be forgiven, looking at only the first two pictures, for asking whether the bodywork did him any real good at all. Left to himself, though, he grows into a more mature state, in terms of his depth and confidence, in the ensuing year. Understanding maturity issues in relationship to bodywork proceeds from this question: Would the boy on the left have developed into the boy on the right in one year without the manual intervention? I think not. The boy in the middle did. Bodywork Is a powerful change agent in the journey from infancy to maturity.

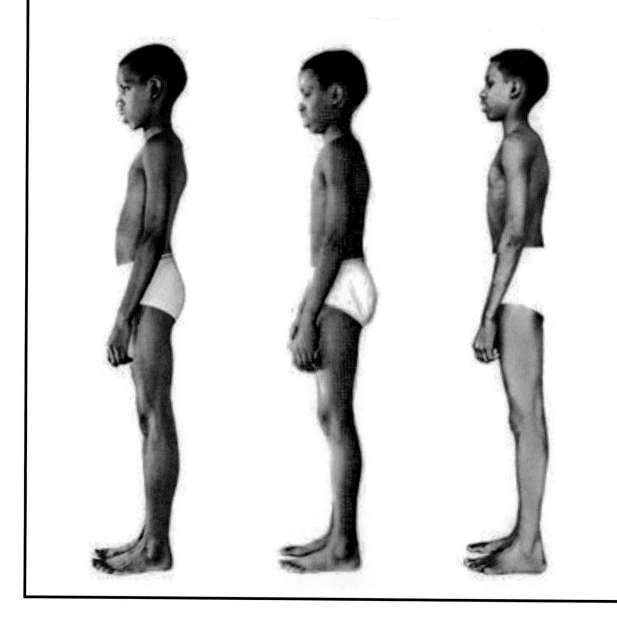

*Photos used with permission of Robert Toporek and the Children's Project.*

Made in the USA
Middletown, DE
23 September 2023

39115803R00084